Designing
and Developing
Multimedia

A Practical Guide for the
Producer, Director, and Writer

Larry Elin

Syracuse University

Allyn and Bacon

Boston • London • Toronto • Sydney • Tokyo • Singapore

Series Editor: Karon Bowers
Vice President and Editor-in-Chief: Karen Hanson
Series Editorial Assistant: Jennifer Becker
Marketing Manager: Jackie Aaron
Production Editor: Christopher H. Rawlings
Editorial-Production Service: Omegatype Typography, Inc.
Composition and Prepress Buyer: Linda Cox
Manufacturing Buyer: Julie McNeill
Cover Administrator: Jenny Hart
Electronic Composition: Omegatype Typography, Inc.

Library of Congress Cataloging-in-Publication Data

Elin, Larry.
    Designing and developing multimedia : a practical guide for the producer, director, and writer / Larry Elin.
      p.   cm.
    Includes bibliographical references and index.
    ISBN 0-205-31427-9 (alk. paper)
    1. Multimedia systems.   I. Title.
    QA76.575. E533   2001
    006.7—dc21
                                                          00-023035

Printed in the United States of America
10   9   8   7   6   5   4   3   2   05   04   03   02   01

To Sally Kita Popielinski
and to the memory of
Lawrence C. Popielinski,
self-sacrificing and loving parents

Contents

4

Game Design   68

10 The Development Agreement   234

Preface

Who Should Read This Book

- *Students.* If you are a student with little or no prior media experience, this book will teach you most of the basic skills you need to produce, direct, and write multimedia.

- *Professionals in other media who wish to step over into multimedia.* If you are approaching multimedia from another media profession, this book will help you identify the key differences and similarities and build on the skills you already have.

- *Multimedia professionals who want to learn how to create products better, faster, and less expensively.*

What This Book Is About

This book is about the *process* of designing and developing multimedia applications from the perspective of the three people who manage, supervise, and document the effort. The producer, who may also be called the project manager, is responsible for managing the development process. The director, who is often the interactive designer, is responsible for the creative vision and supervision of the work. The writer creates and maintains the design documents that guide the work of the development team.

This book is a nuts-and-bolts, practical guide. It describes reliable, successful principles of design and development processes taken from experience gained on interactive multimedia projects at development studios and a major university. The principles apply regardless of product purpose and genre, technology, distribution and delivery system, or revenue and business model. For this reason, the book does not include lengthy coverage of graphic design, software programming, or other topics that change quickly in the rapidly evolving multimedia world. Although described throughout the book in the context of CD-ROM development, the principles and methods of interactive design and process management work equally well for the Internet, Interactive TV, DVD, console game development, and whatever is to come. The concepts are evergreen.

The topics covered in this book include

- Definition of multimedia
- Interactive design
- Components of multimedia applications
- Design of educational multimedia
- Game design
- Interactive design process
- Functional specification
- Development process
- Development agreement
- Phases of product development
- Roles and responsibilities of the producer, director, and writer

The three appendixes provide a sample functional specification and discussions of the multimedia business and the multimedia studio. A glossary of multimedia terms is included at the back of the book, along with a list of references and an index.

The process of designing and developing a multimedia application consists of many tasks, some that are completed serially—meaning one after the other—and others that are completed in parallel—or simultaneously. These tasks and how to complete them are covered in detail. The role, responsibility, authority, and accountability of the producer, director, and writer with respect to these tasks is described.

This book is all about *process*. It's up to you to bring the creative and technical talents that will make you a success in multimedia.

Who This Book Is About

The producer, director, and writer of multimedia are the leaders of the development team and are with the product from its inception to its final delivery. Other members of the team pop in and out of the process as required. They include content experts, the interactive designer, game designer, instructional designer, art director, sound designer, video crew, software engineer or programmer, quality assurance supervisor, artists, animators, talent, researchers, business affairs people, attorneys, public relations director, accountants, and production assistants.

Multimedia is populated with "hyphenates." Many people have the experience and talent needed to perform more than one role. The team, then, should not be thought of as a group of distinct individuals, but rather as a grouping of important functions. For example, the producer, director, and writer may all be the same person in some situations. At other times, the producer may also be the lead programmer and the director may also be the interactive designer. The writer of educational products is very often the content or subject expert.

In the early days of the video game business, programmers designed and developed the games and often generated their own art and sounds, but things have changed. Multimedia products have become very complex undertakings involving huge budgets, large staffs, and all forms of media. In the richness of the final product and the complexity of the development process, multimedia is very much like Hollywood film production. The ever increasing complexity of the products, the rise in costs and extension of development time, and the growing size and diversity of the development team have underscored the importance of methodology, organization, and process.

A Brief Note about Nomenclature

The multimedia industry is a composite of the entertainment, computer software, consumer electronics, video game, telecommunications, advertising, and publishing businesses. Many multimedia applications are for educational and instructional purposes and involve professionals from those disciplines. As a result, there exists some disagreement within the industry about vocabulary. Job titles, such as "producer" and "director," have slightly different meanings in software publishing than in film and television. The title "producer" is only now replacing the software industry's "project manager" in most studios, although the job descriptions are very similar. The writer has a different set of responsibilities in a multimedia studio than in a film studio.

The word *development* means one thing in film and television and something very different in software publishing. In the film business, the word refers to the beginning of the production process. Development occurs when filmmakers engage the director and talent, polish the script, and arrange production financing and distribution deals. After development, a film goes into preproduction, production, postproduction, and distribution. In software publishing, development is the entirety of the product-creation process. Software development includes design, prototyping, asset production, software programming, testing, and disc burns.

Multimedia products are often called titles or applications. Most of the time, this book uses the word *product,* but from time to time the word *title* or *application* is used interchangeably.

In this book, the word *development* was chosen instead of the word *production* to describe the overall process of creating a multimedia product. *Production* is used to describe a particular phase of the product development cycle. The job title "producer" was chosen over the title "project manager." The single word *multimedia* is used instead of the phrase *interactive multimedia* throughout the book.

How This Book Is Designed

This book is designed to be both a text and a reference volume. You can skip around depending on your area of interest, level of previous experience, or where you happen to be on a specific multimedia project. Some sections are appropriate, maybe even critical, for everybody to read. Other sections are of greater interest to the producer, others to the director, and still others to the writer. You will see these icons throughout the book:

PRODUCER

This icon appears whenever the material is of particular interest to the *producer.*

DIRECTOR

This icon appears whenever the material concerns the *director.*

WRITER

The *writer* should look for this icon.

WEBSITE

 This icon indicates that the material in the book has updated or component information at the book's web site. The URL is www.abacon.com/elin.

This book is divided into three parts. Because the producer, director, and writer of multimedia must be fluent in the fundamentals of interactivity and nonlinear storytelling before attempting to create a product, the first part of the book is devoted to interactive design. Part 1 provides the reader with general concepts of interactive design, the grammar and vocabulary of interactivity, and a step-by-step approach to the design process. Part 2 then leads the reader through the development process, during which interactive design takes place. This part includes a discussion of the client–developer relationship. Part 3, the appendixes, includes sample documents and a description of the multimedia industry and the infrastructure and practices of the multimedia studio.

Part 1

Part 1 provides the reader with the proper grounding and context for the rest of the book by dealing extensively with interactive design. Interactive design is the beginning and central idea that drives and determines the development process that follows it. Therefore, it is the first and most important concept to cover. The reader may undertake further exploration of the subject because there is a wealth of empirical knowledge and theory. A list of recommended books is provided at the end of every chapter; this list is updated periodically on the web site.

Part 1 continues with chapters on interactive design for the general multimedia product, for education and training, and for games. A chapter on the design process follows. Part 1 concludes with a chapter on writing the design document called the functional specification. The reader who is interested only in the design of multimedia will have a good foundation on which to build after reading Part 1.

Part 2

Part 2 is about the development process, and this part is organized as a time line. Successful development occurs during a series of phases. In multimedia, the phases of development are the discovery phase, during which a developer and its client reach an agreement to create a multimedia product; the design phase, during which the product is fully designed and a functional specification is written; the prototype phase, during which a working version of the product is produced for evaluation;

and the production phase, during which the product is completed through gold master. Each phase has specific, clearly defined deliverables, tasks, milestones, and approval stages. Each deliverable requires the services of certain development personnel to accomplish assigned tasks, in a specific order and for a budgeted length of time. Whereas most development resources pop in and out of the scene during these phases, the producer, director, and writer are always there. As each phase is covered, the specific roles of the producer, director, and writer are discussed in detail.

The Appendixes

Appendix A includes a portion of a functional specification for a CD-ROM product developed by students at the S. I. Newhouse School of Public Communications at Syracuse University. This document serves as a good example for other students, as it demonstrates excellent style and structure and describes a multimedia application that two students were able to build in a single semester.

Appendix B discusses the multimedia industry—how the various segments are structured, what the principal businesses are, and how revenue is generated. After a rocky start, parts of the industry have settled down, consolidated, and matured. Various market segments are discussed, including entertainment, corporate training, and education.

For each market segment, the following points are discussed:

- Purposes and objectives of the offerings of the segment
- Distribution system for delivering the offerings to the users
- Venue (location) where users typically experience the offerings
- Technology (hardware and software) needed to experience the offerings
- Extent to which the segment offerings use video and sound
- Extent to which the offerings are interactive
- Dominant business model that generates revenue for those businesses in the segment

Producers will be most interested in this appendix because they are usually responsible for determining the products to develop, with whom to publish and distribute, the kind of agreement to negotiate, the time to release a product, and the cross-marketing opportunities to pursue.

Appendix C examines the multimedia studio. This appendix includes sample organizational charts—both administrative and functional, with job descriptions—including each position's responsibilities, authorities, and accountabilities. Producers, directors, and writers should read this appendix, but the producer and director who manage all of the resources employed in development should take particular interest.

The Web Site: www.abacon.com/elin

The companion web site contains additional examples, sample documents, and downloadable templates. There is a syllabus for a course that can be taught using this book, which includes lecture notes and assignments. The sample documents include development contracts, letters of intent, budgets, database layouts, approval forms, change orders, top level designs, functional specifications, and bug-tracking forms. The web site includes links to product demos and samples that illustrate concepts described in the text and to other important multimedia sites.

Acknowledgments

While writing this book over the past year, I got help, encouragement, and constructive criticism from many people whom I'd like to thank and acknowledge here. First of all, my gratitude goes to my editor, Karon Bowers, who championed this book at Allyn and Bacon, and to her able assistants Jennifer Becker and Scout Reilly, who held my hand through the process.

My sincere gratitude goes to those who reviewed the book in progress. They will see in the results that I honored their suggestions. Thanks to David Donnelly, University of Houston; Bob Hoffman, San Diego State University; Brant Houston, University of Missouri; Ed Lamoureux, Bradley University; John Newhagen, University of Maryland; Brian Ott, Colorado State University; and Bill Siska, University of Utah.

Several colleagues at the S. I. Newhouse School of Public Communications at Syracuse University read and critiqued the manuscript and gave me valuable content and structural advice. Professors Joan Deppa, Richard Breyer, and Peter Moller, all experienced authors, made special effort to keep me on course. Professor Breyer, the chair of my department, also took care to lighten my course load during the critical final months. Professor Stephen Masiclat spent a great deal of time guiding my research and directing me toward seminal work by others in the field. Graphics majors Eric Koby and Daniel Adler created all of the diagrams, icons, and tables in the book under Stephen's art direction. Research assistant Leigh Todd Budgen gathered and synthesized a mountain of information on several topics included in the book. Arlayne Searle was always cheerfully available to help with last minute printing, shipping, and other chores. Special thanks go to Dean David Rubin, who encouraged me to write this book, even though he knew I was wrong when I pointed at my head and said, "It's all up here."

Professor Philip Doughty of the School of Education at Syracuse University and Dr. Sylvia R. Smith of Mosaic Organizational Performance Group reviewed and helped me polish the chapter on designing for educational and instructional purposes. Sylvia was kind enough to contribute a case study.

Many industry people lent a hand when I asked for it. Very early on, Kevin Gillespie, Tom Zahorik, John Sutyak, and Joe Gammal of Hasbro Interactive showed strong support for the book and provided their ideas and critique. Hasbro Interactive graciously provided sample documents, pictures, and diagrams used in the book. J. Dianne Brinson and Mark F. Radcliffe contributed the entire chapter on the development agreement, reprinted in this book with minor editing, from their book *Multimedia Law and Business Handbook.*

Other support came from Alex Davis, Tom Erlewine, and Dan Krivicich of Electronic Vision; Michel Kripilani and Susan Weyer of Presto Studios; and Louis Castle and Aaron Cohen of Westwood Studios. They all provided anecdotes and information, as well as images from their products. Paul Symczak and Janis Manning of GTE, Margaret Adamic of Walt Disney Enterprises, and Shawna Toussaint of The Learning Company cleared rights to images used in the book.

My students played a major role by creating the need for the book and then by contributing material, ideas, and feedback. Special thanks go to Christopher Liston and Rebecca Treacy-Lenda, whose CD-ROM project on cancer appears throughout the book and in the appendix. Thanks also to Alethia McCullough and Kate Leonard, who contributed images from their class project on HIV. My Fall 1999 class read the manuscript as their required text and provided a steady stream of feedback that helped me fine-tune it in the final months. Thank you, Aline Al Rayes, James Biddle, Sylvia Borenstein, Arul Chib, Hillary Cutter, Andrea Goodrich, Katherine Gregory, Mohan Kumar, Kevin Lappin, Nina O'Brien, Matt Pothier, Lindsay Rowan, Scott Schilling, Rohini Tulsian, and James VerHague.

Of all these wonderful people, none were more nurturing than my wife, Kathryn Benson. Thank you, love, for your support, encouragement, and confidence in me.

Design

Multimedia and the

People Who Make It

In this chapter, you will learn about

- The definition of multimedia
- The interactive nature of multimedia
- The multimedia audience
- The multimedia designer
- The roles of the producer, director, and writer

The first step in understanding multimedia (and the rest of this book) is to define it and to differentiate it from linear media, such as television and film. There are four characteristics of multimedia that set it apart from other media: it is interactive, it is personal, it is digital, and it utilizes a computer. These characteristics cause the process of design and development to be very different from and far more complex than the process for most other media.

This chapter explores the audience for multimedia and redefines it as users, rather than viewers—an idea that engenders profound new challenges as we design multimedia experiences.

Finally, the chapter studies the people who make multimedia applications and bullets the special talents, skills, and gifts they must have to do their jobs properly. It looks carefully at the producer, director, writer, and interactive designer and examines their roles in the design and development of multimedia.

Multimedia Defined

Scholars and professionals, not to mention the general public, struggle with the definition of multimedia. Schweir and Misanchuk (1993), describing interactive multimedia instruction, say it is, by its very nature, invertebrate: "You poke it, and it slithers away." And multimedia for instructional purposes is just one of many incarnations of what is stowed under the same umbrella term of *multimedia*. There are the Internet, CD-ROM products of all stripes, kiosks, and console games. Many people experience all of these, three of them right at home. What is striking is that there appears to be, at first blush, more differences between these multimedia applications than similarities.

The Internet offers an online experience that takes the Web surfer anywhere in the world, at any time, for information, communication, commerce, community, and entertainment. Although bandwidth and certain technical hurdles *currently* limit the sensory experience, for the most part, to text, still graphics, audio, limited animation, and even more limited video, the Internet does provide access to what seems like an unlimited amount of data. CD-ROMs, on the other hand, provide an offline experience that limits access to the data stored on a 650-megabyte disc (although the DVD holds significantly more, and there are hybrid discs that allow the user to access the Internet concurrently). However, the sensory experience they provide is richer. Audio, video, and animation are robust, and interactivity is rarely affected by the latency problems endemic on the Internet.

Does the user's experience make a difference? Can experiences as different as a database search through Lexis-Nexis for magazine articles on 17th century French poetry, using the kiosk at the Loews Hotel on Lexington Avenue to find a good sushi restaurant, and spending 40 hours with the computer game *Myst* all be multimedia?

The Internet is a communications medium. There is a race to discover exactly how to turn it into a revenue source, and Internet firms are exploring advertising, subscriptions, and e-commerce schemes. CD-ROMs are retail products. Software publishers behave just like book and music publishers, which shrink-wrap their products and stock them in stores. Consumers buy CD-ROMs, and the differences between retail and wholesale and between wholesale and development costs provide revenue for all concerned. Does the business model make a difference? Are the e-commerce site www.Amazon.com, the public relations/marketing site www.Chrysler.com, the educational retail CD-ROM *Mavis Beacon Teaches Typing*, and the subscription CD-ROM *Launch* all multimedia?

In common, everyday language today, the answer is yes. This is true largely because all these applications share certain characteristics that are generally accepted as defining multimedia.

Tony Feldman, in his book *An Introduction to Digital Media*, arrives at this definition: "Multimedia is the seamless integration of data, text, sound, and images of all kinds with a single, digital information environment" (1997, p. 24). That definition falls just short of one that is useful for the purposes of this book. It is *interactivity* that characterizes multimedia as we know it today and which characterizes all of the experiences mentioned above. So add this phrase to the end of Feldman's definition: "which can be accessed interactively by the user."

We have had multimedia in linear, non-computer-based forms for quite some time. Several years ago, I attended a showing of *The General,* a silent film starring Buster Keaton as a Civil War hero who foils a Confederate plan to penetrate Union lines. The film was shown in the La Paloma Theater in Encinitas, California, which had been built in 1923, just prior to the sound era. In those days, theaters featured an orchestra pit in front of the stage. Film distributors sent sheet music with the film prints so local musicians could play the score for the film in real time. They also sent instructions for a sound maker—what we call a Foley artist today—to add sound effects such as thunder and gun shots in sync with actions on the screen. Filmmakers often added text frames within the body of the film to reveal key story points, though *The General* was so well crafted it didn't need any.

The General was a multimedia event. While the picture ran, a 27-piece orchestra located right in front of the audience played the original music composed for the film. Two sound effects creators were off to one side, banging hammers against sheets of metal, slamming doors, and, yes, clomping coconut shells against hardened soil in a wooden box. It was wonderful. I remember suspending all my conscious thoughts and being swept away by the story on the screen and the mood of the music.

On another occasion, I attended a multimedia presentation sponsored by a major automobile manufacturer for its dealers. In a cavernous ballroom, the dealers and their spouses were treated to a magnificent feast served by attractive young waiters and waitresses. The place was festooned with bunting and balloons. Full-size model cars were suspended from the ceiling in a way that made them look like they were floating. Spotlights roamed the room Hollywood-style. Several bands played simultaneously at opposite corners of the room. One entire wall of the room was a mosaic of screens; on the opposite side of the room, a battery of slide, movie, and laser projectors stood waiting. During the meal, there were several speeches and awards presentations, most greeted with polite applause and the constant din of silverware clinking against china.

When the multimedia show started, it was breathtaking. Suddenly, the room was immersed in perfectly synchronized music, lasers, and simulated fireworks that turned out to be colored streamers. The waiters and waitresses were suddenly dancers and singers. The slide and movie projectors threw their light across a hundred yards of darkness and painted that huge wall of screens with images that moved, dissolved, blended, and seemed to explode off the screen. 3-D computer-generated graphics tumbled on the screens to introduce the new model year while real cars paraded onto the ballroom floor. The dealers were pumped—standing and applauding wildly. The show was a phenomenal success. Even I got excited.

Those two shows are good examples of what was once thought of as multimedia. They featured sound, picture, text, and graphics, usually presented to a large audience in some linear, synchronized manner. Today, multimedia still employs sound, picture, and graphics, but it is distinguished by four characteristics. In common use today, the word *multimedia* refers to experiences that are interactive, personal, and computer-based. Multimedia is now digital, not analog or live media as in the two examples. These attributes are the "drivers," the main influences, for the design of multimedia. The producer, director, and writer must understand how these characteristics bias the design of multimedia applications. Throughout this book, I use the term *multimedia* to refer to interactive, computer-based products that are rich with sound, pictures, and text and that are commonly distributed on CD-ROM, though the principles discussed in this book apply well to other product forms, such as broadband interactive television and the Internet.

Multimedia Is Interactive

One of the biggest leaps—especially for linear thinkers such as filmmakers, story-tellers, authors, and even musicians—is this idea of interactivity. I teach multimedia development to college students who are majoring in television and film. They struggle with this notion of interactivity because they are taught in every other class how to lead a viewer around by the nose. "You have to grab them in the first scene." "You have to build and reveal character from scene to scene." "Do not have any action or dialogue that does not drive the story forward." In interactive multimedia, there may be no "first" scene, there may be no progression of scenes, and there may be no "forward" motion to worry about. When designing linear media (even linear *multi*media), the designer assumes and maintains control of the viewers, who become passive receptors of the message. When designing interactive media, the whole idea is to turn control over to the viewers and cause them to become engaged and active participants. Mark Dillon, head of Internet services at GTE and a multimedia pioneer, used to refer to this as designing a product with which the user can carry on a dialogue.

The Audience Redefined

The first step over this conceptual speed bump is to redefine the audience. Multimedia does not have *viewers*, it has *users*. If the multimedia application is a game, it has *players*. The word *viewers* suggests passive onlookers who expect the presenter to control their experience. Viewers *want* someone to control their experience because a hearty portion of their delight comes from the surprises the storyteller presents them with. I had no idea the waitress pouring my coffee during the car extravaganza would suddenly start belting out a song and dancing down the aisle. It was marvelous! What kind of movie experience would an audience have if the filmmaker didn't shock it with unexpected action? The phone rings, parents come home early, a car blows up, an old lover shows up at the door, the newborn is a girl, the volcano erupts. Sometimes these events are predictable based on previous scenes, but they are still delightful. Viewers thrive on the scenes that reward their story sleuthing and anticipation. It's what motivates them to continue watching.

Users, on the other hand, are motivated by something else altogether. Users are active, goal-oriented participants who want to control their own experience. They expect the interactive multimedia designers to provide them with the means to achieve their goals. Users take delight in their experience when it is clear that the designer has anticipated all those things they may want to do and has provided them with the means to do it.

What Users Want

Users want control. The challenge of multimedia, then, is to establish a dialogue with users, which enables them to access the domain knowledge of the multimedia application in an active, self-paced, self-guided manner. The language chosen must be easily learned by users—so easily that users master it after a short time. Donald A. Norman, in his book *The Psychology of Everyday Things,* discusses design principles that apply to multimedia applications as well as everyday things. Among his most important directions are to "make it easy to determine what actions are possible at any moment" and to "make things visible, including the conceptual model of the system, the alternative actions, and the results of actions" (1988, p. 188). With some imagination, you can see these are things we all try to do when we engage other people in conversation. We afford them a chance to respond by letting them know what to respond to, what responses are appropriate, and how we may respond to *their* actions. When we provide others with what Norman calls affordances, they have control of their experience.

A good example of this concept from the world around us is the automobile. Its purpose is to provide us with personal transportation. The car, therefore, must be capable of moving forward and backward and to turn right and left under the control of the driver. These are *features* that the car must have to fulfill its purpose of providing *personal* transportation. The dashboard, the controls, and the seats are designed by correctly anticipating everything the driver may want or need while using the car. The gauges and dials are meant to provide the driver with a view to the inner workings of the car. They are placed where the driver would most naturally look to find them. The steering wheel, pedals, and gearshift are designed to give the driver control over the car's behavior. They are placed where the driver would most likely reach for them, and they are shaped in ways that communicate how they operate. The seat positions the driver so he or she can see and reach everything provided to control his or her experience. The dashboard and the control devices—the interface—provide the driver with *functional control.* All cars perform the same basic purpose and, except for expensive bells and whistles on some models, have the same dashboard and controls. The biggest difference from one car to the next is the aesthetic presentation, what you could call the *look and feel,* of the cockpit.

Unlike automobiles, multimedia applications differ, one from the next, in terms of content, features, functional control, look and feel, and structure. These are terms we'll get into very deeply in a few pages. The inner workings of multimedia applications are unique, and as a result the dashboard—or *interface*—is customized for every product. Every multimedia product requires a different collection of gauges and dials to provide the user with a view of its inner workings. Applications require a custom set of devices to provide the user with control over the behavior of the product. Nearly every product has a "look and feel" designed specifically to set it apart from others. When you design a car, you know you need to include a steering wheel, gas pedal, brake, speedometer, gas gauge, and so on. When you first set out to design a multimedia product, you can't be sure what you may need to include. You have to invent a new language, a new interface, to establish the dialogue.

The Multimedia Designer

The multimedia designer is responsible for establishing contact between the user and the application. Multimedia projects originate at all kinds of shops—from two-person operations to medium-sized studios to huge corporations. Many multimedia products are developed at pint-sized operations affectionately called "two guys with a Mac," referring to the Macintosh computer they use to develop their applications. There are probably thousands of these operations scattered all over the world—most, if not all, of them creating products on a work-for-hire basis for outside clients. There are hundreds of studios employing 10 to 25 people, and under 100 studios employing 50 to 100. These small-to medium-sized studios are often more entrepreneurial. They may create products for clients on a work-for-hire basis but also develop their own properties, meaning they invest their own resources and money to create products that they wholly own. Large corporations such as Sega, Sony, Disney, Fox, Mattel, and Hasbro own intellectual property and publish interactive multimedia consumer products featuring their brands. Many corporations create multimedia applications for training, marketing, and public relations. There are companies that specialize in publishing educational applications for both home and school. Some of these companies produce their products internally, and others engage outside developers—such as the medium-sized studios or the tiny ones mentioned above.

Within these settings, a wide assortment of professionals are responsible for designing multimedia products. Their titles, backgrounds, qualifications, focuses, strengths, experiences, and sensibilities vary. Depending on the size, the core business, and the product specialty of the company, application design may be the responsibility of the producer, the instructional designer, the writer, the creative director, the graphic designer, the game designer, or the lead programmer. Some have produced, written, or directed in other media, such as print publishing, music, film, TV, or computer software. Some have spent years earning degrees in instructional design, man–machine interface design, computer science, or programming. Others have taken crash courses in Macromedia Director, Authorware, or other off-the-shelf authoring tools. Many have simply immersed themselves in the multimedia culture.

Design Is a Process

Although one person may be the central figure in the design of a multimedia product, and may even have "Interactive Designer" emblazoned on a business card, one person can rarely do the whole job alone. The design of multimedia products is influenced by marketing, pedagogical, technical, aesthetic, graphic, legal, and business forces. The designer must know, understand, and respect these forces while sculpting a design from a virtual lump of clay. In actual practice, interactive design is an iterative *process* involving a team that includes the producer, director, writer, various designers, technical consultant, marketing director, content experts, and the client. When a company I managed produced animated storybook products for Disney Interactive, there were often 8 to 10 people in a room at DI having conference calls with our producer, director, and writer working through design issues. That may seem excessive, but the design would not have been fine-tuned properly if we had been on the phone with only one of them.

During the design phase, other members of the team lend their special expertise to the design. The degreed instructional designer, for example, is a valued expert who plays an important role in the design of educational products. The software engineer acts as the technical consultant, providing an often sobering view of the programming challenge. The art director, sound designer, and marketing manager all add their individual sensibilities, talents, and knowledge to the design process.

A Case Study

A good example of this creative process comes from Tom Erlewine, then art director at Electronic Vision, a multimedia studio in Athens, Ohio. Electronic Vision teamed up with Ohio University to produce an educational CD-ROM called *How to Make Your Movie: An Interactive Film School*. The web site provides a link to the makers of this CD-ROM. Pictures from this product are used as examples in this book. In response to a query about their creative process, Erlewine described the following:

> *How to Make Your Movie* was created by a tightly woven team. Three principal players contributed to the design of the program and its interactivity. Here are the titles and how we interacted in the process:
>
> Rajko Grlić was the director and author. Rajko wrote the content of the program and conceived its format. The idea of "breaking into" a run-down school building to

go through the film professor's notes is all his. Rajko knew nothing about multimedia at the outset and still knows very little. He would describe an interaction as if he were directing a scene.

FIGURE 1.1

Tom Erlewine, Rajko Grlić, and executive producer Dan Krivicich (left to right) at work on the CD-ROM *How to Make Your Movie: An Interactive Film School.* Multimedia design and development are a team effort and an iterative process.

Tom Erlewine was the art director and program designer. Tom designed the majority of the graphics for the project and oversaw all the graphics to maintain a unified feel throughout. As program designer, he worked closely with Rajko both to understand what was intended and to challenge each part of the program from a user's viewpoint. Ideas would be talked out, sketched out, and even argued about until best solutions were found. Following Rajko's concept of a photographic "noncomputer" interface, Tom designed interactions that delivered the technology without abandoning the wrinkled-paper look.

Several programmers were tried on the team at the outset, but their skills did not produce the desired results. In working with these programmers, Tom learned the capabilities of the authoring system, although he is not a programmer himself. In his role of program designer, this was necessary in order for him to serve as the liaison between the abstract wishes of the author and the concrete necessities of the programmer.

Finally, Daric Christian joined the team as programmer and assistant art director. He contributed the required programming skills plus much more: He is also an accomplished photographer and PhotoShop artist. This hybrid of skills made Daric ideal for the project. What Tom and Rajko had established as the intent of each interaction would then gain from Daric's input. Sometimes ideas had to be adapted to the realities of programming, and sometimes Daric's insights would spark revisions to the ideas. At these times, all three would challenge the idea until the best working plan was arrived at. (Erlewine, personal communication, January 28, 1999)

The Roles of the Producer, Director, and Writer

The producer, director, and writer are key, central figures in the design and development of multimedia. These are their roles in the process:

The Producer

 In a nutshell, the producer, who may also be called the project manager, is focused on the *business* of development. The producer manages time, money, people, and resources. At many companies, but not all, the producer is responsible for the success of the entire product, even its packaging, marketing, and how and when it gets reviewed by the press. The producer may be responsible for clearing rights; negotiating contracts with publishers, talent, and subcontractors; licensing new software; buying equipment; hiring or terminating staff; contact with clients; and reporting up to a board of directors. On the other end of the spectrum, the producer may find himself or herself personally delivering a "gold master candidate" to the airport at 2:00 A.M. on a Saturday.

When the producer carries that load, success is measured in four ways. The product itself must (1) be of commercial quality, (2) be completed on time and within budget, and (3) do well on the market. Finally, (4) the producer must manage the development *process* properly, resulting in a strong relationship with both the client and the development team. There are many cases in which products are of a high commercial quality but are over budget or late to market, which affects their performance in the market. There are many instances in which the product is of good quality, on time, on budget, and sells well but the development process was mismanaged. The client relationship is left in a shambles or the development team is a quivering blob of protoplasm after spending countless nights and weekends working to meet poorly conceived development goals.

These responsibilities are not unlike those of film producers, but the multimedia producer must have many more skills to do the job well. The multimedia producer must know

- The multimedia business—who the players are and how they make their money
- Multimedia products—what's been done, what was successful and why, and what was not successful and why not

- Legal issues—contracts, copyright law, First Amendment issues, licensing, sub-contracting work, work-for-hire and freelance law, and many other terms and conditions

- The development phases—the deliverables, milestones, and "prize" for each of the four phases

- The production process—every task, the order in which they are completed, and by whom

- Development planning—determining the critical path, scheduling of resources, having backup and contingency plans

- Interactive design—what is a good design, what features are needed for a competitive or effective product, how the design affects schedule and budget

- Art, animation, video, and sound production—who does them, how long things take, and how much things cost

- The technology—the hardware platforms, software, what's possible, what's not

- Budgeting—determine the staff and resources needed to complete every task, use the burdened rate, and develop a budget

- Record keeping—creating and maintaining the paper trail, including all memos, work orders, change orders, additional cost estimates, client approvals, and status reports

- Progress tracking—on a daily or weekly basis, measure progress versus cost. Generate reports and modify development plan or product design to fit budget

- Focus testing—obtain and process criticism and implement modifications to enhance the product

- Quality assurance—regression testing and bug fixing prior to product release

- Promotion and marketing—get the product in front of the public with the best possible word of mouth, press, reviews, and promotional tie-ins

The producer is an organized, detail-oriented, forward-looking leader. The producer must be in front of the development at all times, anticipating every development task and possible glitch. The producer is the steady hand that manages the business process with such assuredness that the creative and technical processes flourish.

The Director

The director, who is very often the interactive designer, is responsible for establishing, articulating, and supervising the creative vision of the product. This role is very similar to the role of the director in filmmaking. Not too long ago, multimedia *producers* were responsible for the creative direction of the product in addition to all of the day-to-day business activity—a huge job all by itself. Borrowing some wisdom and experience from the film industry, many companies now divide the roles. This will likely be the prevalent trend from now on, particularly as computers and television converge and the line between content developed for one and content developed for the other blurs.

The director is responsible for interpreting the interactive, graphic, and sound design of the product. The director is "on the set" during the entire development process. On a day-to-day basis, he or she directs the activities of the development staff in such a way that all the components are created at the proper time and in the proper manner so they form the intended product. The director must know not only what needs to be created—such as discrete graphic elements, animated scenes, sound effects, and video clips—but also *how* to create them. Among the many skills and knowledge a director must have are

- Multimedia products—what's been done, what was successful and why, what was not successful and why not, what production techniques were used
- The development process—every task, the order in which they are completed, by whom, and how
- Interactive design—what is a good design, what features are needed for a competitive product, what the design implications are in terms of graphics, sounds, and software
- A sense of aesthetics—a knowledge of graphic design, style, layout, color, texture, and line
- Art, animation, video, and sound development—who does it, how long things take, and how all the pieces come together when they're completed
- 2-D and 3-D animation development and computerized ink and paint systems.
- Lighting, blue screen, and chromakey techniques for video
- Voice and sound recording and Foley and needle drop sound effects
- Music composing, arranging, mixing, and development
- Editing sound and picture
- The technology—the platforms, their performance, what's possible, what's not
- The ability to plan and execute—to instruct, nurture, and direct the development staff so each member's efforts contribute directly to the successful completion of the product

The Writer

The multimedia writer writes for many audiences. When writing for the Internet, the writer usually creates content that will be consumed by the public, or an external audience. The document *is* the product, and there are a number of techniques and styles that have become standard practice for the Internet writer. This book does not discuss writing for the Internet, but it does recommend a couple of books at the end of this chapter for the Internet writer.

Throughout CD-ROM development, the writer is responsible for generating a number of key documents for an internal audience, as well as some that accompany the product and others that are included within the product. These documents run the gamut from creative proposals, which are designed to generate interest in the product, to technical software specifications to "release notes" that accompany CD-ROM "burns" to the client. Some documents resemble those common in film and television. The concept document, for example, includes many of the elements of the film proposal, such as audience, genre, subject, and market need. It is targeted at the same readership—executives, clients, marketing and sales people, and others who can green-light the next phase. The top-level design is analogous to the film treatment. It describes the product in greater detail, further developing the story, the characters, the look and feel, and the product's most compelling features. Other documents are unique in structure and content. The functional specification, for instance, is a combination script (in the movie sense) and technical definition (in the software development sense).

Among the documents the writer creates are

- Concept document or product proposal
- Top-level design
- Functional specification
- Needs analysis and evaluation report (for educational products)
- Learning objectives (for educational products)
- Game design
- Narration and dialogue scripts
- Script questions for focus tests
- Text that appears in the product itself
- Release notes
- Copy for packaging
- Copy for manual and/or liner notes included with product
- "Readme" files

At some studios, the writer is the interactive designer; at others, the writer fleshes out and fills in many of the interactive design details. Either way, the writer is always a key member of the development team. Writing begins when the product is just a glimmer in someone's eye and ends when the product is finally in the class-room, or shrink-wrapped and on the retail shelves. This involvement contrasts sharply with the role the writer plays in film and television. The film writer's in-volvement usually ends when the screenplay has gone through its final draft and preproduction is about to begin. At that point, the director assumes creative control of the production and there is usually very little additional writing. This is one reason many film writers have gravitated toward multimedia—they get to stay involved.

Another reason is that multimedia demands many of the skills film and television writers have. These skills include

- A creative flair
- A sense of humor
- The ability to listen to and interpret ideas from colleagues
- The ability to create believable characters
- The ability to write dialogue
- The ability to describe settings, locations, and action
- The ability to organize concepts and create structure
- A willingness to revise and modify
- Flexibility—the ability to write in many different styles depending on audience, genre, subject, and purpose

The multimedia writer must also know

- Multimedia products—what's been done, what was successful and why, and what was not successful and why not
- How to write the specific documents required for multimedia development
- The development process—what documents are needed, by whom, and when
- Interactive design—what is a good design, what features are needed for a competitive product, and how to describe them. The vocabulary of multimedia.
- Art, animation, video, and sound development—what's possible, what does it look like, and how it can be used to tell the story
- The technology—the platforms, their performance, what's possible, what's not, and how to describe it
- Computer software—terminology, general capabilities, and what information is useful to the software engineers

Chapter Summary

The term *multimedia* has taken on new meaning over the past several years. Implicit in the term is an application, product, or experience featuring text, graphics, animation, video, and sound displayed on a personal computer to a user. The experience is interactive, which means the user takes control of the event and becomes not a passive onlooker but an active participant.

This puts new demands on the people who design and develop multimedia. Designers must anticipate what the user may want and then provide the means for the user to have that experience. They must create a product with which the user can carry on a dialogue. Unlike in many other media, these facts determine that the design and development process of multimedia is a collaborative team effort, involving experts in management, direction, writing, interactive design, game design, instructional design, art, sound, video, programming, marketing, and legal issues. Taking the lead of this team is the producer, who must manage the business; the director, who keeps and directs the creative vision; and the writer, who chronicles the design.

Recommended Reading

Feldman, Tony. *An Introduction to Digital Media.* Routledge: London, 1997.

Norman, Donald A. *The Psychology of Everyday Things.* Basic Books: New York, 1988.

Sammons, Martha C. *The Internet Writer's Handbook.* Allyn and Bacon: Boston, 1999.

Schwier, Richard A., and Misanchuk, Earl R. *Interactive Multimedia Instruction,* Educational Technology Publications: Englewood Cliffs, 1993.

Principles of
Interactive Design

In this chapter, you will learn about

- The vocabulary of interactive design
- The notion of a multimedia application as a system
- The components of interactive design: content, features, controls, look and feel, and structure
- The user interface
- The metaphor

In this chapter, you are introduced to the main characteristic that distinguishes multimedia from other media: interactivity. After reading this chapter, you should buy, borrow, or download as many multimedia products as possible. Study them. Compare what you experience with these applications with the interactive design principles you discover in this chapter and in the recommended readings you'll find at the end of this chapter.

The interactive design concepts discussed in this chapter are *general* concepts—applicable to a wide variety of multimedia applications. In subsequent chapters, interactive design concepts that are genre or end-user specific are presented.

By the end of this chapter, you should understand that multimedia applications are made up of five components: content, features, structure, functional control, and look and feel. Together, these components make up a media *system,* rather than a message *sequence,* as in linear media. Designing for this medium means learning several new skills, including the ability to consider these five multimedia components simultaneously and to integrate them into one comprehensive design. Of these components, *structure* is the most important to learn and conceptually the most difficult to master.

Interactive Vocabulary

To begin, it is necessary to learn some concepts and terms. These are not presented alphabetically, but rather in an order that allows you to build a high-level, conceptual understanding of interactivity. These terms are used throughout this chapter and the book.

Hypertext.   The term *hypertext* is attributed to Ted Nelson (1974), a computer visionary who conceived of a vast, interconnected database of all the world's knowledge. He called this concept Xanadu. In Nelson's concept, documents in an enormous, textual database would be linked to each other by contextual and temporal associations, making it possible for users to explore the entire virtual library effortlessly. Today, the term refers to chunks of content made up primarily of text and to the embedded command that is attached to a word or phrase in that content. The embedded command allows the user to link (or branch) to another, related chunk of content located somewhere else. *Hypertext*, then, is one word that describes both the content and the interactivity resident in an electronically stored document.

Hypermedia.   *Hypermedia* describes the same experience as *hypertext*, but it is used when the linked elements are made up of media other than text, such as sounds, pictures, and graphics.

Link.   Link is used as both a noun and a verb. When two digitally stored documents or chunks of data are connected, the connection is called a link. Jakob Nielsen (1990) says links are "frequently associated with the specific parts of the nodes (chunks of data) they connect, rather than the nodes as a whole" (p. 2).

When a user actively moves from one chunk of data to another, he or she links. The document from which the user links is called the "anchor node," and the document the user links to is called the "destination node."

The word *branching* is often used instead of *linking*, especially to describe a connection between whole nodes, rather than between specific words or text in a node. The term *branching* is used most often when referring to connections made between nodes in an offline environment, such as within the confines of a single CD-ROM. The term *link* is more often associated with connections made between nodes in an online environment, as between two URLs on the World Wide Web.

Nodes.   The term *nodes* was first used to refer to the linked documents in a hypertext environment. Now that interactive multimedia has evolved to include more than linked documents—not only does the content include more than text, but also the interactivity includes more than links—*nodes* is used to apply to chunks of both content and software.

Interactive and Linear Nodes.   Nodes can be either *linear* or *interactive*. Users may access a *linear* node and not be required to interact. For example, they may simply link to a document or an image or watch a movie clip in a ballistic, or non-interruptible, way. Or they may access an *interactive* node, where they may be required to initiate some action or respond to some prompt from the application before anything else happens. Sometimes a node is referred to as a *screen* or a *page*. However, these terms suggest that a node is a static and largely graphic or textual presentation, which it is not. Software event nodes are not graphic in nature.

Users starting an application may access an interactive node where they are prompted to sign in. Upon hitting the return key, a *software event* is initiated. The software compares each user's entry to names of previous users stored in a database. If there is a match, the code branches the user to another interactive node, where the application prompts, "Do you wish to continue your previous session?" If there is no match, the code branches the user to a *linear node* that shows an introduction. The software event took place in the blink of an eye, out of sight, but it determined for each user what would happen next.

Examples of typical interactive and linear nodes include

- Bumpers—usually a linear node showing the company logo when a product is first started. This experience is very similar to the bumpers at the beginnings of films

- Title—a linear node featuring the title sequence of the product

- Sign-on—an interactive node where the users type in their names

- Introduction—a linear node where a narrator or on-screen guide introduces users to the product

- Main menu—an interactive node providing users with a jumping-off point for the rest of the product; similar to the homepage of a web site

- Submenu—another menu somewhere else in the product

- Search—an interactive node that allows users to type a keyword; the software then searches the content database for references to that word

- Activity—a node that may include interactive toys, such as a virtual coloring book for children

- Level—an interactive node in a game where the user must overcome some obstacle, solve a puzzle, or defeat an enemy to advance to the next level

- Score—a linear node that displays the top 10 scores achieved by previous players of a game

- Reward—a linear node that shows, for instance, a movie clip of a ship exploding and sinking. This is your reward for successfully finding your opponents' destroyer with your torpedo

Branching.   Users move from one node to another by branching. Branching may be initiated by the user or by the application software. A user who decides to access another node in the product by clicking on a button or a hyperlink branches in a deliberate, conscious way. At other times, the product may be programmed to branch the user to another node automatically after the program displays something to the user. At the start of many products, for instance, there is a bumper screen displaying the logos of the companies that developed the product, followed by the product's title screen, followed by the main menu screen. Children's animated storybook products often follow this sequence. The product automatically branches the user from one of these nodes to the next after a certain amount of time or after an animation or graphic plays. However—and again, this is pretty commonplace—if the user clicks his or her mouse at any time, the program branches to the next node immediately.

Node Map.   A node map—also called a flow diagram—is a graphical representation of the nodes and how they are linked to each other. It is a road map showing every place the user can go and the path to get there. A detailed node map can look very complex, especially if all events and possible paths are included.

Node maps are terrific, indispensable graphic tools for the interactive designer. The designer can see in an instant if he or she has provided the user with the means to reach and exit every node. There are several examples in this book—a simple one a little later in this chapter.

Navigation.   Early interactive designers recognized that users quickly "lost their way" when linking from one document to another, especially in a hypertext-rich environment, and they began pondering the problem of navigation. The term *navigation,* of course, refers to "finding your way." The problem of navigating through a large and complex, interconnected collection of nodes is more difficult to solve when the links are between Web pages or databases on the Internet. This is because the various destination nodes are linked not under the watchful eye of a single designer, but by many designers. In fact, the Internet is the result of interactive design by a committee now numbering in the millions.

The designer of a self-contained multimedia CD-ROM application can solve the problem in a number of ways because he or she has complete control of the structure, the look and feel, and, very importantly, the modes of navigation through the product.

There are three modes of navigation commonly designed in multimedia products:

■ *The Browse Mode* allows the user complete freedom to branch everywhere to explore the product. The Internet and information retrieval systems behave this way. The popular game *Myst* is designed with this type of navigation.

■ *The Customization Mode* allows users to provide information about themselves or parameters about their interests; the application then narrows their experience, sets certain parameters, or links them to appropriate nodes. Many self-help, reference, and information products are designed this way. Games that allow users to indicate what level of play they want—easy, medium, or hard—behave this way. A Web browser affords this customization.

■ *The Guided Tour Mode* gives the user interactive experiences in a linear, predetermined order. Vannevar Bush first conceived this idea in 1945, when he developed the idea for what he called the Memex system. Though never built, the system was an accurate premonition of the hypertext environment that evolved over the next 50 years. Nodes of animated storybooks are arranged in a linear way, even though each node has interactive events within it. Many of the most popular games—especially those in which players advance through levels—are designed this way.

As you can tell, it is possible to design a product with one, two, or all three types of navigation.

Multimedia as a System

A novelist tells a story using words. A writer may ask himself, "How do I connect these words together in such a way that I create the most entertaining and meaningful experience for my reader?" A filmmaker tells the same story using pictures and sounds. She wonders, "How do I use camera, lighting, dialogue, music, and editing to create an engaging and moving tale for my audience?"

The multimedia designer creates an experience for users using text, pictures, graphics, audio, databases, computer software, and hyperlinks to other multimedia environments. The multimedia designer asks, "How do I organize and present all of this information so the user can control it? Should this be a game or a reference product? How will I use graphics, text, animation, video, sound effects, music, and narration to impart information? What should the buttons and icons look like and where should they be located on the screen? How will the overall experience of the user be rewarded?" The multimedia designer does not create a sequence of events, as the novelist and filmmaker do, but rather a functioning *system* of events and control, of action and reaction. Interestingly, the software written to cause a multimedia product to operate properly is often called an engine, further supporting this notion of a system.

Components of the System

The functioning multimedia system is made up of component parts, just like any machine or device. Even though many radically different types of applications are called multimedia, all have the same component parts: content, features, structure, functional controls, and look and feel. These will be discussed shortly. The nature of the component parts for a particular application is fixed (or at least heavily influenced) by various "drivers," or determinants, such as the application's venue, purpose, target user, subject, and genre. These drivers are not *part* of the system but play an enormously important role in the design of the system components.

Component Drivers

Drivers are forces that have a direct influence on the nature, or makeup, of the five basic components of a multimedia application.

■ *Target Users*—All multimedia products have a target, or intended, market— that group of users who are most interested in the subject matter and genre. There are products designed specifically for children, teens, and adults. Some are designed for very small, niche groups. More than any other consideration, the target user influences design decisions related to the components of the multimedia product.

■ *Venue*—Where and how a multimedia application will be used. Possible venues include CD-ROM on a personal computer, a web site on a personal computer, a console game played on a big-screen TV, a WebTV application on a home TV, or a CD-ROM-equipped kiosk at a museum. Each venue presents design challenges that will determine one or more of the components of the system.

■ *Purpose*—All products have a clearly defined purpose, or goal. Educational products have learning objectives, games are designed to entertain, while many web sites are designed for informational and promotional purposes, others for commerce. The purpose of the application will drive design decisions related to the components.

■ *Subjects*—All multimedia products are *about* something. They all have a *subject*. There are informational multimedia products about family planning, gardening, and horses; educational applications about geography, spelling, ancient history, and law; and entertainment products about Monopoly, Barbie, and sports.

■ *Genres*—All consumer multimedia products fall into one or more product categories, or *genres*. The genres are games, education, reference, information, and office utility. *Tonka Garage* is a best-selling game product for children about fixing, building, destroying, and racing cars. *Triple Play Plus Spanish* is an educational CD-ROM that teaches Spanish using voice recognition software. *TurboTax* is a best-selling office utility product that allows users to calculate and file their income tax returns.

There are other drivers that are more product specific. Client needs, budget, time line, and marketing issues (such as branding or licensing) are just a few. The designer must be aware of all of the drivers before and during the design of the application's basic components.

Multimedia Components

All multimedia products, regardless of user, venue, subject, or genre, are made up of the following components. These are the "moving parts" of the system. Some of them, like the engine of a car, are behind the scenes or under the hood. Others are clearly visible and give control of the system to the user.

■ *Content*—The body of knowledge, information, concepts, ideas, the story, or the game. In software terms, content is the database. If the subject of an application is horses, the content may consist of the history of all breeds, the story of the domestication of horses, famous thoroughbreds, and tips on the care of horses. Content is represented or displayed to the user in the form of text, pictures, graphics, animation, video, and sound.

■ *Features*—The special interactive characteristics or capabilities the product has. Conceptually (because technically, not very simple), the simplest example of a feature is a link. More complex examples are artificial intelligence, the ability to search a database, or the ability to print a screen. A feature in a product about horses may be a search engine that allows the user to specify characteristics he or she desires in a horse; the application then recommends a breed that most closely matches the user's preferences. Features are made possible by software programming.

■ *Structure*—How the content and the features are organized to create a working, interactive multimedia system. The structure determines how the content is divided up—usually into small, logically organized nodes—and how the features enable users to move from one node to another or from one central location to all others, or to otherwise interact with the content.

Taken together, content, features, and how they are structured make up the *multimedia application*—that part of the system that sits behind the screen, out of sight until the user chooses to access and use it.

■ *Functional Control*—The means by which a user actually controls the product (what the "dashboard" consists of and what controls are provided) and how the product responds to the user. Control is provided with virtual (onscreen) devices, such as buttons, pulldown menus, sliders, and hypertext links, and real (physical) devices, such as the mouse, the keyboard, and the joystick.

■ *Look and Feel*—How the entire title is presented graphically and with sound. There are countless artistic and stylistic ways to present any subject, and this concept could best be thought of as the thematic approach, to borrow a film term.

Taken together, functional controls and look and feel make up what is known as the *user interface*. The user interface is the perceptible part of the system—the visage with which users carry on the dialogue and control their experience.

The interactive designer must consider all of these components simultaneously while developing the overarching design of the product. These components are intricately linked: the nature of one often determines or affects the nature of the others. It is the designer's responsibility to mold the components together into a compelling and "do-able" interactive experience for the user.

Unfortunately, whatever you may know about the structure of linear media will be little use to you when designing multimedia. But there is good news: Of the components above, two are common to all other media. All media have content and, because we experience media through our senses, all media exhibit a look and feel, even when it consists only of sound or text. So you may be two fifths of an interactive designer already!

Even though the designer must consider each component as linked to and interdependent with the others, they are presented here serially. The best place to start is with the design of the components of the application—the content, features, and structure. Design what the product consists of and what the user can do with it. This exercise leads naturally to the determination of the user interface, which consists of the controls and the look and feel. But do not stop there. The process is iterative, meaning that the designer starts with certain design decisions, which then evolve as he or she makes others. Let us first get clear on what these components are and how they fit into the design puzzle.

Content

Content refers to the subject matter, body of knowledge, information, concepts, ideas, story, or game in the multimedia product. Content is displayed or represented to the user with images, text, sounds, animation, graphics, video, and data that make up the user's audio/video experience. Because these elements are stored digitally in one or another special *file* format, every discrete element is called an *asset*. A background graphic, a video clip, a sound effect, and a block of text are all assets.

Mammoth Micro Productions, of Golden, Colorado, designed and produced a CD-ROM game about Izzy, the mascot of the Olympic games held in Atlanta in 1996. The game is an animated adventure quest, but it also includes some historical and statistical information about past Olympic games and biographical stories about past Olympic medal winners. That's the *content*. The product's assets are hundreds of hand-drawn images, which include backgrounds, props, and characters, and more than 100 animated scenes and hundreds of photographs, video clips, and audio clips. The product contains thousands of assets. Most products do.

The Objective of the Application.   The most important determinant of the content of a multimedia product is the objective of the title and the needs of the users. Clearly, if the objective of a multimedia application is to teach seventh-grade mathematics, the content should consist of all those ideas and concepts that survive a needs analysis and meet educational standards. Then, the designer must acknowledge real-life constraints that limit the content.

Cost, Rights, and Disc Space. A huge constraint on the quantity and quality of content is cost. The designer can include only the content he or she can afford. All content—in the form of the assets that represent it—must be either created or acquired. Assets are created by artists, animators, videographers, writers, researchers, and photographers. Assets can be acquired from existing sources, typically through licensing arrangements. Labor and licensing are expensive.

Another constraint is intellectual property rights. The designer may not be able to acquire the rights to certain content. For the Olympic games product, Mammoth was unable to obtain the rights to use video of certain athletes who demanded too much money for the license to use their pictures.

A third constraint is disc space, or storage capacity. A CD-ROM can hold a little less than 650 megabytes of data, and every asset will take up some of that space. The double layer DVD-18 holds far more—17 gigabytes of data. Application software also takes up space. The more space available for an application, the more content (and its associated cost) the designer can use. This may or may not be a constraint for a web site. It depends on the client server space. A more important constraint for the content of a web site is bandwidth and individual asset file sizes.

Because content—its acquisition and development—is usually the most costly and time-consuming component of multimedia, consider it first when designing. If the development budget is known, it is possible to determine, at least generally, one of the five components immediately.

Create an Asset Breakdown. It is helpful to create an initial asset breakdown and to put it in a table, as in Table 2.1. As the design evolves, so does the list. As the designer develops the product's features and look and feel, more or fewer assets may be needed. Eventually, the producer will add columns to the list and break down the content even further, into individual assets. The list will eventually include all the pertinent information for all assets, including file names, file sizes, dates when created, and revisions.

The asset list in Table 2.1 is from the product *Tonka Search and Rescue*, produced by Media Station, Inc., of Ann Arbor, Michigan, for its client, Hasbro Interactive. Hasbro approached Media Station with a broad idea of what their product would be about and what content it should include. The Media Station producer estimated the necessary assets based on an analysis of the content of the proposed product. An experienced multimedia producer can study the quantity of assets to ascertain whether the proposed product is too big or complex for the proposed budget or schedule.

Table 2.1 Asset Breakdown	
Asset Type	**Amount**
Audio (narration)	42 minutes total (3 voice talent performing 7 voices)
Audio (sound effects)	25 effects (engines, brakes, squealing, etc.)
Audio (music)	Main theme, fanfares, victory tune—5 mins. total)
Animation (graphic)	25 scenes @ 10 secs. each
Video (archive)	None
Video (to be shot)	None
Text	3 new fonts for Print Shop
Graphics (backgrounds)	30 background screens
Graphics (sprites)	250 small sprite graphics for games
3-D objects	3-D vehicle database for game—14 different vehicles
Other graphics	50 license plates, 20 buildable objects, 9 newspapers and awards

Features

The term *features* refers to the specific *interactive* experiences or capabilities the product offers. Features directly affect the user's overall experience and determine how sophisticated and rich the interactive dialogue is. Features are not necessarily unique or new, and many have been in common use for quite some time. The basic features of a multimedia product are most often determined by its genre, rather than by its subject. For example, an educational product about horses is likely to have features different from those of a game about horses. When the goal or objective of the product is to provide information, it may have still other features. At your next opportunity, go the the web site. You will find some recommended multimedia products in a number of genres. See how the features differ from one to the next.

Examples of Features.   The hypertext link is the most commonly experienced feature. This feature enables the user to link to another node or to another location within the same node by clicking on text that has been embedded with software. The entire World Wide Web is based on the link, which can connect any URL to any other. Within many web sites and in most multimedia CD-ROM products, there are numerous other, more complex features. For example, web sites such as www.eBay.com and www.Amazon.com allow the user to purchase products or services. Credit card commmerce requires software far more complex than that required to establish a link.

In the product *Tonka Search and Rescue,* players may sign in at the beginning of the game by typing their names on an ID badge displayed on the screen. From that point on, while the game is being played, the current player's name shows up on various awards. The player may print these awards. This is a feature of the product, one that the target users—children age four and up—enjoy immensely. Another feature of this product is the ability to print and then manually construct paper toys.

A product rich in instructional and educational features is *How to Make Your Movie: An Interactive Film School,* produced jointly by Electronic Vision and Ohio University. This highly interactive product allows users to learn and practice lighting, shooting, and editing a film in a virtual studio. One of the many compelling features includes an exercise in a lighting studio, during which users may click on a light meter and move it around the room. As users maneuver the meter over the screen, the reading on the meter changes. As the reading changes, so does the suggested exposure of the shot.

FIGURE 2.1

In this activity from *How to Make Your Movie: An Interactive Film School,* the user can click on the light meter and move it around on the screen. When the camera aperture opens or closes to match the reading, the exposure changes.

The *Rand McNally TripMaker* enables users to find out how to get from one place to another by the shortest possible road route. The user types in the point of departure, such as Needham, Massachusetts, and the destination, such as Columbus, Ohio. The product calculates the best and fastest route and produces a map, a list of directions, and an estimate of the total driving time.

Determining Features. The designer determines which features to include in a product by evaluating the product objective and the users' needs. Educational products, for example, have learning objectives and adopt one of a number of teaching methods to achieve those objectives. The designer may include tutorials and stringently orchestrated modules through which users must traverse. Or the designer may provide an open, user-paced learning experience. Either way, the features are chosen with an eye toward creating an educational environment, usually with measurable results. Entertainment products, such as games, include features designed to make the game fun and stimulating, sometimes even addictive.

Features and Genres.   Table 2.2 identifies features typically associated with some popular multimedia genres. Study existing products and identify the outstanding features they have. Add them to the list. Invent your own and add them. If you come up with the "next big thing," you could have a hit on your hands!

Table 2.2 Features and Genres					
Features	Games/ Adult	Games/ Children's	Reference	Education	Office Utility
Multiplatform		Yes	Yes	Yes	Yes
Single or multiuser	Yes	Yes		Yes	
User sign-in	Yes	Yes		Yes	Yes
Customize world	Yes				
Personalize experience	Yes	Yes	Yes	Yes	Yes
Searchable database	Yes		Yes		Yes
Tutorials				Yes	
Drills				Yes	
Tests				Yes	
Artificial intelligence	Yes			Yes	
Control difficulty	Yes	Yes		Yes	
Link to online	Yes		Yes	Yes	Yes
Replayable	Yes	Yes		Yes	
3-D real-time	Yes				
Scoring	Yes	Yes		Yes	
Rewards	Yes	Yes		Yes	
Print screens		Yes	Yes	Yes	Yes

Competition as a Driver of Features. Product features are often driven by market forces, notably competition. A new product must have at least the features present in competitive products. Even in educational application development, in which learning objectives are the primary concern, the products are still released in a competitive environment. Kaplan and The Princeton Review developed competing CD-ROM products intended to help high school students earn better test scores on the SAT exam. The Princeton Review developed and released its product first, and it proved successful. Kaplan studied the competition and detailed the features it had to include in its product in order to measure up to the existing product. Kaplan's product, quantitatively and qualitatively at least the equal of the competition, is likewise very successful. A study of multimedia packaging reveals that the marketing message on the back of the box almost always highlights the product's features, so consumers can compare the product to others.

The Cost of Features. The cost of implementing features in multimedia products is most often felt in the engineering or software development part of the budget because they have to be programmed. A feature also determines certain assets: in particular, the assets that put the feature in front of the user. For example, if the designer decides to include a multiuser feature and that users will sign in at the start, then the art director must design a graphic background. The writer and sound designer must write and record a voice-over explaining to the users what to do next. The producer may have to license, or an artist may have to create, a type font that spells out the users' names on the screen as they type on the keyboard. The sound designer may have to find a sound effect to use when the users hit the "return" key. All features create tasks that must be completed by many different people.

Structure

Of all the components of interactive design, the most important and difficult to master is structure. *Structure* refers to the underlying organization of the product's content and features. Without a good structure, it doesn't matter what content, features, and functionality the product includes. It doesn't matter what it looks and sounds like. Without good structure, the product is unusable or, at a minimum, extremely frustrating.

The content of a multimedia product can be a database, or a game, or a story, and the purpose of the title can be to reference the database, play the game, or enjoy the story in a user-controlled environment. The designer must organize the content so that users can access the data they are seeking, play the game at the level they desire, or experience the story at the speed they feel comfortable with. Most of the time, this entails chopping up the content into small parts in some logical way and then providing features—in the form of computer software—that stitch it back together under the direct control of the user.

Structure, then, defines all of the linkages of a system. This is an unfamiliar and sometimes confusing concept for filmmakers, journalists, writers, musicians, and other linear communicators who organize *their* thoughts, *their* messages, *their* art, and then present them to an audience that consumes them in the order and in the volume *they* predetermined.

The feature film screenwriter, for example, is familiar with the three-act structure. Act I is called the setup, during which the audience meets the protagonist and finds out what his or her conflict is. Act II is called the confrontation, when the protagonist engages in crisis after crisis to overcome the conflict. Act III is the resolution, when the protagonist either does or does not overcome the conflict in a final scene known as the climax. The three-act structure can be diagrammed as in Figure 2.2. Notice that it is a linear sequence of events that has a beginning, a middle, and an end.

FIGURE 2.2

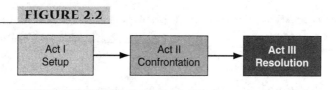

Every multimedia application must have its own, unique structure based on its particular content and features. The structure of the multimedia product defines an organization of ideas *and* events. To illustrate this key difference between the structure of a linear presentation and the structure of a multimedia system, let's look at a very simple example.

A designer designs a multimedia product about horses. The objective is to allow the user to see a picture of either a large plow horse (A), or a riding pony (B), depending on how the user responds to an audio prompt. After 10 seconds, the picture goes away and the audio clip plays again. The structure can be diagrammed as shown in Figure 2.3.

Notice that the structure of the multimedia product includes not only the visible images of the content—the pictures of the two horses—but also invisible events taking place behind the scenes. The software events are the features of the application. The first feature is to receive the response of the user, analyze it, and display the correct image. The second feature is to determine when 10 seconds have elapsed, to remove the image, and to return to the start point.

One can easily imagine how much more complex the structure of the application becomes if the designer includes additional content—let's say, 100 breeds of horses—and additional features. However, even this simple example clearly demonstrates the notion of a system, rather than a sequence, and causes one to ponder where the middle and end of this experience really is.

FIGURE 2.3   A Node Map

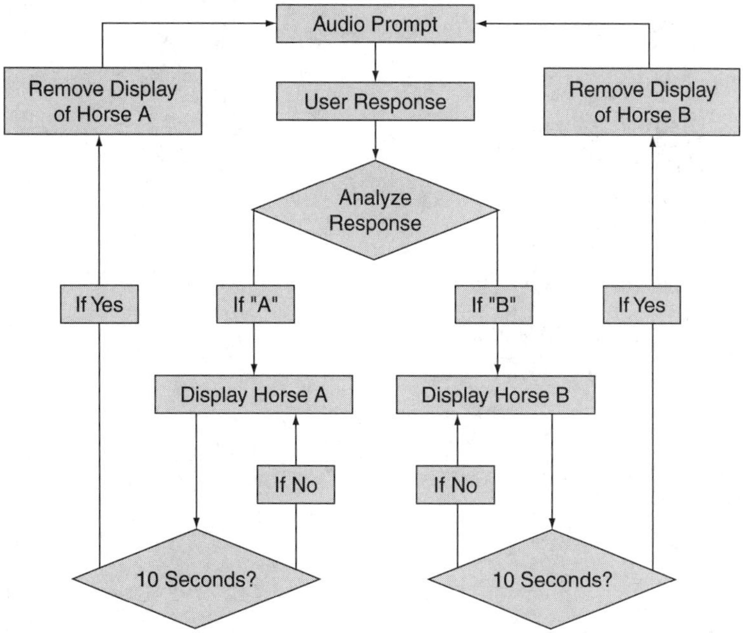

Example of Structure

To get an idea of how a designer thinks about structure on a grander scale, let's study another example. Suppose you are designing an educational product to teach 9- to 11-year-old children about the principles of flight—lift, thrust, control surfaces, and supersonic flight. You also want to cover the history of aviation, so you decide to include a section that includes the myth of Daedalus, the early drawings of Leonardo da Vinci, hot air balloons, all those wonderful Rube Goldberg-like inventions of the late 19th century, the Wright brothers, and so on. You think you should separate military aircraft from those designed for peaceful use. You decide you need a section on space flight and on those high-altitude, subspace commercial flights that are just around the corner. This is the content of your product.

You look at the content carefully, and what pops out at you is that all this information falls into a number of definable categories. What you see is technology, history, uses, and the future. After further scrutiny, you cull some of those hilarious old films of early aviators pedaling like crazy and falling straight down off the edge of a ramp. You make another category out of those and call it "aviation bloopers." You are convinced the user would want to access the content this way.

After you research the subject thoroughly, you arrive at a comprehensive list of subcategories that fall under the five main categories. Here's what you see when you outline the material for just one category:

1. Technology
   a. Thrust
      a.1. Propellers
      a.2. Jets
      a.3. Turbofans
   b. Lift
      b.1. Wings
         b.1.a. Biplane
         b.1.b. Single wing
         b.1.c. Canard
         b.1.d. Swept wing
   c. Control Surfaces
      c.1. Elevators
      c.2. Stabilizers
      c.3. Tail
   d. Fuselage
      d.1. Open cockpit
      d.2. Closed cockpit
      d.3. Aerodynamics
   e. Forces
      e.1. Drag
      e.2. Gravity
      e.3. Centrifugal force

There's even more material under each of the subcategories, but you get the idea. By the time you're through, you will likely have more than 100 individual chunks of subject matter that you want to make available to your user. You divide and subdivide the content as logically as possible. You anticipate what users would want to learn and how they would expect to find the material. You put yourself in their shoes. You start to structure your product.

Content, features, functional control, and the look and feel you choose will ultimately affect your structure and the node map that accurately depicts it. At this *earliest* of stages, it may look like the node map in Figure 2.4.

Notes on the Node Map.   The node map is also called a flow diagram, and you can see why. It graphically shows how the user can move from one chunk of content to another. In the early stages of design, construct your map to help you get a sense of how your subject matter is best organized.

FIGURE 2.4　Simple Node Map for Product on Flight

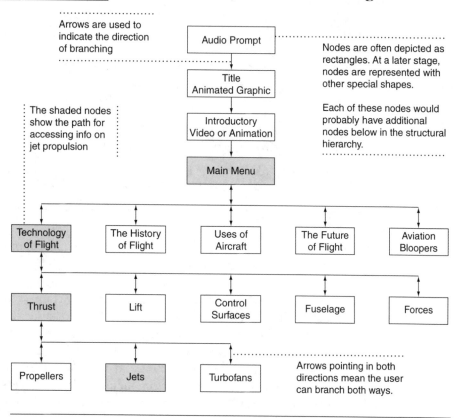

As the design evolves, you begin to include each and every node, using other graphical shapes to represent the type, function, or event of each node. Other shapes often used are shown in Figure 2.5.

Functional Control

Functional control refers to both the real and the virtual devices users use to control the interactive experience—their half of the dialogue. The devices are active, are alive, and obey the command of the user. The most common response from the application to users' use of a device is to change the content or makeup of the current screen in some way. Selecting the blue, underlined hyperlink on the typical Web page, for example, nearly always replaces the existing screen image with another. Another node of content database replaces that which was previously there. Over the Web, that content could come from a server located anywhere in the world. In multimedia, that new node more often than not includes some combination of text,

FIGURE 2.5

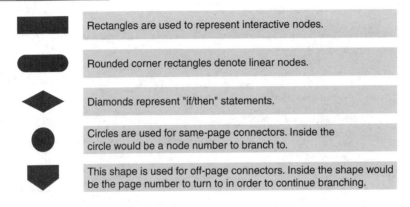

Rectangles are used to represent interactive nodes.

Rounded corner rectangles denote linear nodes.

Diamonds represent "if/then" statements.

Circles are used for same-page connectors. Inside the circle would be a node number to branch to.

This shape is used for off-page connectors. Inside the shape would be the page number to turn to in order to continue branching.

sound, pictures, animation, video, software, and additional functional devices so users can continue with their experience.

Real and Virtual Devices. Designers give users functional control via real devices—such as the keyboard, the mouse, or the joystick—and via virtual devices displayed on the screen. Virtual devices include graphic representations of buttons, arrows, sliders, dials, levers, and hypertext. Virtual devices are displayed on the screen and are typically activated by pointing and clicking on them with the mouse. With some virtual devices, such as a button, the user clicks it once, simulating the action of pressing a physical button, such as the "on" button of a microwave oven. With other devices, such as a slider, the "click and drag" technique is used. The user clicks on the slider with the mouse, holds the mouse button down, and then drags the mouse to control the slider. This, as you can tell, simulates the action of moving a volume slider on a high-end audio mixing board with your finger.

The Hotspot. Another type of virtual device is the "hotspot." A hotspot is an area of the screen that behaves like a button but does not look like one. There are adventure games in which the player controls a character on the screen. The character is constantly faced with choices, such as taking this fork or that one on a road, picking up a leather bag, opening a door, and so forth. The player controls the character's action by clicking on the road, the leather bag, or the doorknob. These are hotspots—areas on the screen that have been programmed to behave like buttons.

Features Determine Functional Control. The application's features determine what functional controls are necessary and appropriate. If the multimedia product features a two-player quiz game, how do the players indicate that they want to an-

FIGURE 2.6

A screen from Hasbro Interactive's *Tonka Search and Rescue*, which has buttons, a lever, a dial, and a hotspot. These virtual devices enable the child to display other kinds of graphics on the monitor, dial through them, print the one that is displayed, or branch back to the previous screen.

swer the current question? How do they assert control? It's up to the designer to arrive at an entertaining and effective solution. For this specific example, one tried-and-true method is to give each player a specific key on the keyboard to hit. The first player to hit his or her key gets to answer the question. It's up to the designer to decide how to do *that*, too.

Look and Feel

Look and feel refers to the art direction and sound design, which, when taken together, create the product's ambiance. The graphic design of your product is the users' first impression. It's the first thing they experience: They see it on the box. In fact, many multimedia products are purchased, or not purchased, based on what the packaging communicates about the look and feel of the product. As we discussed, cost often drives content decisions, the competition drives many decisions about features, and the features largely determine the functional controls. The target market drives look and feel. You must correctly understand your users' tastes and needs and design a graphic appearance that resonates with them.

FIGURE 2.7

This screen, from the best-selling *Disney's Animated StoryBook, The Lion King CD-ROM,* is covered with hotspots users discover by running the cursor over the image. When the cursor is over a hotspot, the cursor's appearance changes from a black paw print to a white one. This signals users that something will happen if they click here. When a user clicks on this hotspot, the baboon character lifts the baby lion.

FIGURE 2.8

Rajko Grlić, the producer, director, and writer, and Tom Erlewine, the art director and designer, at Electronic Vision use a beat-up, cluttered, inner-city film school as the locale for their product *How to Make Your Movie: An Interactive Film School.* This design resonates with passionate, devoted film students—the target market for the product.

Look and feel consists of many separate elements which, when combined, create a certain Gestalt—something larger than the sum of the parts. Think of it as the product's idiosyncrasy. Descriptions of these elements follow.

Graphic Design.

■ *Style*—such as modern, art deco, postmodern, Western, Eastern, African, industrial, cartoon, space-age, businesslike, etc. Of course, there are variations on all of these. When the designer selects a style, he or she tries to identify with the intended user.

■ *Color*—such as bright, primary, muted, pastels, earth tones. The product can leap off the screen like a box of breakfast cereal or recede into it like a brooding mystery. Color creates mood.

■ *Texture*—There are a million textures, most found all around you, such as warm wood, puffy clouds, cool metal, hot metal, hard marble, color wash, and shiny plastic. Textures can be used effectively to set tone—businesslike and formal or casual and relaxed, cool and pretentious or warm and inviting.

■ *Line*—The design, placement, and orientation of your graphic elements may suggest a jagged, broken, horizontal, vertical, or curved line. Line can generate feelings of tension and conflict or order and control.

■ *Lighting*—such as low-key light (deep shadows) and high-key light (bright, evenly lit) set the mood of the scene or screen. Dark, deep shadows are heavy and mysterious, while bright lights are light-hearted and gay.

Icons and Controls.

■ *Icons*—graphic signs and symbols that wordlessly inform the user. Icons can be used to label a screen, a button, or another graphic. Icons contribute not only by communicating useful information, but also by amplifying the product's style.

■ *Buttons, sliders, dials, levers*—These control devices not only serve a useful purpose, their design contributes to the product's overall graphic appeal.

Type Font.   Type specialists choose type fonts for their effectiveness as communicators of style and attitude. Type fonts must also be chosen based on the platform and the venue in which the application will be used. Is the user 10 feet away, using WebTV to access the application, or 15 inches away from a kiosk in a crowded, brightly lit airport terminal?

Screen Layout.   Screen layout refers to the allocation of screen real estate to the visual elements. The designer may decide to reserve certain areas for buttons and controls, screen titles, pulldown menus, video windows, icons, and other graphics.

Screen layout is the blueprint of the screen showing where these areas are, how big they are, and what will be there.

Sound Design.   Sound effects, music, and voice contribute to the overall mood of the product. Consider the different statement the designer makes with a product featuring the music of Led Zepplin versus one featuring, let's say, Mozart. Or if the sound effect heard after pressing a button is a clothes dryer buzzer instead of a pleasant wind chime. Narration by James Earl Jones is dignified and serious and commands more respect than narration by the cartoon character Beavis.

The User Interface

Combined, functional controls and the look and feel of the application make up what is called the user interface. Brenda Laurel (1990) calls this the "contact surface," although she and other contributors to the book *The Art of Human–Computer Interface Design* suggest we should all be looking for a better definition. Sitting behind the interface, out of view of users until they choose to visit, are content and features, carefully structured so users can use the interface to do exactly what they want to do.

The Metaphor.   The most effective user interface takes advantage of what users already know or sense about the world around them. When an interface is effective because it employs images, sounds, or other design elements and behaviors the user is familiar with, it is a metaphor. The interface of the Apple Computer, later copied by the designers of the Windows interface, makes use of the desktop metaphor. The interface surface is designed to look and behave like the desktop of a physical office space. It includes a trash can icon, which is used for throwing things away. Data is stored in locations represented by icons that look like file folders. This metaphor works not only because the average user is familiar with the presentation, but also because the presentation fairly accurately represents how the system actually works. In other words, the interface design (what it looks and behaves like) and the system design (how the underlying software works) mirror each other. Norman (1988) notes that the proper design of all things involves providing users with a good conceptual model, one that enables them to understand the designer's intention by presenting it through the system's design, which, in the case of multimedia, is represented by the user interface.

Figures 2.9(a) and (b) are sample screens from a CD-ROM created by multimedia students at the S. I. Newhouse School of Public Communications at Syracuse University. The target users are people struggling with cancer. Cancer patients are encouraged to keep journals during their treatments, so they would be familiar with the look and feel and with the control surface provided by the designers. This

FIGURE 2.9

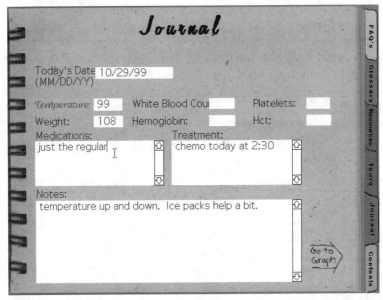

(a)

(b)

In a student-developed CD-ROM for cancer patients, users can keep a journal in which they record daily information about their condition. The CD-ROM then creates charts and graphs showing the daily fluctuations, as shown in (a) and (b).

© 1999 Christopher Liston and Rebecca Treacy-Lenda.

multimedia product is an electronic journal that includes many additional features, including a tool that allows the user to keep track, over time, of his or her temperature, white cell count, and other health indicators.

Anticipation, Intuition, Consistency.   When you design a user interface, your job is to anticipate correctly what users may want or need to do at every particular moment of the interactive experience and to provide them with the means to do it. You must empower them to take control of their experience. You must provide them with devices that are intuitive and consistent. There is no greater glory in interactive design than to create an experience users have never had before, but are still familiar with. Robert Abel, one of the most talented and successful graphic designers of the 1970s and 1980s, admonished us to create an experience that reminds the audience of something it has never seen before. Norman (1988) says a design should make sure that (1) users can figure out what to do and (2) users can tell what is going on. Creating an interface that accurately reflects what is going on just below the surface would seem to be the best way to do that.

The interface is intuitive when the user can infer how to assume control of the product by which devices are provided, what they look like, and where they are located on the screen. A right-pointing arrow with beveled edges—an icon we have all seen on VCRs—almost certainly means "forward" to a user. A left-pointing arrow probably means "go back." Control is consistent when the designer establishes a pattern of functionality and sticks with it. If the designer establishes those arrows, he or she should continue to use them and make sure they always cause the product to behave the same way. Locate the arrows in the same place on the screen every time they are needed. It is counterproductive to provide users with an interactive dialogue and then make it frustrating by forcing them to learn a new vocabulary every time they want to communicate.

Let's take the dashboard example one last time. If you can drive one car, you can probably drive any car. Slip into the driver's seat. The steering wheel is in front of you. The speedometer is straight ahead. The ignition key is to the right, probably on the steering column. The turn signal is a short post sticking out on the left side. The gas pedal is below your right foot, the brake to the left of that. The gearshift is on the raised section between your right thigh and the passenger seat. If the shift is pushed all the way forward, it's in park. Even though there is a world of qualitative difference between a Dodge Neon and a Mercedes Benz, both cars serve the same purpose. The design of the interface, therefore, is consistent. If you were to rent an unfamiliar car and the manufacturer had moved the ignition switch to the ceiling behind the sun visor, you'd be pretty ticked, wouldn't you?

Appropriate for User and Genre.   User interface should be intuitive and consistent. It should also be appropriate for the user and the genre of the product. If the users are preschoolers, create buttons that are large and obvious and do not rely on text to indicate what they are for. Don't use text if the product will be sold internationally.

In Figure 2.10, from *Disney's Animated StoryBook, The Lion King CD-ROM,* buttons are depicted as sign posts. Words on the sign posts are supported by icons so young readers can connect the purpose of the button with both the English word and a pictorial representation. The buttons themselves are large and easy to identify. This is an age-appropriate design.

FIGURE 2.10

Disney's Animated StoryBook, The Lion King © Disney Enterprises, Inc. All rights reserved.

Volumes have been written about user interface design: far more than can be presented in this book. The reader should expand on the general concepts presented here by reading the books recommended at the end of this chapter.

Chapter Summary

Despite the fact that all multimedia applications are unique, they are all comprised of five basic components—content, features, structure, functional control, and look and feel. We discussed the genres and user segments of multimedia products, and the role they play in driving design decisions.

Content is the body of knowledge, concepts, and ideas that make up the subject matter of your product. The driver for how much content you can include in your product is cost, although the physical limitations of the medium also constrain you. Features are the interactive experiences you provide your users, which allow them to access the content. Features include games, activities, and the abilities to customize, to search a database, and to print the screen. More often than not, and perhaps regrettably, the features you include in your product are determined by the competition. Structure is the organization of the content and features in a logical way.

Multimedia designers use terms such as *nodes, node maps, branching,* and *navigation* to describe the structure of their products. When we divide and subdivide content into chunks of knowledge, ideas, concepts, or games, we call these chunks nodes. Giving the user the means to access and leave a node is called branching. A diagram that shows the structure of the nodes and how one navigates through this structure is called a node map.

Functional control is the term for the real and virtual devices you provide the user so they can control the product. The keyboard and mouse are real devices. On-screen buttons, sliders, and dials are examples of virtual devices. The features you choose for a product determine the functional controls you include so the user can control them.

Look and feel is the graphical and audio style, or ambiance, of the product. This concept refers to how the product appears, not how it behaves. User preferences often determine the style of graphics and sound.

Well-designed user interface is consistent and intuitive and anticipates what users want and how they expect to find it.

We've covered a lot of ground, yet we've only begun to scratch the surface. That underscores the complexity and enormity of multimedia design and development. Most of what we've talked about in this chapter is conceptual. It's best to look for these concepts in existing products. An exercise you may want to try is to buy a product—ideally one you'd like to keep and use—and see if you can reverse engineer the interactive design. Identify the users, the subject, and the genre. Make a list of the content, the features, and the functionality. Describe the look and feel and try to create the node map that graphically depicts the structure. This exercise will help you prepare for a later chapter, which deals with the very practical side of interactive design—the process.

Recommended Reading

Head, Alison. *Design Wise, A Guide for Evaluating the Interface Design of Information Resources.* Cyberage Books: Medford, NJ, 1999.

Laurel, Brenda. *Computers as Theater.* Addison-Wesley: Reading, MA, 1991.

Laurel, Brenda, et al. *The Art of Human–Computer Interface Design.* Addison-Wesley: Reading, MA, 1990.

Nelson, Ted. *Computer Lib/Dream Machines,* Revised Edition. Microsoft Press: Redmond, WA, 1987.

Nielsen, Jakob. *Hypertext and Hypermedia.* Academic Press: Boston, 1990.

Norman, Donald A. *Things That Make Us Smart.* Addison-Wesley: Reading, MA, 1993.

3

Design for Instructional and Educational Multimedia

In this chapter, you will learn about

- The background and skill set of the instructional designer
- Types of computer-based instruction
- Criteria for using multimedia to solve learning problems
- Design parameters for educational multimedia
- Learning theories and how they may be applied to multimedia applications
- Multimedia education venues and the characteristics that impact design

In this chapter, we cover design issues for instructional and educational multimedia. These are treated as a special case, as these particular applications of multimedia require special design considerations unnecessary in other genres. Unlike entertainment products, such as games (which are covered in the next chapter), the primary focus of educational multimedia is to impart knowledge, skill, or concepts to the user. It is important to point out quickly, however, that many educational applications do utilize game concepts. Instructional applications have specific pedagogical purposes: for example, to teach an academic subject at a particular grade level in a school setting, to train a new employee about a new manufacturing process, or to instruct the public about an exhibit at the historical museum. In each case, multimedia is used to facilitate learning, and this requires the input and guidance of an expert in the field: the instructional designer.

As a key member of the design team for educational and instructional multimedia, the instructional designer determines the learning objective and whether multimedia is appropriate for the solution. He or she gains an understanding of the subject matter and gets a clear sense of what the target user already knows about it. The designer understands the many theories of how people learn and when and how to apply them. The designer knows how to use the power of interactive multimedia to engage learners. Increasingly, and especially when designing applications targeted at the Net Generation (people between 0 and 20 years old), the designer is aware of users' familiarity with computers and multimedia.

This chapter is a broad encapsulation of key instructional design concepts, intended to make the reader conversant with the work of the instructional designer. The producer, director, and writer should understand these concepts in order to work closely and effectively with instructional designers and educators, who bring all of this background with them. There are many good books on the subject of instructional design and using multimedia for learning. Some are recommended at the end of the chapter. What is clear from the research done for this book, however, is that technological developments are transforming just about everything we once held sacred about teaching, teaching methods, students and how they learn, and the role of interactive technology in the process. Don Tapscott (1999), in his book *Growing Up Digital*, sums this up very well when he says, "New media tools offer great promise for a new model for learning—one based on discovery and participation. This combination of a new generation and new digital tools will cause a rethinking of the nature of education—both in content and in delivery" (p. 127). Tapscott's book is a thought-provoking examination of the effect that technology, and in particular interactive technology, is having on children.

Marshall McLuhan said, "The medium is the message," and perhaps he foresaw the profound changes in an entire generation of youngsters that would be brought about by their intimacy with computers, interactive multimedia, the Internet, and even video games. The medium has indeed altered the receiver. The interactive designer of the future is well advised to look long and hard at target users for clues about how to design the educational and instructional multimedia application that will be most effective for those who were reared on the medium.

The Instructional Designer

According to Kerry Johnson and Lin Foa (1989), the goal of instructional design is "to develop better, faster, and more efficient learning tools" (p. 3) so that children and adults can adapt more easily to the increasingly complex world around them. The instructional designer, then, designs solutions to learning problems. The instructional designer is brought into a project first, long before a multimedia design team, to survey the landscape and determine whether the problem is first of all an educational or training problem or whether it is something else. Many apparent educational or training deficiencies turn out to be organizational, management, or cultural problems rather than knowledge or skill gaps. If the designer ascertains that there is an instructional need, he or she assesses the content, the learner, the knowledge or performance gap, and many other factors, and designs an instructional model. Even when the project does call for an instructional design (as opposed to, let's say, a new organizational plan), the solution may or may not involve multimedia. The instructional designer approaches every assignment unbiased and unfettered, with no preconceptions about what may be the problem and what may be the solution.

For the purposes of further discussion, we concern ourselves only with projects that require instructional or educational solutions and call for multimedia as a prime component. In order to create a complete tool or system for teaching and learning, the instructional designer applies theoretical and practical knowledge from many diverse disciplines.

Understand the User

From the social sciences, in particular psychology, the designer develops an understanding of how the mind works: how people assimilate knowledge, process data, and make connections. This, of course, enables the designer to understand the end users and to design a learning environment that best fits their needs and abilities.

Manage Development and Evaluate the Tool

From management and engineering, the designer borrows strategies and methods that make systems analysis possible. The designer is able to define a problem, conceive a solution, develop a system, put it to work, track its use, and evaluate its effectiveness. This enables the designer to manage the process of creating the instructional tool in a professional and workmanlike manner. This is most important on very large projects dealing with complex content and involving many users. Measuring effectiveness, once the tool is in operation, is especially important to the instructional designer. Having used an orderly process to create the tool, the designer can quickly track down any part of it that isn't effective.

Manage the Data

From information and computer science, the designer uses methods for collecting, processing, and managing large amounts of data. Many educational, training, and instructional programs contain enormous volumes of data, related not only to the content of the programs, but also to the students and trainees. The designer may use sophisticated 3-D database programs for collecting and processing data, for example.

Create the Message

From the communication arts, the designer uses media, including sound, text, images, graphics, animation, and video, to craft messages. The designer understands not only how to use these media to communicate in a general sense, but also how each medium contributes to the message itself. The designer chooses a medium based on how well it can communicate a message, on what effect that medium choice will have on the message, and on how the learner will interpret *that* message.

Establish the Interaction

Finally, with interactive multimedia, the designer has access to tools that enable direct, purposeful interaction with users. Interactive multimedia provides the designer with a delivery system that comes closest to one-on-one, personal dialogue between teacher and learner. The designer can adapt the system to meet any learning objective, using any teaching method, to reach any target user.

FIGURE 3.1

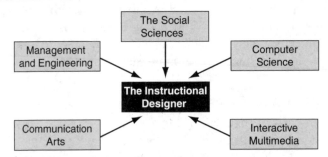

The instructional designer applies theories and practices from many disciplines to develop multimedia learning tools.

The instructional designer is a renaissance person, gifted in both left- and right-brained activity. Using an understanding of behavioral and cognitive psychology, he or she visualizes the learner's perspective. Then the designer participates in the design and development of an interactive multimedia application that connects users with the knowledge domain. He or she lays out an orderly design, development, and evaluation plan to create the teaching tool.

Types of Computer-Based Learning

Instructional designers were early adopters of interactive technology for teaching purposes. Over the years, the instructional community coined a number of terms to apply to the various nuances of computer use (interactive multimedia in particular) for teaching. While designing and developing an educational or instructional application, one or another of these approaches may be chosen, usually based on the learning objective, target users, subject matter, venue, and cost and time considerations.

CACL—Computer-Assisted Cooperative Learning

As the name implies, CACL emphasizes applications that promote collaboration and cooperation, rather than individualism and even competition among students. Research by Johnson, Johnson, Stanne, and Garibaldi (1989) compared the use of cooperative, competitive, and individualistic computer applications and found that cooperative users outperformed the others in a number of significant areas, including the "quality of daily achievement" and the "mastery of factual material." They found that "a dialogue between peers promoted more higher-level reasoning and ability to apply learning than did a dialogue with a computer" (Johnson & Johnson, 1993, p. 147). This seminal work took place before the emergence of the Internet as a cooperative environment, which has since provided a worldwide petri dish for the study of computer-assisted cooperative learning.

CAI—Computer-Assisted Instruction

Applications that fall into the CAI category favor the instructivist method of teaching, which is discussed later in this chapter. Generally, CAI applications tend to be fairly linear presentations of carefully orchestrated lessons. Students are introduced to the content, learn it, master it, and branch to increasingly more complex content.

CAL—Computer-Assisted Learning

A slight twist on the CAI model, CAL switches the control of content presentation from the tight fist of the instructor to the student. CAL applications tend to encourage student exploration, curiosity, and browsing. Later in this chapter, you will read about the constructivist theory of learning, which CAL applications support. Most children's educational CD-ROM products can be considered computer-assisted learning applications because they encourage users to browse and move about and to engage in activities and games in a self-directed manner.

The Criteria for Selecting Multimedia

Instructional designers look at many factors before deciding that multimedia is an important, or even a small, part of the instructional mix. Before getting to the point of deciding to use multimedia, the designer has already decided whether instruction is a suitable solution. Although project-specific requirements may cause other criteria to rear up as well, the designer now evaluates

■ *What.* Does the subject matter lend itself to multimedia treatment? Can the subject matter be best represented with the combination of audio, video, animation, graphics, and text? Is all of this overkill? Conversely, does the subject matter require direct, purposeful contact with real objects or machines? Is a virtual experience OK?

Can the subject matter be broken up into nodes and accessed and experienced in chunks? Is a linear presentation more appropriate? Is the subject matter stable, or likely to be changed or modified over time, and often?

■ *Who.* How many end users are there and what is the demographic and psychographic composition of the group? Is the high cost and time-consuming nature of multimedia development justified by the number of users? Is the group permanent or transient? Will the need (indeed, the users) still exist when the multimedia application is complete? Are the users sophisticated enough to use multimedia? Are the users starting from the same point of departure, or are some of the learners more advanced and others less accomplished than the group as a whole?

■ *Where.* Where and how will the instruction or training take place? In a classroom? At the learner's home? On a factory floor? In a community center? Are the learners together in one place or spread out all over? Will the environment support or obviate the use of multimedia?

■ *How.* What teaching method(s) does the instructional solution call for? Does it conjure up learner collaboration as a team or an individual approach? Is it tightly controlled by an instructor or highly individualized and self-paced? Does the teaching method encourage user exploration? For any particular method, what is the best way to evaluate the learner?

If the subject matter consists of concepts and ideas that are best expressed using graphics, the realism of video, or the visualization capabilities of 3-D computer animation, then an audio/video treatment is appropriate. Otherwise, a paper-based approach may be better; it will certainly be cheaper. If the subject matter can be segmented into nodes or chunks and does not need to be linearly linked like a film or video, then the subject could be structured for a multimedia treatment. If, in addition to the aforementioned, the subject matter is somewhat calcified (old, and very little if anything new is added), then a multimedia treatment on CD-ROM may be appropriate. If the subject matter is exposed to frequent or even periodic changes, additions, or deletions, then an online Internet or intranet multimedia application should be considered.

Multimedia is an ideal teaching agent for user populations large and stable enough to support the cost and time commitment needed for design and development as well as heterogeneous—diverse and variously qualified for the subject matter. Multimedia can be designed to accommodate user groups having a wide range of abilities to handle the subject matter. For example, the application can prescreen users and then customize the learning experience to meet individual needs. Such a feature is expensive, so it can only be justified if there are many users (or very high-priority users such as astronauts) who would benefit from it.

Multimedia is best used for instruction on a one-to-one basis: individual users rather than groups. Very small groups—two or three—may be the exception. This does not eliminate classrooms or other crowded environments as long as each user is able to engage in his or her own personal dialogue with the multimedia application. Another exception to this is when individuals, each with his or her own application, can collaborate over an Internet or intranet connection.

A computer-based training program now in use at Lockheed Martin, the $26.3 billion defense contractor, is a good example of one that meets most if not all of the criteria above. In the past, several defense contractors, including Lockheed Martin, have been investigated and fined for ethics violations, ranging from bribery to conflict of interest. In order to avoid further troubles, the company instituted a training program that utilizes, among other things, an online teaching tool that its 160,000 employees can access anytime, from anywhere. The training courses include role-playing games in which employees learn about security, software license compliance, labor charging, and ethical behavior. Although other factors may contribute to corporate misdeeds, Lockheed Martin's online multimedia training program tackles one potential cause—a lack of knowledge among its employees—head on.

Various teaching methods are discussed later in this chapter, but here it can be said that multimedia is appropriate for learning environments in which self-motivated, self-directed, and self-paced learning is encouraged *at least at some point* in the instructional model. Otherwise, what's the point of utilizing interactive multimedia? If the teaching method and learning objective of the project require regular, measurable, and data-intensive evaluation of the learner's progress, multimedia can do that. The application software can keep track of learner behavior, growth, decision chains, and other activity in real-time. It can provide immediate feedback to both the learner and the instructor.

Design Parameters for Educational Multimedia

Once the designer has established that a particular project calls for a multimedia intervention, he or she considers various design parameters that are distinctive to educational and instructional multimedia design.

Educational and instructional applications do consist of the basic components described in Chapter 2. Content and features, and the way they are structured, make up the underlying application and the functional controls and the look and feel make up the user interface. However, instructional multimedia is unique in its purpose and goal. It is specifically developed to impart knowledge, skills, or concepts to users. This uniqueness of purpose interjects additional drivers into the design process. For an educational product, the instructional designer considers forces that in turn influence and drive the design and development of the basic components.

■ *Instructional challenge.* This is the overall educational or instructional need. It is the *problem* that the multimedia application must solve. Instructional designers may describe the instructional challenge as a "performance discrepancy": the quantification and qualification of a gap between the user's current and desired level of knowledge.

■ *User's profile.* The intellectual, psychological, and physical state of the user. The designer considers what the user already knows about the subject matter, how the user is motivated, and where the learner will use the application. Designers of products in other genres—games for example—are interested in the user but are seldom concerned with what the user already knows about a particular subject.

■ *Learning objective.* What the designer wants the user to know about the subject matter when all is said and done. The learning objective is the *solution* to the problem.

■ *The teaching method* to be used to impart the knowledge, and how the interactive, multimedia environment will be used to support the method. There are many methods, each with supporters and detractors in the educational arena.

■ *The evaluation method* to be used to determine whether the user has learned the subject matter and whether the learning environment is, therefore, effective.

FIGURE 3.2

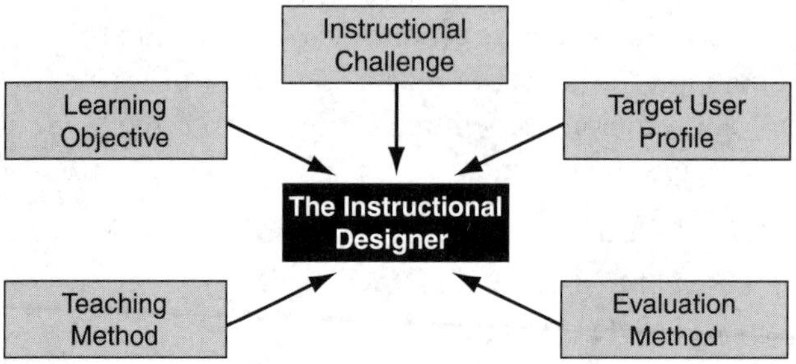

Instructional Challenge

The instructional challenge is the problem the application must solve. Here are some examples:

1. Nobody arriving for the convention can find a hotel.
2. All college freshmen have a problem with grammar, punctuation, and spelling.
3. There are myths circulating about the causes of HIV/AIDS among those most at risk of contracting the virus.
4. People who have just discovered they have cancer need emotional and medical support and access to resources that provide it.
5. We have 40,000 consultants, and all of them must learn about this new tax law.

Instructional designers describe challenge as a "performance discrepancy." The performance discrepancy is the gap between what the target users currently know about a particular subject and what they should know. In a corporate training scenario, for example, the challenge may be that an entire organization is switching from one word-processing package to another. Every employee must learn a new application but not how to use a computer, how to open an app, how to save a file, or how to print. They already know these things from using the old software. In fact, the discrepancy between the employee's current state of knowledge and the desired state may be very small. In a consumer product scenario, the challenge may be to teach European history to seventh graders who have had no exposure whatsoever to the subject. The discrepancy is great. In both cases, the designer identifies the range, or size, of the discrepancy, and the starting point for the instructional discourse. The conclusions drawn from evaluating the instructional challenge lead the designer to define the content.

An Analysis of the Target User

Prior Knowledge.   The designer must evaluate the target users, placing particular emphasis on their prior knowledge of the subject matter. What are the users' frames of reference? For instance,

- I took a calculus course, but that was 25 years ago.
- I've had four years of progressively more difficult Spanish.
- I am completely new to computer science.
- I've heard of HIV, but I have avoided learning more. Diseases disturb me.

This, obviously, gives the designer a starting point for identifying the content. Many multimedia products include features that assess each user and automatically determine the amount of exposure the student already has to the material. The application software then customizes the level of complexity to match the student's skills. The demographic profile of target users plays a role in determining the range of content—where it begins and where it ends.

Motivation.   Instructional designers also consider the psychological state of the users, in particular their motivation to learn. What is it that predisposes them to open themselves up to acquiring new knowledge, skills, or concepts? What is it, they ask, that stimulates learners in this particular situation? Research in this area suggests that when people are motivated to learn, they begin more earnestly, spend more time learning, and work harder at it. So what motivates them?

1. If I take this course, I'll get a raise.
2. If I learn this new management technique, I can get more productivity from fewer salespeople.

FIGURE 3.3

Students from the S. I. Newhouse School of Public Communications and from the College of Nursing (both at Syracuse University) collaborated on a CD-ROM. The product, targeted at women, is designed to survey each user on her knowledge of HIV and AIDS and to educate her based on the results of her responses to questions. Data collected helps researchers determine the commonly held misconceptions about HIV infection in the sample population.

© 1999 Alethia McCullough and Kate Leonard. Used with permission.

3. If I learn more about nutrition, I can lose weight and look 10 years younger.
4. If I learn how to do all this math, my mom and dad will be very proud.

Although these thoughts may cross the minds of users of instructional multi-media, many other factors determine whether or not they stay with it. If they must work very hard to achieve barely measurable results, for example, their desire to continue will quickly dissipate. This is especially true when learners are not volunteers.

Instructional designers struggle with just how to anticipate what will motivate learners, and what will sustain their interest. In the commercial market for educational products, the most successful are those in which the learning is encrypted in entertainment and games. Children play for hours at a time, and return many times, to games such as *Where in the World Is Carmen Sandiego?* and *Math Blaster*. This is not an argument favoring gaming as the basis for instructional design to promote effective motivation. However, Dempsey and Jacobs (1993) do suggest that "[b]y facilitating learner involvement via simulation and gaming and incorporating sound instructional features, learning outcomes should show improvements relative to other training methods that are less engaging or that provide less effective means of instructional interaction." One should look carefully at what motivates learners to play a game. In the next chapter, you will learn about establishing success strategies, avoiding frustration, and rewarding users, all of which can also be applied to educational design.

The Learning Objective

After identifying the challenge and evaluating users, the designer formulates the solution to the instructional problem by defining the learning objectives of the product or application. Here are some examples:

1. We must provide information on all of the hotels within a 20-mile radius of the convention center.
2. We must create a grammar-slammer course that freshmen can complete independently during their first two weeks at university.
3. We must educate those most at risk of contracting HIV and dispel myths that are endangering them.
4. We must provide emotional support and sound medical advice to cancer-stricken people.
5. We must create a distance learning system to teach all of our consultants, while they are on the road, about the new tax law.

The designer defines the broad learning objective of the application and the solution to the performance discrepancy and then determines the details of the instructional model. When designing a product for use in school, or when targeting a specific academic subject, the learning objective may be driven by educational standards set by governing bodies such as the state or federal government, school boards, or boards of regents.

The learning objective determines, first of all, the content—what it is, how much, and how complex. Suppose for a moment that the content is a foreign language, such as Spanish. The designer must determine the level (beginning? advanced?) of Spanish, the breadth and depth of the vocabulary, and whether or not the objective includes reading and writing. If it includes conversational Spanish, does it promote Castillian or South American pronunciation? The learning objective may also drive the determination of the teaching method, as discussed below.

The Teaching Method

Schweir and Misanchuk (1993) identify several different learning environments (so called because they are "organic and malleable" [p. 14]) that support different, mostly traditional teaching methods. Teaching methods are not specific to multimedia, but you will recognize that these environments closely parallel what we have already described as *modes of navigation* in Chapter 2. Instructional designers select the teaching method based on the subject matter, the target user population, the venue (school or home), and other things such as whether the users will be acting alone or in collaboration with others. The selection of the teaching method has a direct impact on the development of interactive features and on the structure of the content with those features.

Schweir and Misanchuk identify the prescriptive environment, in which the instructor assumes control and which includes the all-to-familiar drill and kill method. The prescriptive environment is the "guided tour" mode. Their "democratic environment" is one in which the user takes a more active role in structuring the learning process (such as being able to browse freely). The "cybernetic environment" is one in which the computer actually takes a more active role in structuring the learning experience. The cybernetic environment is comparable to the "customization" mode described in Chapter 2. Although these environments are well represented in educational multimedia products and applications, the work of researchers in this area continues, and other new and innovative approaches are bound to surface. Usually, based on the task at hand—what the learning objective is and at whom it is directed—one of these methods is chosen.

Instructivist or Prescriptive Environment.   The behaviorist B. F. Skinner is behind the notion that behavior is shaped by reinforcements and rewards. Carried over to education, it is thought that for optimal learning to occur, there must be a structure in which carefully planned lessons are systematically and linearly presented to the student, who is rewarded for properly assimilating the material. In this environment, the focus is on the instructor and what he or she intends. It is heavily mediated, meaning the designer takes on an almost intrusive role in the experience of the user. This is the instructivist option.

Using this teaching method, which closely approximates what has happened in the classroom for the past several hundred years, an expert (the teacher) determines ahead of time what a larger number of students need to learn and develops a syllabus. The syllabus consists of specific lessons, or chunks of information, which are parsed out to the students in a specific order. Each tidbit of knowledge builds on the preceding until the student's level of knowledge reaches that of the planned target. Tapscott (1999) calls this "broadcast learning" (p. 129) because it is ballistic, rarely interruptible, and almost always a one-to-many scenario. Although imprinted with the very traditional classroom metaphor, multimedia products that adapt this method can and often do add several features that take advantage of the technology:

■ *The lessons are user paced.* Because the multimedia environment is one-to-one (one computer, one student) the user controls the pace. He or she can stop the lesson, replay it, and in some applications, slow it down.

■ *Users can test themselves.* The multimedia product is designed with periodic tests or challenges. These enable users to identify areas where they may need to relearn and to return to those lessons.

■ *The lessons adapt to the progress shown by the student.* In more advanced versions of this approach, the application tracks the user's progress and skips over material he or she has clearly mastered or repeats material the user has not.

Tutorials and drill and kill are two features very common in multimedia products designed in the instructivist or prescriptive environment.

Democratic or Free Access Browsing. In this teaching method, the burden of learning is shifted to the users. Rather than imposing specific lessons, in a specific order in the mold of a syllabus, the designer structures the application so that users can freely browse or access any information at any time. This method may be non-mediated in that the designer may set up or facilitate the introduction of concepts and then back away, leaving the student to explore without intrusion, editing, or influence. The entire Internet operates under this principle, though most educators agree that merely "grazing databases" is not necessarily learning and is certainly not instructional. Tapscott (1998) disagrees, arguing that on the Internet, "children must search for, rather than simply look at, information. This forces them to develop thinking and investigative skills" (p. 26).

When the application is an offline, mediated product such as a CD-ROM, the designer still maintains a great deal of control, though it may not seem so to the user. Many educational games are designed with this method at the core. In the educational game *Where in the U.S.A. Is Carmen Sandiego?,* users are apparently free to explore anywhere the clues take them after a premise has been established by the game engine. However, in actual fact, the users can only explore the game world (see Chapter 4), obtain the clues, meet the characters, and learn the facts that have been predetermined by the designer.

Cybernetic Environment. Schweir and Misanchuk describe the cybernetic environment, in which the computer becomes a more active participant in the teaching/learning equation. The most common and identifiable example is artificial intelligence (AI), which is used in games, simulations, and very high-end lab experiments. In the most sophisticated AI applications, the software can "learn" new information, process it, and arrive at new conclusions based on its interaction with the user.

Most applications are not AI in that sense, but they are very smart, largely because of the enormous number of calculations they are capable of performing. Deep Blue, IBM's chess-playing supercomputer that defeated human chess champion Garry Kasparov in 1997, is a memorable example.

FIGURE 3.4

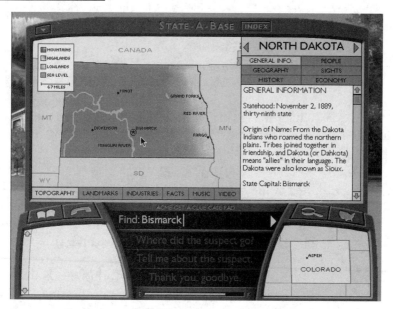

A screen shot from *Where in the U.S.A. Is Carmen Sandiego?*, published by The Learning Company. The user may browse anywhere in the country, but the information provided is predetermined by the designer to maximize learning.

In less famous but more prodigious cases, AI-like technology is used routinely in games, frequently for educational purposes. Many games behave as though they utilize AI but are merely very good simulations. *SimCity,* a game that reacts to the decisions made by the player by either growing or shrinking a city, is credited with teaching children certain tenets of urban design because it behaves dependably and predictably to the building, taxing, bonding, and renovating carried on by the player. To the player, it appears to have a mind of its own, but it is actually responding to programmed if/then statements. The user quickly learns that "if I build a power plant here, businesses will spring up around it, but residences will lose value, lowering my tax rate."

The Constructivist Method.   This method, based on the work of Seymour Papert and, before him, Jean Piaget, the father of developmental cognitive psychology, is diametrically opposed to the Instructivist option. Piaget theorized that children, in their earliest developmental years, construct their own knowledge of the world through observation and experience. This places them as active participants in their learning, rather than passive receptors of information, as in the prescriptive or instructivist environment. It makes the constructivist method a *learning* approach, rather than a *teaching* approach. Children are encouraged to try things and make mistakes heuristically, learning from both the mistakes and the successes. The constructivist method is particularly adaptable to computer technology because it requires an interactive dialogue between the learner and a teacher or teaching device.

In the constructivist model, the learning goes even further than in the cybernetic environment. The user is encouraged not just to learn from the application, but to learn how the application works. In the *SimCity* example above, the user may be tempted to theorize how the series of if/then statements in the software combined with variables and data and user interactions result in a certain image—a new factory—being displayed near the power plant. The user may say, "I see that when I build a power plant, a factory appears nearby. This must be because . . . "

The teaching method chosen by the designer influences the features he or she includes in the overall design of the product. You can see that any multimedia product may include not just one, but combinations, of these methods, and most of them do.

FIGURE 3.5

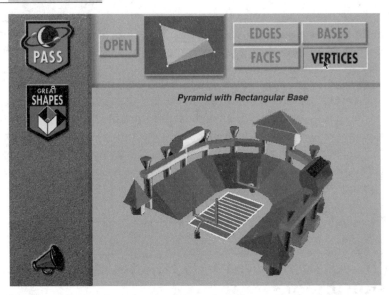

Project Pass, jointly developed by GTE and the NFL, was designed to teach seventh-grade mathematics. The multimedia component utilized both tutorial (instructivist) and self-directed (constructivist) methods to teach students about geometric shapes.

The Evaluation Methods

Just as there are many approaches to teaching methods, there are several approaches to evaluating the teaching method's effectiveness. Furthermore, there are both on-line and offline methods, the former to allow users to understand their own learning progress and the latter to enable the designer to assess the teaching process! Although there are differences in approach and methodology, all evaluation systems are designed toward these ends:

■ *To allow the user to be consistently aware of his or her progress.* In traditional methods, this is accomplished by testing the student and providing him or her with a score, or grade. In heuristic scenarios, the student experiences success or failure and is given the opportunity to try again, gradually learning the "correct" way of doing things.

■ *To allow the system (or tutor, or instructor) to become aware of the user's progress.* Many educational applications are a component of a larger entity, such as a course, a training program, or a curriculum. Regardless of how the user has been kept aware of his or her progress, the system must know "Does the user know more than when he or she started, and if so, what?"

■ *To allow the system to be assessed.* Like all multimedia products and applications, educational products are designed and developed with a lot of hope and promise and no assurance that they are as effective as planned. Developers often create control groups of users and assess the effectiveness of the product by testing users and nonusers before and after the product's release.

Just as for other genres of multimedia, feedback on the design and implementation of the product is important to the designer. Evaluation feedback is important for marketing purposes for all genres. But for educational products, the main purpose and importance is to determine the product's effectiveness at achieving the learning objective. The evaluation method may resemble, in many ways, those methods used for game, entertainment, or utility products, but the purpose, and therefore the structure of the evaluation, differs. An observation made during a focus test, for example, may not be so much, "Did the user like it?"—though that is always important—as, "Did the user understand it?"

Educational and Instructional Multimedia Venues

Instructional and educational multimedia applications are designed to go where the learners are. Depending on the purpose and intended users, the final venue may be the home, school, office, factory floor, or lobby of a midtown hotel. The venue determines many characteristics of the design, including the mode of distribution (online Internet or intranet, offline CD-ROM, or a combination), length of the program, ease of use, display characteristics, the use of audio, functional controls, and look and feel. The venue determines which of three possible contexts the design may adopt: competitive, individual, or collaborative. The following are some typical venues for instructional and educational applications and the design implications that arise from them.

The Home

Instructional multimedia designed for home use takes into consideration that the typical user will probably be alone and using his or her personal computer. The home computer is technically capable of playing a CD-ROM and/or connecting the user via modem or cable to the Internet or intranet. Both the venue and the delivery system carry rather profound implications for the design of the application.

CD-ROM Products. If the educational product is an offline CD-ROM, the user must be self-motivated to use the product. There will be no personal tutor or instructor to provide encouragement, guidance, or other stimulation. The user experiences the educational material in isolation. As discussed earlier, educational products aimed at children are generally constructed as edutainment products, combining games, activities, characters, stories, songs, and other ingredients that motivate the learner with pleasure. The offline CD-ROM must be designed as a robust, interactive multimedia product that can effectively engage the user on its own. The approach is supported by both research and market share.

Home users of educational CD-ROM products cannot be evaluated by instructors (unless some provision has been included that enables an instructor to obtain a record of the user's performance). However, the products can and should be designed to provide users with continuous feedback on their progress. Particularly sophisticated products can evaluate learners' progress and adjust the presentation of content to fit their level of knowledge.

Distance Learning. Most online educational applications are directed at adult learners in a distance learning course. In these situations, the home learner is connected via Internet or intranet to a learning community, an instructor, an institution, and a curriculum. The curriculum may include electronic seminars, collaborative readings and discussions, threaded conversations, feedback, and role playing, all of which are known to be effective motivators. Distance learning applications become what many have called a "cyber-democracy," (Brown, 1998) a learning environment in which the instructor puts content, learning objectives, and a general syllabus into motion, only to watch it take on a life of its own as the students engage in communal research, reporting, criticism, and discussion. The instructor's job often consists of synthesizing student comments, redirecting explorations, and helping with transitions to other topics.

This suggests that online distance learning applications must be designed to encourage and facilitate communication and interaction with others. Certain teaching methods would not find a happy home in such an environment, particularly the instructivist method that puts a premium on linear, tightly controlled lessons.

Home educational products and online applications must be designed for the basic home computer. The designer cannot include features that require special-purpose hardware or software, extremely fast modems, or broadband connectivity. For online applications, in particular, this puts limits on the amount of multimedia that can be included in the design.

The Classroom

Multimedia applications designed for use in schools are, like the home variety, intended for use on personal computers (as opposed to special-purpose hardware) that can play CD-ROMs and connect to the Internet. Like distance learning applications, the school-targeted product is part of a larger curriculum that may include texts, independent research, some time in the classroom, and face-to-face instruction. Unlike distance learning, the participants are gathered together in close proximity, at the same time, and communication between the participants extends beyond asynchronous, text-only communiqués. Real-time group dynamics are introduced in the school venue.

The fact that students are co-located in the school setting introduces certain design parameters. Even though each student may work on a computer, he or she may do so as part of a small team, and the entire class is probably present at the same time. This suggests the design should accommodate multiuser capabilities. Lessons may include collaborative games and activities, especially those that involve synchronous communications.

Corporate Training

Corporate training takes place at the office, on the factory floor, on location (on the job, but away from the office or factory), and at home. Corporate training programs share many characteristics with distance learning programs, the home CD-ROM, and applications designed for the classroom. The design considerations described previously apply here, as well. The chief differences are the profile of the learner population, the motivation of the learners, and the typical content of the subject matter, which lead to still other design considerations.

Corporate training is usually directed at adult learners. Wlodkowski (1989) says that "one of the most widely accepted views in the field of education is that adults are highly pragmatic learners" (p. 48). Research shows that most of the time, adult learners are highly self-motivated, self-directed, mature, and responsible. Even when adult learners are suffering from self-doubt, low self-esteem, and other problems that may cause them to stumble in a corporate training program, they tend to

FIGURE 3.6

Project Pass, designed to teach seventh-grade mathematics by using football as the context, was a complete curriculum. It included a "coach's manual" for the instructors and "playbooks" for the students.

fare better because of what Wlodkowski calls "an innate need for self-determination and competence" (p. 56).

How does this affect design? Unlike children's programs that may require entertainment (activities, games, music, and stories) to engage the user, corporate training multimedia needs none of that, which may actually have the opposite effect on the adult learner. What motivates the adult learner is progress, or success, with the subject matter. Feedback is essential to show the learner continuous progress. As you will read in Chapter 4, such success may be accomplished with games, and simulations are well known to enhance learning among adults. Role playing in both a competitive and a collaborative setting is routinely and successfully used in training courses.

Most corporate training programs are skill or task oriented. The skills and tasks are job, and sometimes company, specific. Multimedia applications designed for one company, to solve one performance discrepancy, are usually useless to another.

A Case Study

Sylvia Smith, Ed.D., vice president and an instructional designer with Mosaic Organizational Performance Group. She works closely with clients such as Sears, Roebuck & Co. to develop effective instructional and training programs. Reprinted by permission.

Dr. Sylvia R. Smith is an instructional designer and the vice president of the Chicago office of Mosaic Organizational Performance Group (previously called McGill Multimedia), a Canadian company that specializes in developing instructional and training programs for a variety of corporate clients. Smith supervises the strategy and implementation of instructional design for Mosaic. Her specialties include instructional design, curriculum development, performance analysis, performance appraisals, and group facilitation. Smith contributed the following case history of a project completed in 1999 that helps illustrate the instructional design process.

Sears, Roebuck & Co. engaged Mosaic Organizational Performance Group in November 1998 to partner in the design of a companywide sales management training program, now entitled Achieving the Competitive Edge. The challenge was to design a program that could assist two levels of managers: incumbent sales managers who had been with Sears for more than six months and new hires who had just begun careers with Sears. The two levels had to be designed so that both the incumbent and new hire sales managers could achieve the same core knowledge base that is now the required standard for all Sears sales managers.

Sales managers are required to make numerous decisions daily dealing with operational, tactical, and leadership issues. Thus, a comprehensive sales management training program required a multilayered delivery process. To accommodate the need for a multilayered delivery process, various formats were incorporated into the program. These formats included multimedia, hard copy, video, one-to-one interaction, and facilitator-led discussions. Regardless of format, the development of each component in the program required a well-defined instructional design process.

The instructional design process used in this project incorporated 10 key steps. The 10 steps are: a needs analysis, performance and learner analyses, goal setting, defining supportive objectives, developing instructional strategies, determining instructional materials, determining instructional delivery process, formative assessment, and, finally, a summative evaluation.

The initial step in designing the sales management training program was to conduct a comprehensive needs analysis to carefully assess the issues and problems to be addressed. During the needs analysis, an instructional designer and project manager conferred with subject matter experts to analyze both the current and desired performance levels. This analysis provided information on elements of the current situation, existing materials, target audience, program expectations, time line, target audience, and topic(s) to be included in the program. After this information was gathered and organized, clear program goals were then defined.

In this project it was decided that two independent overall program goals were most appropriate to meet the unique needs of the incumbent versus the new-hire sales managers.

The overall goal of the incumbent sales manager's version is to offer relevant and useful business-specific information that could be practically integrated into day-to-day work situations. This overall program goal set the stage for the identification of specific support goals and objectives. These program goals and objectives provided the framework to determine the instructional strategies that led to the most appropriate delivery format for each program component. The delivery formats for the incumbent sales managers were threefold: a business-specific planner, a "toolkit" of structured action items, both of which were supported by 16 interactive video modules that provided scenarios for flexible store implementation.

The overall goal for the new-hire sales manager's version is to provide a comprehensive 12-month mentorship program. Just as with the incumbent program, the overall program goal required the definition of comprehensive objectives. During their first 12 months in the job, new hires would be progressively introduced to relevant business-specific information that ranged from technical to leadership skills. Due to the complexity of the new-hire program design, the delivery formats include a multilayered process that contains a business-specific planner, a toolkit, multimedia instruction materials, one-to-one interaction, facilitator-led interactive discussions and an evaluation component. The formative evaluation component for the new-hire sales managers includes a three-tiered performance assessment scheduled during the 4th, 8th, and 12th months of the program. Performance monitoring records for each sales manager are kept in a section entitled "Sales Management Development Plan." This component provides for specific, structured performance feedback to sales managers throughout the program.

A comprehensive project such as the sales management training program requires detailed organization and management throughout the entire design and development process. Defining clear program goals is a critical element of the design process. The program goals act as anchors from which more specific objectives are developed. The instructional design process used in this project built detailed and targeted segments into a comprehensive, clear, and useful training program. This defined and structured training program design is now used in 855 Sears stores, serving as the blueprint for 6,000 Sears, Roebuck & Co. sales managers to achieve a competitive edge. (Smith, 1998)

Chapter Summary

In this chapter, we discussed the unique design requirements of educational and instructional multimedia, beginning with the role of the chief contributor, the instructional designer. It is the instructional designer who determines whether an instructional or educational need exists, the performance discrepancy that must be corrected, and whether multimedia is an appropriate vehicle for the solution. Using knowledge of the social sciences, computer science, management practices, communicative arts, and multimedia, the instructional designer crafts a computer-based tool that achieves the learning objective. The teaching tool may fall into any one of several traditional, computer-based models, including computer-assisted cooperative learning, computer-aided instruction, and computer-based training, to name a few.

Designers rely on a number of criteria to decide whether multimedia should be used to solve the learning objective. Designers evaluate the subject matter and determine whether it can be modularized, or divided up into chunks, and accessed in a nonlinear manner and still make sense. They assemble demographic profiles of the target users and determine if the size, background, motivation, and other characteristics of the group justify the use of multimedia. Designers consider the venue for the instruction and whether it supports multimedia. And finally, they ascertain if the intended teaching or learning method blends into an interactive multimedia delivery system.

Unlike nearly all other genres of multimedia, educational and instructional multimedia applications are solutions to specific problems. The designer must define the instructional challenge, or "performance discrepancy"; the learning objective, or solution to the problem; the teaching method; and the evaluation method. All of these are based on empirical knowledge and have a firm research base to support the decisions. Once defined, these elements guide and direct the design of the multimedia application.

The many venues of instruction and education also contribute to the design of the interactive application. Instruction delivered over the Internet to a largely adult learner population calls for a different design approach than, let's say, a mildly educational CD-ROM intended for the pleasure of children at home.

Recommended Reading

Boyle, Tom. *Design for Multimedia Learning*. Prentice Hall: London, 1997.

Brown, Barbara Mahone (1998). "Digital Classrooms: Some Myths about Developing New Educational Programs Using the Internet." *THE Journal, 26* (5). Retrieved August 12, 1999 from the World Wide Web: http://www.thejournal.com/magazine/vault/a2007.cfm

Dempsey, John V., and Sales, Gregory C., Eds. *Interactive Instruction and Feedback*. Educational Technology Publications: Englewood Cliffs, NJ, 1993.

Johnson, D. W., and Johnson, R. T. "Cooperative Learning and Feedback in Technology-Based Instruction." In Dempsey, John V., and Sales, Gregory C., Eds. *Interactive Instruction and Feedback*. Educational Technology Publications: Englewood Cliffs, NJ, 1993.

Johnson, Kerry A., and Foa, Lin J., Eds. *Instructional Design: New Alternatives for Effective Education and Training.* Macmillan: New York, 1989.

McLuhan, Marshall. *Understanding Media, The Extensions of Man.* The New American Library of Canada: Toronto, 1966.

Papert, Seymour. *The Children's Machine: Rethinking School in the Age of the Computer.* Basic Books: New York, 1994.

Reynolds, A., and Iwinski, T. *Multimedia Training: Developing Technology-Based Systems.* McGraw Hill: New York, 1996.

Schwier, Richard A., and Misanchuk, Earl R. *Interactive Multimedia Instruction.* Educational Technology Publications: Englewood Cliffs, NJ, 1993.

Tapscott, Don. *Growing Up Digital: The Rise of the Net Generation.* McGraw Hill: New York, 1998.

Wlodkowski, Raymond J. "Instructional Design and Learner Motivation." In Johnson, Kerry A., and Foa, Lin J., Eds. *Instructional Design: New Alternatives for Effective Education and Training.* Macmillan: New York, 1989.

Game Design

In this chapter, you will learn

- The similarities between games and stories
- Why people play games
- Success strategies for games
- Three important guidelines for designing a game
- Game concepts and components
- Concepts common to all types of games
- Genre-specific concepts
- Game genres and their characteristics

In this chapter, you are introduced to design concepts for multimedia CD-ROM games. You will learn the guidelines, underlying success strategies, and features used by game designers. In professional settings, experienced game designers take the lead role in the design of game products, and they often take on the additional role(s) of producer, director, writer, and/or technical director. As a producer, director, or writer, you may work closely with game designers on projects, and you must have a clear understanding of the design concepts they employ. Refer to Chapter 2 to review the discussions of the drivers and components of interactive design, which also apply here.

In subsequent chapters, you will learn about development processes that the producer manages, the tasks the director supervises, and the documents that the writer creates.

What Are Games?

Researchers in mathematics, politics, war, economics, philosophy, and other disciplines apply a "bag of analytical tools" called game theory to understand how decisionmakers (players) interact (Osborne & Rubenstein, 1994). In their book on game theory, Osborne and Rubenstein define a game as "a description of strategic interaction that includes the constraints on the actions that players *can* take and the players' interests, but does not specify the actions the players *do* take"(p. 2). In other words, a game is the description of a playing field, objectives, rules, certain constraints, and behaviors possible within the playing field. Players are free to move within these boundaries while attempting to find the strategic solution or best possible outcome in their own self-interest. This definition applies very well to both entertainment and educational games developed for the multimedia market.

Games Are Pervasive

Multimedia games are the largest segment of the retail market. Many other multimedia products incorporate games or game theory as a component of their overall design. Even educational applications use games as an integral part of the learning application. Knowledge Adventure, publisher of the *Math Blaster* series of educational CD-ROM products for children, published on its web site a treatise on the connection between game play and learning (http://www.knowledgeadventure. com). "What is it about good games that makes them powerful tools for learning? In fact, good games mirror good instruction. They include the same basic components: motivation, modeling, practice, evaluation, and active learning."

How important are games? They are an economic force. *USA Today* reported in the spring of 1999 that computer games would reach $7 billion in total sales before the end of the year, greater than the predicted Hollywood box office ($6.5 billion) (Snider, 1999). Games have affected society in other, unexpected ways. Don Tapscott, industry visionary and author, devoted his keynote address to the Electronic Entertainment Expo in 1999 to a discussion of the social, cultural, and political impact of computer games. Among other things, he credited the computer games market with being a primary driver of the technological advances currently available with all personal computers, such as fast processors, accelerator cards, math coprocessors, and video cards.

Games are the earliest form of interactive entertainment. Roman soldiers played dice and medieval kings played cards. Our grandparents played *Monopoly*. They interacted with each other! Multimedia began as a game industry—some even call it a game *culture*—more than 30 years ago. A long succession of technological and creative advances have taken the game industry from early text-based, online games such as *Dungeons and Dragons* and *Zork* through early graphical games such as *Pong* and side-scrollers such as *Pac-Man* to today's real-time 3-D flight simulators and virtual reality games.

The platforms have changed (from early video game consoles like Atari to Pentiums and 128-bit console games), and the graphic look and sound capabilities have evolved and improved steadily. However, the real value of a game is in its underlying design. In fact, enjoyable games endure and many old games are re-released year after year with very little change to their underlying game design. Hasbro released several successful board and card games—the same ones played by our grandparents, *Risk, Monopoly, Yahtzee,* and *Scrabble* among them—as multimedia products. Why? Because multimedia is an ideal medium for repackaging what is essentially great interactive entertainment.

Similarities between Games and Films

As a filmmaker and game designer, I am struck by the similarities between storytelling and game design. Well-made character-based films often feature ordinary people doing extraordinary things, or extraordinary people doing ordinary things. In *Shoes of the Fisherman,* Anthony Quinn plays a prisoner in the Russian gulag system who becomes the Pope. In *Kindergarten Cop,* Arnold Schwarzenegger plays a tough cop who winds up babysitting a room full of preschool children. Games are like that, as well. The player, of course, is the main character. Well-crafted games enable perfectly ordinary teenagers to defeat powerful enemies (Satan, for instance, in a game called *Diablo*). Puzzle games like *Tetris* can confound even MIT graduates.

A well-structured film begins with a setup that reveals a conflict the main character must overcome. So do good games. By the end of the game's introductory sequence, the player knows what his or her goal (conflict) is and goes about trying to attain it. The second act of a well-written screenplay has the main character encountering and dealing with one crisis after another, leading up to the resolution of the conflict. In the process, the main character is transformed by this experience. Games force the player to deal with one challenge after another—each more troublesome than the previous—until he or she resolves the conflict. Players are transformed by games—more often than not by becoming better game players than they were when they started.

Games and Education

As discussed in Chapter 3, educational applications are designed to impart knowledge, skill, and concepts to the user. Years of research by psychologists, sociologists, teachers, and instructional technologists have resulted in a vast store of theory and empirical data on how people learn and what teaching models best facilitate learning. The studies continue, but this much they agree on:

■ People need to be motivated to learn. Volunteer learners ("I want to take this course.") are more motivated than those who are compulsory learners ("I have to take this course.").

■ The best learning model is one that enables students to build on previous knowledge. In educational circles, this is called scaffolding. Ultimately, the model should allow learners to apply what they have learned to new situations— ideally, to real-life occurrences.

■ The more concrete the initial experience, the more likely students will understand abstract concepts. This is especially true for children. "Don't go near the outlet, you'll get a shock," means nothing to three-year-olds until they actually experience one. (Don't try this at home.)

■ Some people learn better visually (observing), others kinesthetically (doing).

■ Either way, people learn better when they can practice what they learn and can evaluate and recognize their own progress, which also contributes to a higher degree of motivation.

As you read this chapter, you will discover there is a very close correlation between game design and the generally accepted principles of instructional design. Multimedia games are designed to motivate players to start and continue playing, largely through a combination of success strategies, scaffolds (or levels) of play, and constant feedback. Once drawn in, game players amplify their learning by constantly practicing and applying new skills to advance through the game. Some games, particularly simulations, enable players to apply what they have learned to near-real-life situations. Short of direct, purposeful experiences, multimedia games provide virtual experiences capable of teaching abstract concepts. Multimedia games are multimodal. Players must learn and engage the game both visually and kinesthetically. This facilitates learners regardless of how they learn best.

Why People Play Games

There are countless reasons people play games, but the most seductively simple is that games are *fun*. What makes a game fun? Well-designed games serve our conscious and subliminal needs for dominance, superiority, competition, challenge, learning, applying knowledge, skill development, self-esteem, collaboration, teamwork, destruction, and building—all in a benign, risk-free environment. Depending on one's state of mind and psychological and emotional needs, one may enjoy any game that provides one or more of the above.

These diverse game outcomes have one common thread—*success*, or the possibility of success. When players are successful playing a game, it is rewarding. When the game is rewarding, it is fun. The objective, then, of any game, is that it should be fun and entertaining. When games are designed for educational or instructional purposes, the objective should still be entertainment. Learning and enjoyment are not mutually exclusive, and the most successful educational applications support this. The Learning Company's *Carmen Sandiego* series is so popular with children that it spawned its own animated TV series. Visit the web site for links to game reviews, game developers, and game publishers.

FIGURE 4.1

Children playing The Learning Company's *Where in the U.S.A. Is Carmen Sandiego?* encounter entertaining characters and situations while learning about the country's geography.

Success Strategies

When the designer designs a game, an early decision is how players will be rewarded. How will they achieve success? There are a number of *success strategies.*

■ *Win over an opponent.* Most games involve a winner-take-all scenario in which the fun of the game is successfully vanquishing an opponent. In multimedia games, the opponent is sometimes the computer.

■ *Meet a challenge.* Some games involve not beating an opponent, but rather overcoming some obstacle or challenge. Flight simulators present the challenge of successfully taking off, flying, and landing.

■ *Solve a problem.* Some games, like certain immersive puzzle games such as *Myst* or *The Journeyman Project,* present the player with a problem or puzzle, which tests players' knowledge, memory, or detective work.

- *Heighten a fantasy.* Some games help a player fantasize. Everyone daydreams and fantasizes, but a well-executed game heightens the virtual experience. A flight simulator, for example, can actually cause a player to sweat.

- *Learn a skill.* Success in some games is achieved by learning and applying a new skill. Many children's activity games teach children about colors or shapes then challenge them to play a game in which this new skill is tested.

- *Form a social unit.* This success is the opposite of vanquishing an enemy. The fun is derived from forming a team with others and then participating in an activity that may involve winning, meeting a challenge, solving a problem, or learning a skill. Rotisserie baseball leagues are a little like this.

Any game can be studied to determine the strategy that makes it rewarding. The designer's decision regarding the strategy is driven by, and in turn affects, the chosen venue (platform), target user, subject, genre, and other influences. For example, a game that has, as its underlying strategy, the formation of a social unit is appropriately developed for a networked, online venue like the Internet where many players can meet. MUDs (multiuser domains) are cyberspace meeting places where games involving the formation of social units have been played for years.

Guidelines for a Game

In the process of developing the game idea, the designer keeps in mind the following guidelines.

Few Rules, Infinite Play

The game should have very few rules but provide game players a huge variety of game experiences and outcomes. Checkers, chess, poker, and goh are examples of games having relatively few rules but unlimited possible experiences and outcomes. When the ratio of rules to outcomes is correct, the game is considered "elegant."

Easy to Learn, Difficult to Master

When a game has few rules to learn, players begin experimenting with their skill and enjoyment of the game immediately. If, at the same time, the game is endlessly challenging, players continue to test themselves with the game. Every popular, enduring game embodies this guideline. Goh, for example, is a game most people can learn to play in a few minutes. Mastering the game, however, can take a lifetime.

Short-Term Rewards

Players should be rewarded continuously and consistently while playing the game. Short-term rewards include scoring, advancing through levels (holes on a golf course, for example), or winning "hands," as in a card game. Short-term rewards in some children's multimedia games are as simple as an audio clip that announces, "Good work!"

These three guidelines are the key to getting players to try the game and continue to play it. Think of the games you play and see if these guidelines apply.

Game Features

You recall from Chapter 2 that all multimedia titles are systems consisting of the application (content, features, and structure) and the user interface (functional controls and look and feel). Perhaps more so for games than for other forms of multimedia, features play a key role. Features are the interactive capabilities or characteristics of multimedia and are at the very heart of game play. Whereas most any reference product or informational web site can feature little more than a search engine and hyperlinks, multimedia games rely on very robust forms of interactivity, including real-time simulations, artificial intelligence, multiuser functionality, and highly customizable experiences. As a result, a comprehensive array of game features has evolved over the years and continues to grow.

A type of natural selection is at work in the game industry. Game consoles and multimedia platforms evolve and mature. With each generation, new and better capabilities are introduced and exploited in game design. Games appear utilizing these features and are accepted or rejected by the market. As time goes on, successful games are imitated, unsuccessful games are forgotten, and all games begin to fall into one or more of the surviving genres.

The emergence of genres leads one to look at the specific characteristics and features that typify successful games. Producers, directors, and writers should understand these concepts, as they drive the designer's thoughts about what should or should not be included in a game design targeted for a particular genre and its players.

Features Common to All Games

Goals.   Every game presents a goal or objective for the player to achieve. The goal may be to score a lot of points (*NBA Jam*), defeat an enemy (*Diablo*), discover a hidden secret (*Myst*), build a self-sustaining city (*SimCity*), or learn math (*Math Blaster*). The goal of a game is analogous to the conflict in a screenplay: It's the one big thing the main character—the game player—must overcome. The player must know what the goal is and how to attain it. Many games feature an introductory sequence: a linear movie that reveals the story behind the game and tells players what they must do to succeed.

Challenges.   Challenges are obstacles that the player must overcome to attain the goal. These are the roadblocks or "fiery hoops" the player has to get over, around, or through. Challenges can be "minions," which are the minor enemies players may have to defeat while working their way toward the "boss" enemy usually found at the end of a game level. Challenges can be the series of questions the player must answer while competing with friends in *You Don't Know Jack.* Norman (1988) admonishes that "challenges should not be confused with frustration and error" (p. 208). There is a thin line between challenges that lead to enjoyment and those that lead to disappointment.

Rewards.   Whenever players overcome a challenge, they expect to be rewarded. Examples of rewards are a musical riff, a congratulatory audio cue, or a numerical score that increases. In the old arcade game *Asteroids,* players were rewarded with the sight and sound of the asteroid vaporizing every time they blasted one.

Rules.   Rules define the results, or consequences, of actions initiated by players. The rules of physics are programmed into the behavior of a flying or driving simulation game. When players drive their cars into a turn too fast (action), they spin out (results). The rules of baseball are included in the rules for a sports game: three strikes are an out, three outs end a half-inning, and so forth. Rules such as these may be known either cognitively or intuitively by players before they start playing. In such an event, the designer is counting on players to have a certain base knowledge, upon which players build by playing the game.

Other game rules are determined by the game designer. The designer of a multimedia baseball game determines such things as "if the player swings at this type of pitch within this time frame, then the ball will be hit to right field." Rules such as these must be learned by players while playing the game, usually heuristically, by trial and error: "If I swing now, I think it'll go to right field."

The game designer's most difficult task is to arrive at the shortest set of rules (see the guideline "Few Rules, Infinite Play" in this chapter) that will provide the richest game experience possible. The designer must make sure that rules never change—that once a rule is learned by players, players can apply that knowledge to attain the goal and build on that knowledge to increase their skill.

Point of View.   Players see the game from either the first- or third-person point of view. The first-person point of view gives players a view of the game through the eyes of a participant who is literally (actually, virtually) in the game world. The third-person point of view gives players an omniscient view of the game world—from above and behind the action.

Worlds.   All games are played over a background or in an environment. The term *world* refers not only to the graphic appearance of the game field, but also to the

FIGURE 4.2

A first-person view of the action from the game *Lands of Lore,* developed
and published by Westwood Studios, an Electronic Arts company.

layout, size, physical features, attributes, and behavior of the world and to the things
in the world. In a baseball game, the game world is the baseball field. Players may be
able to see the entire game world all of the time, perhaps from the third-person perspective of the umpire behind home plate. In a strategy game, such as *Command &*
Conquer, the game world is a large expanse of land, only part of which can be seen
by the player.

Levels.   Levels are specific locations in the game world where a portion of the
game is played. Players must meet and overcome challenges in a level before moving on to the next level and eventually achieve the main goal. So the term *level* refers
to time, place, and achievement. Typically, subsequent levels are more challenging
than the current one. In educational multimedia design, the notion of "scaffolding"
or the "learning ladder" is tantamount to the level in game play. The learner must
master one level before advancing to the next.

Fast Twitch.   The "fast twitch" game depends on rapid and continuous kines-
thetic response from the player. Eye-hand coordination is the principal skill required
to succeed. In sport, ping pong is a fast twitch game. In multimedia, fast-twitch

FIGURE 4.3

A view of the game world from the strategy game *Command & Conquer,* developed and published by Westwood Studios, an Electronic Arts company.

games are driving, flying, fighting, and sports games (including ping pong). Players are engaged in a real-time event while playing these games and must make split-second decisions to stay in the game. Success depends on experiential cognition.

Slow Twitch. The "slow twitch" game does not depend on instantaneous responses from players. Chess, for example, is slow twitch. In slow twitch games, players are not engaged in a real-time event. They may take time to ponder the next interaction and base their decisions on things they have have learned while playing. The slow twitch game genres include board, strategy, children's activity, adventure, role-playing, and immersive games. Success depends on reflective cognition.

Features Common to Most Genres

Winning and Losing. Not all games are about winning and losing, but when they are, the designer must determine how a player can win and how hard it should be and how a player loses and how easy that should be. The designer determines the combination of skill, luck, good decisions, sound strategy, eye-hand coordination, timing, or other game elements that contribute to winning. Will the combination translate into a success strategy for the player? Will the game be fun?

Backstory. Strategy and role-playing games often include what is called the backstory, or history, of what happened in the game world leading up to the moment the game player came on the scene. Sometimes the backstory is very elaborate, including beautiful, cinematic development of planets, cultures, conflicts, and characters. The notion behind this is that players become immersed in the fantasy and more passionately involved in a competitive game. Interestingly, the *goal* of the blockbuster game *Myst* is to discover the *backstory* of the game world!

Characters.   Multimedia games may or may not include characters. Puzzle games such as *Tetris* have none, while Disney's Animated StoryBook CD-ROMs such as *The Lion King, Pocahontas,* and *Hercules* are built around characters. When they do appear in a game, characters have the following functions:

- ■ *Star.* In animated storybook products, including the classic *Grandma and Me* and all those wonderful Disney products, the character is at the center of the product and all activity orbits around it. The game is a story about the character.

- ■ *Host or guide.* The character acts as the players' sidekick, mentor, host, or guide, usually serving the purpose of explaining to players what to do next, how to do it, and providing encouragement. Tonka Joe is the child's buddy while he or she plays with *Tonka Construction, Tonka Search and Rescue,* and *Tonka Garage* products. Tonka Joe introduces the game, then reappears continuously during the game to accompany the player from one challenge to the next.

- ■ *Player's persona.* The character is the player's "game piece." The player controls the character's every action. In the adventure games *Kings Quest* and *Phantasmagoria,* the player assumes the roles of characters in the game, taking them from one location to another and directing them to open doors, pick up items, use tools and so forth.

- ■ *Player's team.* The player selects a group of characters from a larger pool and uses this group to play the game. In role-playing games (RPG), the player usually selects a team of characters—each with special attributes—and winning the game is a matter of employing these team members correctly to solve problems.

- ■ *Player's enemies.* Enemy characters are among the challenges faced by players. Players must fight, shoot, or kill enemy characters to attain the goal. The minor enemies are called "minions," the major enemies are called "boss." Minions who are particularly easy to defeat are called "fodder."

- ■ *Bystanders.* Like extras in a film, bystanders are just hanging around in the game world. In some particularly violent shooting games, bystanders are routinely caught in the crossfire.

As in screenwriting, characters are developed to be believable, interesting, and worth caring about. Writers try to develop multidimensional characters whose actions can, after a while, be predicted as the viewer becomes familiar with them. In games, designers assign characters *attributes* and *behaviors,* which essentially accomplish the same thing. RPG, strategy, sports, fighting, shooting, and killing games depend very much on the attributes and behaviors of characters, because players' success depends on their ability to understand, utilize, and control characters and to take advantage of the weaknesses of the enemies.

Attributes.   Character attributes relate to the character's physical appearance, physical or mental prowess, and/or supernatural abilities. Combatants in a fighting game, for example, may have powers that include great upper-body strength, elastic arms, leaping ability, or the ability to throw fire. Designers also determine how long these powers last and what circumstances cause them to diminish.

Behaviors.   Character behavior relates to how the character acts or reacts to situations that occur during the game. Combatant characters may be designed to attack constantly whenever an enemy is within a certain distance. Others may be designed to run away under the same circumstances. Behaviors can be designed to change as the game situation changes. For example, the same character programmed to run away may charge the enemy mindlessly if he or she has been given a particular weapon, given power-up (see the next section), or cornered.

Power-Ups.   Some games require the character to obtain "power-ups" in order to have the strength to overcome another challenge. Power-ups can be super-charged fuel for a car in a racing game, extra ammo in a shooting game, or food for the whole team in an RPG.

Payoff.   The big reward at the end of a successfully played game is the payoff. In the *Tonka Search and Rescue* game, the child player is rewarded with a newspaper with his or her name in the headline that he or she can print out. The newspaper celebrates the child's accomplishment. All games must end with some kind of payoff, just as all films end with some kind of resolution or climax.

Genre-Dependent Features

Multiplayer.   More than one player can play the game, either as opponents or as a team. Competitive games such as strategy, fighting, and sports games are often multiplayer. Some games do not lend themselves to the one-on-one competitive genre. Puzzle games and immersive games, such as *Myst,* tend to be single-player.

Turn-Based Multiplayer.   The game is played by more than one person, and players take turns controlling the game, as in a board game such as *Monopoly.*

Artificial Intelligence (AI).   AI is a discipline in computer science that attempts to teach a computer to learn. In the game industry, the term is used to describe a

FIGURE 4.4

The interactive board game *Monopoly,* published by Hasbro Interactive and developed by Westwood Studios, features multiplayer, turn-based play. Players can compete with each other over the Internet.

game that behaves as though it has a mind of its own. The player competes against the computer. The computer makes game-playing decisions just as a human opponent would.

Randomness.   Some aspects of the game are determined randomly by the game engine, causing every game session to be unique. The game *SimCity,* for example, randomly generates a completely unique terrain—or game world—when a new game begins. That causes the game to be a unique experience every time it's played.

Real time.   The game actually *generates* graphics and sounds "on the fly," while the game is played, at the rate of 30 frames per second (sometimes less, sometimes more).

Simulation.   The computer generates graphics and sounds in real time, based on various parameters, databases, tables, algorithms, and input from the player. The resulting view is usually a believable result matching what the player would expect to see in real life. Flight simulators behave this way. As the player controls air speed, wing flaps, and other control surfaces, the view through the cockpit window changes accordingly and realistically.

Customizable.   Players can set parameters of various kinds at the beginning of the game, and these parameters determine the game experience. Many games allow players to select their own personas, construct their own weapons, or pick their team. Other games allow players to set a level of difficulty.

Competitive.   Players either win or lose the game. A goal is established and obstacles must be overcome. Failure can occur. Many children's activity games, such as those in Disney's Animated StoryBook CD-ROMs, do not allow children to lose the game.

Game Genres

There are at least a dozen identifiable game genres. In the list below, several genres are combined because they share the same success strategy and features. Players are rewarded in the same way.

Children's Activity

These games are designed for young children and are exemplified by Animated Story-Book products developed by Disney. It is difficult to think of some products in this genre as games because they are often designed to be linear stories with some interactive experiences. Many titles include a game as a "page" in the storybook. The games are generally noncompetitive. There may be scoring, but it is designed to be a short-term reward for players, not an indication of winning or losing the game. The fun comes from learning and accomplishing some goal. Children's activity games often have an educational objective. The child may be challenged to match colors or to match an animal's sound with its picture. For older children, the education is played down and the activity is played up. *Barbie Fashion Designer,* for example, is a game to design and create—out of real cloth by using a color printer—new clothes for a Barbie doll. These games tend to be single player and slow twitch. Because they are designed for children, they have animated characters, music, and songs.

Role-Playing Game (RPG)

In an RPG, players are often assigned a mission or goal, and, as the name suggests, they assume the role of a character in a fantasy world. Using a customization feature, the player selects a group of companions with special gifts to join him or her on the mission. The game can be won or lost, and winning is determined by how well the player uses the team's gifts to overcome various challenges that confront him or her. The enjoyment derived from playing an RPG is gained by assembling the team and working with it to accomplish the mission. These games may be multiplayer—sometimes played by large numbers of people over the Internet—and are generally slow twitch. They are viewed from the third person and can be re-played many times with different results.

Immersive

In immersive games, players do not assume the role of another character and are usually alone—there is no team of gifted specialists. Players explore a fantasy world from a first-person point of view and gather knowledge that enables them to solve a mystery or puzzle. There may or may not be an antagonist, or enemy, to deal with. *Myst, Time Lapse,* and the *Journeyman Project* are good examples of this genre. These games are slow twitch and time consuming but not replayable—once the player has solved the mystery, that's it.

FIGURE 4.5

The Prayer Hall in *The Journeyman Project 3: Legacy of Time,* developed by Presto Studios. This is an immersive game in which players explore rich, tantalizing locations, looking for clues to a mystery.

Adventure

Adventure games are similar to immersive games, but the view is usually a third-person view. Players control one character as a "game piece," causing the character to move from place to place and look for the solution to a mystery or puzzle. *Kings Quest* and *Phantasmagoria,* both written by Roberta Williams, are classic examples.

Strategy

Strategy games are competitive, win-or-lose conflicts usually pitting players against the computer. AI is a feature of strategy games. Online versions enable players to compete against one another in staged conflicts. In the most popular products—such as *Command & Conquer* and *Warcraft*—players are given command of an army and resources—equipment, money, time, raw materials—which they deploy and utilize to their own advantage. Meanwhile, the computer or the opponent is doing the same thing. Eventually, the two (or three) battling armies meet. The outcome of the conflict depends on the choices made by each player and the computer. During the battle, the player maneuvers his or her army on the battlefield and makes command decisions. Some versions of strategy games allow players to toggle between different views of the battle, from a high-level, omniscient view to a first-person view on the field of battle.

Sim

Sim games (taken from the word *simulation*) are noncompetitive, single-player games. Sim games feature a cause-and-effect style of artificial intelligence. The games are designed to enable players to make decisions and to see the results of those decisions immediately. The success strategy is to learn a new skill and to apply that knowledge to achieve a new, more challenging goal. *SimCity* and a number of derivative products are examples. In *SimCity*, the computer creates a random terrain replete with mountains, trees, rivers, and oceans. Players are given money with which to build a city. As players decide how to spend money—on roads, factories, homes, or marinas—the effects are seen and heard immediately. Seen from a third-person point of view and in real time, the city either grows and prospers or runs out of money and falls into disrepair.

Sports

Sports games have been designed around all major and many minor sports. In some sports games, players compete against the computer by controlling one or all of the members of their team. In other sports games, such as golf, players compete by themselves against the course, the elements, and their own lousy swing. Depending on the sport, the game play may be fast twitch (basketball) or slow twitch (golf). The newer and better-selling competitive games combine many features of other genres. In some products, players select a team based on real athletes with various skills, similar to the RPG. The computer does the same thing, similar to a strategy game. Graphically, the games are real-time, 3-D simulations of actual sporting events. Players can switch between different third-person views of the game.

Driving and Flying

These games are single-player, fast-twitch, real-time, 3-D simulations that boast a number of success strategies. They may be competitive, present challenges, involve learning and applying new skills, and heighten a fantasy. They are very popular—often topping the charts of best-selling multimedia titles. Typically, players are the driver or pilot of a vehicle and can toggle between different views—from behind the wheel of the vehicle to ¾-view from behind the vehicle. The player controls the vehicle using some combination of the mouse, key strokes, a joystick, and virtual controls in the interface. Because the vehicle reacts predictably as it would in real life—turning, banking, spinning out of control, and so on—players can learn to drive or fly with greater skill.

Shooting, Fighting, and Killing

In these games, players are pitted against opponents whom they must shoot, fight, or kill. These games are wildly popular because they appeal to so many success strategies—competition, challenges, fantasy, skill, and, increasingly, teamwork. These games feature single- and multiplayer (online), fast-twitch, and real-time 3-D simulation. The games are randomized to provide limitless game play without repeating scenarios.

A game is distinguished by how well its components, principally its features, have been gathered together and presented to the player. All games within a genre are composed of the same basic features. They all employ the three simple guidelines. They all aim to reward players with the same success strategy.

Game Tweaking

Unlike nongame multimedia products, which must conform to the functional specification, games must be *tweaked*, or adjusted. Tweaking refers to the continuous fine-tuning of game play right up to the release to manufacturing (RTM) of the gold master. Game designers begin with some idea of the game play that will deliver a fun and enjoyable experience, but only after the game has been assembled and tested by focus groups do the creators know what they have. The creators make changes to the game based on feedback from the testers and adjust the game-design document to match the changes made to the product. As Louis Castle, executive vice president at Westwood Studios comments in an email interview with me, "The (design) documents are relied on extensively throughout development, but it is a real task to keep them up-to-date all the time. Often the specifications change in an amendment or clarification document without the master document being updated until there is some form of formal review" (June 19, 1999).

What gets tweaked? Scores of things, usually related to how the game feels when played, although sometimes an additional piece of art or a sound is needed to strengthen or improve the game. *Feel* means the speed, pacing, and timing of events. In a quest game produced at Mammoth Micro Productions, the team tweaked such things as the number of times the villain appeared unexpectedly, how many gold coins were seeded randomly in the game world, how quickly players needed to use their power-up, and many other variables. It took extra time and cost, but it was worth it.

The producer, director, and writer should be aware of the tweaking phenomenon. The producer should plan for it in the budget and schedule. The director should plan for it with personnel, making certain that at least one artist and one sound designer is available right up to the last minute. The writer should be prepared to create one final revision of the design document while everyone else is celebrating.

Chapter Summary

Games were the first manifestation of interactive multimedia and continue to dominate the market. Many applications have games as important components or use game theory as the basis for the interactive experience established for the user. People play games because they are fun. The enjoyment comes largely from the rewards of success. Games typically present players with goals which, when attained by successfully overcoming challenges and obstacles, produce conscious and subliminal rewards. Popular games actually bear a remarkable resemblance to screenplays—possibly explaining why some games and stories endure and resonate with people universally.

There are a number of concepts the producer, director, and writer need to know about games in order to work collaboratively with game designers. Among the concepts are the three guidelines for a good game: Have few rules but infinite game outcomes; make the game easy to learn, but difficult to master; and finally, reward players regularly and consistently.

Multimedia games fall into one or more of a dozen game genres. What distinguishes one genre from another is, first of all, the success strategy. Players may experience success by beating an opponent, learning a new skill, or solving a problem or puzzle. The fighting-shooting-killing genre is about defeating an opponent, the children's activity genre is about learning new skills, and the RPG genre is about solving a problem or puzzle. Fighting games usually feature 3-D real-time graphics and fast-twitch action. Strategy games are slow twitch and feature artificial intelligence, customization, and simulation.

Part of the game development process includes a step called tweaking, during which the finished game is fine-tuned for optimum game play.

Recommended Reading

Binmore, Ken. *Game Theory and the Social Contract.* MIT Press: Cambridge, 1994.

Dombrower, Eddie. *Dombrower's Art of Interactive Entertainment Design.* McGraw Hill: New York, 1998.

Osborne, Martin, and Rubenstein, Ariel. *A Course in Game Theory.* MIT Press: Cambridge, 1994.

Tapscott, Don. *Growing Up Digital.* McGraw Hill: New York, 1998.

The Interactive

Design Process

In this chapter, you will learn about

- Writing a concept document
- Performing a competitive analysis
- Writing a top-level design
- Performing a cost/benefit analysis
- Writing the functional specification

In this chapter, we cover the design *process,* a series of iterative steps during which a product concept is gradually refined until the goal—the final design document—is achieved. Because there is such a wide variety of multimedia applications for many purposes and markets, it is inappropriate to call the process described in this chapter hard and fast. The design process for some applications may require more steps. For example, the interactive design process discussed in this chapter is actually nested within the instructional design process for training or education. Instructional design includes steps that are taken prior to determining the need for a multimedia solution and evaluation steps that are taken after the entire instructional solution is deployed. Conversely, there may be fewer steps involved for some applications. For an entertainment product, an external client may approach a developer with a refined product concept. The design process may have already started, before the producer, director, and writer are involved.

Some steps may not be necessary at all, may be performed in a different order, or may be replaced by other steps called for by the specific project needs. For example, designers of multimedia games for the commercial market must conduct a competitive analysis (Step 2 in this chapter). Many times, this is the first step taken rather than the second. Designers of instructional multimedia solutions for use by specific clients for specific problems may not conduct a competitive analysis at all, but rather use the time to search for an existing product that will serve the purpose.

The sensible approach taken in this chapter is to discuss the general case and all of the attendant steps and to make reference to the possible exceptions. The five steps commonly taken in the interactive design process are (1) writing a concept document, (2) performing a competitive analysis, (3) writing a top-level design, (4) performing a cost/benefit analysis, and (5) writing the functional specification.

These five steps move the concept from an early, unrefined idea to a very detailed blueprint in a logical, professional, workmanlike manner. The steps ensure that the product is, first of all, a worthy one—it has a market and it can meet the users' needs and demand. Second, the steps ensure that the product is as good as or better than any competing products—critical in the competitive marketplace. The steps enable the design team to craft a product that can be completed for the target budget and within the schedule. Finally, these steps make it possible for two parties—the product developer and the client—to arrive at a design they agree on.

During the design process, we apply the design *principles* that we covered in previous chapters. You will learn that three documents are written during the design process, and there may be multiple versions of each. The writer writes all three documents with input from the producer, director, interactive designer, and others on the team. The producer and director use the documents to socialize the concept and obtain input and feedback, to prioritize and fine-tune the features, to develop preliminary development plans and budgets, and to reach contractual agreements with the client or potential partners. You will learn that the goal of the interactive design process is the final design document, called the functional specification.

The Design Team

Typically, the producer, director, writer, and interactive designer form the nucleus of the design team. Joining them in order to contribute expert advice and input are the content expert, instructional designer, art director, sound designer, lead programmer or technical director, and quality assurance manager. The makeup of the core team may be different, depending on the nature of the product. Instructional designers take a lead role on educational products, while game designers and technical directors are key on game products. The marketing manager also has a voice in this process and, in fact, is often the first heard when developing commercial products. Initially, the marketing manager provides valuable market research. If he or she cannot sell the product, it should not be made! During this process, the marketing manager observes and comments on the product design, especially on its competitive advantages or shortcomings.

When the product is educational or instructional, the concept team must include a subject matter expert and an educator or instructional designer. GTE and the National Football League collaborated on the development of a multimedia product, which was part of a curriculum designed to teach three standards of seventh-grade mathematics. This project used football as the context for teaching students about geometry, probability, and statistics. The project team included over 30 seventh-grade mathematics teachers from Seattle, Washington, and Dallas, Texas. The teachers developed the lessons, which were adapted for multimedia by an interactive designer. Ultimately, *Project Pass* received high marks from teachers and students and won several multimedia awards.

Step 1: Write a Concept Document

Purpose of the Concept Document

 The first step in the design process is to "put a stake in the ground" and write a one-to-two-page concept document. It is also called a *proposal*. The concept document describes the proposed product, its subject, target user, and genre and touches on the components discussed in Chapter 2. Concept documents for instructional applications include the learning objective, how the product will achieve the objective, and the evaluation method or plan, as discussed in Chapter 3.

The principle audience for the document is the development team. The document's purpose is to give the team a shared experience—something it can discuss and brainstorm. At one company I managed, we had just licensed a well-known cartoon character and needed product concepts featuring the little critter. Our writers (and contributors throughout the company) wrote more than a dozen. Concepts are reviewed, embellished, critiqued, saved, and sometimes thrown away.

The reviewers of a concept document read it and try to answer these questions:

- *Marketing:* Can I sell this product? Is this new, or just a "me too" product? Does it sound exciting? Does this fill a need in the market, or is this a solution in search of a problem?

- *Instructional Designers:* Is this designed in such a way that learning objectives can be achieved? Does the design enable us to measure the application's effectiveness?

- *Creatives:* Is this product cool, or what?

- *Production:* Is this within our capability? Do we have the artists, animators, sound engineers, videographers? How does this fit within our current development load for the year? What could this cost us?

- *Engineering:* What kind of new software code will this take? Can we use any of our current engines? Is there software out there that we could license? Are there hardware issues?

■ *Legal:* Do we have to worry about acquiring rights? Are there other contract issues?

■ *Management:* Is this product consistent with our strategy? Does it move us forward or does it defocus us? How will we be positioned if this product is a success? How will we be perceived if it fails? Can we really make money? Are our resources better used elsewhere?

Contents of Concept Document

To address these questions, the contents of the document include the following:

■ *The target market.* Describe the age, sex, interests, educational level, occupation, marital status, geographical location, and any other pertinent information about the target user. The description could be as broad as "Males aged 13 to 19" or as specific as "All employees in the West Coast office who will be using the new intranet server to obtain sales projections."

■ *The subject of the product.* Describe what your product is about. Weather, football, seventh-grade math, movie trivia, Indian food, cats, or the half-life of uranium.

■ *The need.* If the product is intended to serve a specific need, such as to solve an instructional problem at a corporation or provide travel directions at a kiosk, state the need. The concept document may reference another, previously created document, such as a consultant's recommendations or a needs analysis compiled by an instructional designer.

■ *The educational or instructional objectives.* If the product is intended to have specific results when used, identify them, and indicate how those objectives will be achieved and evaluated.

■ *The genre of the product.* If the product will be offered commercially, this is important. There are a small number of generally accepted "genres" in the multimedia industry. The genres are used by sales tracking organizations such as PC Data to group multimedia products together, rank them by sales, and publish the results. Categorizing products by genre also enables retailers to stock their shelves in a somewhat organized fashion and for shoppers to find what they're looking for. These genres are: Education, Games, Information, Reference, Office Utility. The product the concept describes should fit into one of these genres. If the concept combines genres—such as game and education—this may be called "edutainment."

■ *The theme of the product.* This is the creative approach, which includes the way the product looks, sounds, and behaves. Describe its uniqueness and its *attitude.* Describe what is special about this product and what marketing hooks it may have. Try to indicate its breadth and depth. Compare it to other products.

■ *The target platform (PC, Macintosh, PlayStation, etc.).* This section should include an initial estimate of the requirements the finished product may have for memory and processor speed. Identify any special-purpose hardware or software the end user may need to use the product.

It is fascinating what happens when a concept appears on paper. Suddenly, the fog lifts and an abstraction becomes concrete. A colleague—a writer—once remarked that stones now thrown at an idea have someplace to land. This is a good thing. Committing an idea to paper and making it subject to criticism and tweaking empowers the entire team and builds the community needed to complete the product.

Because concept documents are concise, several can be created and compared with one another, enabling the team to gravitate toward the best product or the best version of the proposed product.

Before Writing a Word

Before the writing process begins, the designer ponders the who, what, why, and how of the product or application. These primary elements must have practical connections to each other. Otherwise, the concept document will be seriously flawed.

Determine the User.   All other decisions related to the concept document begin when the intended user is identified. It's surprising how often this simple tenet is skipped, ignored, or forgotten, even in professional product development. Based on the profile of the target user, the subject, genre, theme, and design components can be determined. Sometimes these things have not already been determined by the client or by a previously completed needs analysis. If not, and if you are designing a product over which you have a great deal of control, select the target user based on these criteria:

■ The affinity and familiarity of the design and development team for that group.

■ The core competencies (audio/visual and software programming) of the design and development team. Play to the team's strengths.

Market Segments.   If you are designing a product for the commercial market, and not for the private internal use of a client, then be aware of the market for your product. The CD-ROM consumer market is segmented primarily along age and gender boundaries. There are many other considerations to use in the design itself, including the educational level, income level, ethnicity, race, and religion of the target users. However, publishers of multimedia products watch buying trends very carefully and have found a close correlation between the age and gender of the target user and the genre of the product he or she is most likely to buy. Games are a classic example. Louis Castle, executive vice-president of Westwood Studios, a very successful game publisher and developer, says in an e-mail interview with me,

> Multimedia *entertainment* is bought predominantly by young males. I hate to take a gender stance, but it is hard to argue with the statistics. Games are made for young males, so young males buy games. I think it will take a good deal of time before the games have interfaces and social features that will reach more statistically normal ratios of female to male buyers (Castle, personal communication, June 19, 1999)

Once the team has identified the target user, it is possible to narrow the focus of the product design to the genre that that target user is known to buy. Table 5.1 shows this relationship. Note that the buying trends represented in this table are not absolute. There is a great deal of crossover. Young teens, for example, buy products designed for adults in much the same way that adults attend movies meant for teens.

Table 5.1 The CD-ROM Market				
Age	**Gender**	**Genre**	**Examples**	**Features**
3–6	Boys and girls	Education and games	*Grandma and Me, Reader Rabbit*	Animation, music, fun activities, characters, preschool education subjects
7–12	Boys and girls	Entertainment and games	*Barbie Fashion Designer*	Activity, multiplayer, role playing, sports, brand identification.
13–18	Mostly male	Games	*Quake, Doom*	Destruction, violence, real-time 3-D graphics
19–up	Males and females	Games and instructional	*Myst, Command & Conquer*	Strategy, simulation, self-improvement
35–up	Males and females	Games, office, information	*SimCity, Mayo Clinic, Rand McNally TripMaker*	Immersive games, efficiency improvements, quick reference

Young Children. Children as young as three years old are known to use computers and play with CD-ROMs. At this age, the child is usually playing alone or with a parent. Because parents make the buying decisions for children this age, the products tend to have some perceived educational value for the child. Products often teach cognitive skills such as colors, shapes, farm animals, beginning reading, and language skills. Others teach psychomotor skills. Many products targeted at this market are "edutainment," meaning they are both entertaining and have some educational value. Typically, these products feature animation, music, and games. Children, after all, spend most of their time watching cartoons and playing with toys, and children's multimedia products are often derivative of established brands, such as Disney's feature animation characters or Hasbro toys. Other successful products, such as The Learning Company's *Reader Rabbit* series of CD-ROM products, are so well crafted that word of mouth among parents have put them at the top of the charts.

FIGURE 5.1

Reader Rabbit educational CD-ROM products from The Learning Company are typically at or near the top of the sales charts. They feature engaging characters and well-executed animation, which appeal to children in the target age range.

Children.   Between the ages of 7 and 12, children are more social. Because they've been in school, they are magnetically attracted to their friends. They are learning to play sports, board games, and card games, all of which involve obeying rules, playing fairly, and socializing with others. At this age, children learn about multimedia products by word of mouth. They become active participants in the buying decision with their parents. Products designed for this age group support the children's maturing social sophistication. Games tend to be multiplayer and foster friendly competition or collaboration. The products continue to feature animation, but the humor may be a little more edgy.

Educational products targeted at these users are based on accepted norms of child development and learning by this age. For example, the designers assume users can read and write and have had math, geography, and science courses in school. *Where in the U.S.A. Is Carmen Sandiego?* is one of a series of educational products published by The Learning Company. It is by far the most popular geography product for fourth, fifth, and sixth graders. The creative concept behind the product is that a mysterious woman named Carmen Sandiego is stealing national monuments and is on the run from pursuers, who include the young player. In the process of locating the thief, players visit locations all over the country and learn about geography. The designers assume players can read at a sixth-grade level, are familiar with the United States, and know how to access the Internet, where additional resources and maps are found.

Teens.   The game market consists almost exclusively of male users, 13 to 18 years old (and aging). With more hormones than they know what to do with, many males in this age group are playing rougher sports, watching R-rated movies, and dealing with the angst of puberty. They are fashion conscious and stay current with popular fads, music, and language. They are comfortable in group situations. Although many different kinds of games are purchased by these users, some have become hugely successful. The most popular are "shooters," "fighters," "driving," "flying," and team sports games. The most common feature of these games is real-time, 3-D animation. These games tend to be fast twitch and demand rapid, sometimes furious hand/eye coordination. The games provide immediate graphical and audio feedback to the user.

Adults.   On the older end of the age spectrum—19 and above—is a heavy use of CD-ROM games, instructional, and informational products. Adults have started their careers and families. Many have realized education is a life-long endeavor and begun exploring topics not covered in their formal school days. Games popular with this age group tend to be more cerebral. Role-playing, simulation, and strategy games are popular. *Myst, Riven, SimCity,* and *Command & Conquer* are examples. Adults also seek out products that will help them be more efficient. An example is the *Rand McNally TripMaker,* a product that enables the user to find the shortest and best automobile route between any two places.

Select a Subject.   This is where, at first glance, the sky is the limit. However, once the designer has targeted users, the field of subjects suitable for that market narrows (and, of course, the reverse is true). To complicate matters, not all subjects are suitable for CD-ROM. The Internet is a more appropriate venue for information, news, data, and other subject matter that changes occasionally and does not require audio and video to impart. Remember that it may take a year to design and produce a CD-ROM product, and once manufactured, the CD-ROM is a calcified pool of data—the contents cannot be adjusted. On the other hand, the CD-ROM can deliver audio and video without the latency and contention problems endemic to the Internet.

Use these criteria to select a subject:

■ *Choose a subject that resonates with the target user.* If the users are children ages three to six, consider uplifting stories, fairy tales, or a product featuring developmental education. If the users are adults over 40, consider self-help and guidance. Explore popular culture. What books are hot sellers? What movies or TV shows are people talking about at work? What major cultural, sporting, or political event is coming up next year? These may point the design team in a general direction.

■ *Choose a subject the design team knows something about.* Content experts and consultants are available for almost anything, but the project's best interests are served if it does not become completely dependent on one.

■ *Choose a subject the developer already owns.* What brand or property does the company have the rights to? Can the rights be acquired? Successful properties in other media already have "legs," and it has been demonstrated that brand recognition moves products in multimedia. For example, products from Hasbro, Mattel, and Disney and anything with *Star Wars* on the box fly off the shelves.

Select a Genre.   Once the target users and subject have been selected, determine an appropriate genre for the product. In film, almost any *subject* can be written as a drama, romance, comedy, or action thriller. Likewise, almost any multimedia subject can be fashioned into a game, an educational title, an informational title, or a hybrid of two or more genres. The *Carmen Sandiego* family of CD-ROM titles combine education with storytelling and games. The products, with the subject of geography targeted at elementary school children, could also have been designed as informational or reference CD-ROMs.

Use the following criteria to determine the genre for the product:

■ Choose the genre most popular with the target user. See Table 5.1. This is the safest method, but if the design team has another idea and feels very strongly about it, well, go with it. There is more art than science to making these design decisions. To this day, I have an enormous amount of respect for the designers who thought a *game* about urban development would be popular and successful. *SimCity* is still my favorite game.

■ Choose the genre the development team is best equipped—figuratively and literally—to create.

Theme. Theme refers to the overarching creative approach of the product. A description of the theme covers, in a general way, how the product looks and sounds, how the product behaves, what features and controls it has, and how the user experiences the product. Very often, a few words or a short sentence can capture the theme of a product, in the manner of a premise for a book or film. For example:

- An easy-to-use reference volume with multiple links to related scholarly treatises.
- A fun and engaging, activity-filled product children will love to learn with.
- A real-time 3-D simulation that makes the user feel like he's really flying.

Determine the Platform. The target platform refers to the home computer that the product will run on. PCs and Macintoshes were, at one time, so different that it was very difficult to create a product that could run on both machines, but that technological hurdle is all but gone. Many products are produced in such a way that they run on both PCs and Macintoshes. However, some cannot. Windows 98 for the PC, for example, provides multimedia programmers with certain built-in capabilities which, if used for a product, may eliminate the Macintosh as a viable platform. The technical expert on the team should be able to determine whether the product has this effect.

Determining the platform is partly a matter of determining how robust a machine the product requires the user to have, and that is generally determined by how complex the product is going to be. Certain features that are designed into the product could put enormous stress on the typical home computer, so designers must be aware of the consequences of every creative decision. Determining platform system requirements requires looking ahead a little bit and deciding—usually in consultation with the technical expert—how much memory the product will need to run and what processor speed will provide the best performance.

If the designer is designing a product for a market niche that is always looking for something graphically spectacular, the design may require certain accelerator boards or certain sound cards or other platform embellishments. Because the average customer will not buy a product that requires him or her to go out and reconfigure his or her home computer, the designer must be willing to reduce the size of the potential market. If the designer adds some kind of exotic feature that attracts the hard-core game player, he or she may lose the mainstream buyer.

Sample Concept Document

 Remember the "Principles of Flight" example used in a previous chapter? The following is a sample concept document based on that idea, incorporating the points made in this chapter.

Concept Document
for
Flight Fanatic

The Complete Multimedia Guide
to the Art, Science, and History of Flight

Prepared by
Students' Software, Inc.

Flight Fanatic, The Complete Multimedia Guide to the Art, Science, and History of Flight is a CD-ROM edutainment product targeted at the 9- to 11-year-old. In this product, you can browse freely to six different and distinct sections where you learn the principles of flight, learn the history of flight, meet some important aviation personalities, watch hilarious videos of early "fixed wing" experiments, learn about peacetime and wartime uses of aircraft, and in a special game section, *you can design and fly your very own aircraft!*

Your host is a new animated character, Patterson Wright, Orville and Wilbur's younger brother. Pat, as he's called, overslept that morning (some say he was up all night *flying*) when they made their famous flight at Kitty Hawk, so he got left out of history. He went on to become a cigar-chomping, barnstorming stunt pilot, full of vinegar and tall tales about flying. In every section, Pat acts as your guide, narrator, and online help.

Flight Fanatic has a distinctly hip, pop, current "Nickelodeon" look. It seamlessly blends colorful and fun graphics with black-and-white newsreel footage, animated reenactments and real-time 3-D graphics. Kids will immediately take to the look. It's what they already watch on their favorite TV channels.

Flight Fanatic is both educational and entertaining. You learn how thrust, lift, and control surfaces work together to carry a fixed wing aircraft aloft and bring it back down again. You learn about the forces that work against flight, such as drag and gravity. You learn about man's early attempts to fly—some mythical, some legendary, and some just plain ridiculous. You learn how we use airplanes for everything from delivering rescue supplies to disaster areas and the mail across the country to delivering cruise missiles in time of war. You laugh out loud at the archival footage of turn-of-the-century attempts at flight, including Victorian inventors pedaling bicycles equipped with wings off cliffs. As you complete each section, you get closer to earning your "flight license" and the right to enter the restricted "test flight" area.

The real payoff comes when you earn your wings and can apply your newly acquired aviation knowledge in the test flight area. There, you get to construct your own airplane by selecting from a menu of wings, fuselages, propulsion engines, and controls. When you take off in your new plane, it behaves as it actually would with the parts you picked! You can fly your plane and toggle between two points of view: third person—watching it from outside—and first person—watching from behind the stick in the cockpit.

Flight Fanatic, The Complete Multimedia Guide to the Art, Science, and History of Flight combines the best of education and entertainment, providing you with solid aviation science, genuine historical fact, and an appreciation for all the uses aircraft have in our day and age. All this is brought to you by an entertaining host with graphics, sound, and endless game play.

Because this title includes a heavy dose of video, animation, sound, and a flight simulation engine, the title is available in Windows 95 for the PC, only. The minimum system requirements are 200 MHz Pentium processor, 16MB RAM, 40MB free hard drive space, and 4X CD-ROM drive. The flight simulator does not require a joystick, but one is supported.

Notes on the Concept Document. Note that the document just flows along, yet the points are made in a particular order that allows the reader to "get the picture" by the end of the first paragraph. The subsequent paragraphs build on it, adding more detail in an order the writer thinks important. Write the concept in the second person, present tense—a little like a commercial. Write it as though the product already exists and the reader is playing it. Write enough to get the reader excited, but don't include every last detail. Hold a few good ideas out and be prepared to talk about them when the idea is "pitched"—orally described in a conference-room setting. Give the readers a chance to add their ideas. On this title, for example, it might be interesting to let users print out their own flight licenses and pictures of their airplane designs. Perhaps the title could include a collection of buildable paper airplanes users can print out and construct.

Socialize the Concept Document

Circulate the concept document internally. Management, marketing, development, technical, art, sound, and QA people should all see a copy. The writer will find out quickly if there is any interest. If there is, call a meeting and get ready to go to Step 2. Don't waste any more calories if the idea gets shot down early, often, and by everybody—just go on to the next concept.

Step 2: Perform a Competitive Analysis

Purpose of Competitive Analysis

After the concept document is written, circulated, reviewed, and edited, research the market for competitive products. Sometimes, a concept document is written as an outcome of a competitive analysis, so this step would have already been taken. If the proposed product is designed for internal use, and not for the open market (as in the case of a training program), the competitive analysis may be completely unnecessary.

The objective of this exercise is to determine whether the product has any competition in the marketplace, and if it does, how the proposed product stacks up. The producer and/or marketing manager must evaluate competing products both quantitatively (objectively) and qualitatively (subjectively).

The quantitative analysis may include sales information. How many units sold through? At what price? At what retailers? Who handled the distribution? When was the product released? What were the components of the marketing campaign? Was the product cross-promoted with a film or television show? Was there heavy advertising?

Obtain competing products and evaluate them qualitatively for production value. Assess the graphics, animation, video, and sound quality. Measure the content. Make a list of the features. Make value judgements about the product. Use your evaluation to make creative, technical, and business decisions about your product design.

Sources of Product Information

There are five primary sources of information:

1. Check the shelves of all the local multimedia retailers and see what is stocked. Talk to sales clerks and find out what's selling, what isn't, what they are re-ordering, what they are returning. Most of the time, they are happy to help. Buy and play with as many competitive products as possible.

 2. Next, check the Internet and visit the web sites of the major multimedia publishers, where they advertise products they are currently publishing or announcing. Often, publishers put demo versions of products on the Web and allow users to download samples.

3. There are numerous independent game reviewers. Some publish newsletters and magazines. Buy these magazines. All reviewers have web sites. Game developers and publishers routinely send prerelease versions of games to these reviewers. A good review can result in thousands, even millions of sales in the game market. See what these reviewers are saying about competitive products.

4. Subscribe to PC Data, a sales tracking organization. It publishes an extensive breakdown of multimedia products and ranks them by sales figures. PC Data is at www.pcdata.com.

5. Attend Electronic Entertainment Expo, also known as E3, held in late May or early June. The venue moves around. It has been held in Atlanta, Georgia, and in Los Angeles. This gigantic conference attracts publishers, developers, distributors, and retailers. Hundreds of products are unveiled and displayed. There are ample opportunities for networking and getting the latest information on all products. Visit its web site at www.e3expo.com.

The Competitive Matrix

 When the producer or marketing manager has gathered information about the competition, he or she builds a matrix like the one in Table 5.2, filling in the information. This enables the producer to organize and study the qualitative product data. The categories used to evaluate the *Flight Fanatic* product are listed in Table 5.2. Competitive matrices are product-specific, so a matrix comparing two educational products would be quite different.

Table 5.2 The Competitive Matrix			
Asset Type	**Our Product**	**XXX Publisher**	**YYY Publisher**
Branded characters	No	Yes	No
Original music	Yes	Yes	No
Number of songs	2	0	0
Celebrity voices	No	Yes	No
Number of backgrounds	12	24	18
Multiplayer	No	No	Yes
Number of activities	10	24	18
Control level of difficulty	No	Yes	Yes
Video	Yes	Yes	Yes
Sign-in	Yes	Yes	Yes
Number of games	1	0	2
Scoring for games	Yes	Yes	Yes
Printing option	Yes	Yes	Yes
Keyboard control	Yes	Yes	Yes
Mouse/Joystick	Joystick and mouse	Mouse	Joystick and mouse
Clickables	Yes	Yes	Yes
Click and drag	Yes	No	Yes

Finding out that the brilliant concept arrived at last week has been done already can be a sobering experience. The results of the analysis can be a mixed bag of good and bad news. What's worse? Discovering that the concept has ten failing competitive products or twenty successful ones? The competitive analysis should be used as a tool to improve or discontinue the product design.

Step 3: Write a Top-Level Design

The Purpose of a Top-Level Design

The concept document is analogous to the "premise" in the film and television world. The top-level design is the multimedia equivalent of the film treatment. The top-level design is a document, usually about five to seven pages long, which describes in greater detail the five key components of the product. The results of the competitive analysis and feedback from readers of the concept document are used both to broaden the project's scope and to tighten up design particulars. Content, features, structure, functional controls, and look and feel are more fully developed.

Because the top-level design is more descriptive of the product than is the concept document, it can be used to conduct initial paper focus tests with potential users. Focus tests at this stage can be used for formative evaluation of the design. Furthermore, the producer can analyze the top-level design and acquire enough information to develop a preliminary budget and development plan. Along with a budget and plan, the top-level design is used as the basis of initial agreements between development collaborators such as publishers and developers.

Sample Top-Level Design

Here is an example of a top-level design for the Hasbro Interactive product *Tonka Search and Rescue,* developed by Media Station, Inc., (MSI) of Ann Arbor, Michigan. As you read this document, look for the five components discussed in Chapter 2— content, features, structure, functional control, and look and feel. You will find all there, blended together in good, readable prose.

Top-Level Design

Tonka Search and Rescue CD-ROM
Ver. 3 1/21/97

INTRODUCTION

Tonka Search and Rescue is an exciting activity-based CD-ROM that puts you right in the driver's seat of Tonka toy vehicles. In this title, you're in charge of the Emergency Dispatch Center, where incoming calls from all over the world are reporting natural disasters—and people who need help! It's your job to pick the right vehicles and get there as soon as possible to search for folks in trouble and rescue them.

Seated at your dispatch center control monitor, you'll be confronted with five different emergencies. The dispatch center will be like a big plastic toy in itself, with colorful buttons, dials, and blinking lights. Like a 911 center for little kids! All of the emergencies will involve people in trouble, but not in life-threatening situations. MSI and Hasbro can select the specific missions from a growing list of terrific possibilities attached or brainstorm others during the design phase.

When you see a rescue mission you're ready to tackle, you select it from the dispatch center. Also from the console, you select the right Tonka toys for the job from your motor pool of vehicles. You have a rescue Helicopter, Boat, Fire Truck, Ambulance, Tow Truck, Bulldozer, Backhoe, Dump Truck, Crane, Tractor Trailer, and Snowmobile or Snowcat to choose from, among others. You may use the Bulldozer to clear debris from the site and then cart it off in a Dump Truck. You may use the Helicopter to carry people away from a volcano threatening to blow, or the Boat to rescue a dog from the top of a house in a flood.

There to help you is Tonka Joe, an emergency rescue expert who can tell you about every mission and how you can use every vehicle to save the day. Once you get to a rescue site, another rescue expert will be on hand to direct you. There will be a different rescue expert at each site—each with his or her own personality.

When you're done with a rescue mission, you can print a copy of a Special Edition of the newspaper that headlines the story of your daring rescue efforts, including a stock photograph of the event. When you complete all five rescue efforts, you'll receive a special commendation award, which you can also print out and frame.

You can also print out buildings from the missions on card stock and then fold and tape them together. Or you can print out natural obstacles such as boulders that you can load into your real Tonka trucks. You can also create and print your own Tonka Truck decals, traffic signs, and even vanity license plates for your Tonka toys.

Tonka Search and Rescue will use MSI's software engine to provide the following improvements and upgrades over Hasbro's prior Tonka product:

- Easier and more accurate driving control of the vehicles, but using the same basic cursor control of the Construction product
- Better control of the vehicles' various functions (e.g., digging, dumping, hauling, lifting)
- More realistic driving and lifting—objects can be picked up and dropped down
- Print-out newspaper featuring player's daring rescues
- Ability to customize Tonka truck decals and even license plates and print them out!
- Ability to print buildings or natural obstacles on card stock that can be built and used with Tonka toy trucks

DESIGN OVERVIEW

Sign-On Screen

The player may sign on by typing his or her name and hometown. This information is used for saving games and, later, for printing "newspaper" articles
about the player's search and rescue exploits. The player's name is used in
the headlines, article, and picture caption. The hometown is used in the newspaper masthead. After inputting his name and hometown, the player can start
a new series of rescue missions or load a saved game.

The Emergency Control Center

The Emergency Control Center is the main interface screen. Tonka Joe
guides the players' understanding of the Control Center, so even if they can't
read, they can use the buttons and dials on the screen. There is a TV monitor
that shows with pictures and sound the different rescue missions where help
is needed. There are buttons for selecting the missions they want to respond
to and the vehicles they wants to take with them. There is a button for quitting
(players are asked if they want to save their game).

*Note: The Emergency Control Center is a double-wide screen. The other half
of the screen is the Print Shop, which is described later. Players can
pan to the print shop by moving the cursor to the right side of the
screen and keeping it there while the pan takes place. They pan back
by moving the cursor to the left side.*

The player is told that there are search and rescue missions everywhere,
and the player will be invited to review each situation by switching the channel
and seeing and hearing what's going on. Voice-overs and slides will play on
the monitor to bring the player up to date on the missions. The player is told
what kind of work needs to be done, informed about what kinds of Tonka vehicles will probably be needed, and asked to select the mission he or she
wants to tackle first.

After selecting a rescue mission, the player selects and dispatches vehicles to the scene. The player can find out more about each vehicle and what
it can do before selecting it. Once the player's team is on the way, he or she
joins them at the site and takes control of each vehicle as needed. Tonka Joe
is there to help.

Once the player is ready to go to the rescue site, he or she zooms through
the display screen right to the site shown there, and the rescue mission begins.

Alternative Main Interface

The Main Interface screen could be a map, similar to the map in the Construction Product. The map would show all of the rescue sites from a perspec-

tive view, and Tonka Joe would explain the situation at the site when the player selects it. The player would then branch to the site, as in the current product. Also selectable from this interface would be the Garage and the Print Shop.

Available Vehicles

- Front Loader
- Crane
- Tractor Trailer
- Bulldozer
- Backhoe
- Helicopter

- Ambulance
- Fire Truck
- Boat
- Dump Truck
- Tow Truck
- Others to be determined

Humor

We have humorous vignettes at each rescue mission to keep the activities light and fun. Most of the humor is unexpected animated gags performed by the rescue guys and gals, the rescuees, or Tonka Joe. Some of the rescue missions themselves are big gags—see some of the suggestions below. Whenever possible, the player can set off explosions to demolish rocks or other obstacles and haul the debris away.

The Rescue Sites

Each rescue site is two screens wide, and players can pan back and forth by moving and keeping the cursor at the right or left side of the screen. Players can even stop in the middle. Viewed from above, the vehicles are 3-D and will look like the toys the player has on the floor of his living room. At the site are the vehicles the player has selected. The player may select any vehicle and use it as needed for that particular rescue. The player selects the vehicle by clicking on it once, and then clicking on the location he or she wants it to go to. Clicking twice causes a vehicle to do what it does—a bulldozer will dig a bucket full of dirt, a crane will lift the load under it, and so on. In general, the rescue missions will not show people in deadly peril; rather, they are "inconvenienced" by the natural disaster. It will always be the objective to help people. Table 5.3 shows a list of six possible missions from which to select five. This list can be expanded during the design phase, and rescue missions can be selected and refined.

Characters

The main character is Tonka Joe who, as in the previous product, is the player's guide and mentor. He appears at the main user interface screen to tell the player what needs to be done and describe how he or she can use the various Tonka vehicles for that mission. There is one secondary character at each rescue site to tell the player exactly what needs to be done. At the end of the mission, that secondary character congratulates the player and guides

Table 5.3	Possible Rescue Sites		
Rescue Site	**Situation**	**Solution**	**Tonka Toys Needed**
Bridge	Swollen river, bridge out, people stranded	Build dike to hold back river, build bridge, save people	Bulldozer, Truck, Backhoe, Crane, Tractor Trailer
Town park	Cat caught in tree	Bring in fire truck, raise ladder. Cat jumps to other tree—this goes on a few times. Finally get cat down—it's a mountain lion!	Fire Truck
Flood	People trapped on rooftops	Bring rescue boat to flood, launch it, ride out to people, rescue	Pickup Truck, Boat, Boat Trailer, Ambulance
Forest	Lost expedition	Search with helicopter, locate group, clear road to them, bring out people	Helicopter, Bulldozer, Truck, 4-Wheel-Drive Rescue Vehicle
Volcanic island	Eruption threatens town	Dig channel for lava flow, divert from town, rescue people	Bulldozer, Backhoe, Trucks, Rescue Helicopter
Zoo	Loose gorilla—people trapped in souvenir shop	Bring in crane and a big cage on top of a tractor trailer. Try to lower over roving gorilla. Bait with bananas?	Crane, Tractor Trailer

him or her back to the dispatch center (or other interface screen), where the player can print a newspaper at the print shop or take on another assignment. There are minor characters at every rescue—including the rescuees who need help and the player's team of rescue guys and gals. We anticipate the look of this animation to be similar to the Tonka Construction Product.

Newspaper Coverage

After every successful search and rescue mission, the game automatically publishes a front-page story about the player and his heroism. This newspaper page features the name of the player's hometown at the top; the date (taken from the system clock); and the player's name prominently in the headlines, the caption for a stock picture of the rescue, and the canned article describing the player's exploits. The player can print this newspaper page out.

The Print Shop

From the Print Shop, the player can print out a copy of the Special Edition of the newspaper after each rescue mission. When the player has finished all five missions, he or she can print out a special commendation award.

The Print Shop allows players to create their own Tonka Truck decals by using a predetermined set of graphic elements such as circles, stripes, lettering, patterns, and textures. Players can print these out and apply them to toys or hang them on the walls. Players can also make their very own vanity license plates for their Tonka trucks. Type in your plate message and print it out!

Players can print a high-rise, a suburban home, the Mayan Temple, the bridge, and even natural obstacles such as big boulders on card stock and, using scissors and tape, build real, desk-top versions.

The Garage

The Garage is an activity center where players can customize several Tonka vehicles. Players can put oversized wheels on a truck or a new plow on a bulldozer. They can also put a new coat of paint on one of their rescue vehicles; when they go out on the mission, it has its new color!

Product Features

- Five exciting rescue missions
- Up to fourteen vehicles
- Double-wide, scrollable backgrounds
- Fun-to-use emergency dispatch center
- Intuitive user interface for controlling vehicles similar to Construction Product
- Humorous animated vignettes
- Short-term rewards (newspaper articles) after each mission
- Ability to create and print Tonka decals
- Ability to create and print vanity license plates
- Ability to print and construct buildings and other structures
- Printable Special Edition newspapers for each mission
- Ability to print a commendation award

Notes on Top-Level Design

Because the introduction is the only section some executives read, it is written in a promotional style, using second-person, present tense. This style tends to draw readers in and make them feel as though they are briefly experiencing the action described. Subsequent sections shift to the third person and refer to "the user" or "the player" or "the child." This is fine. The style here is more informational, allowing readers to disengage emotionally and dispassionately evaluate the description of the product.

The top-level design is written with the intention that it be evaluated, broken down, and later modified. The producer reads it carefully, evaluating the "scope of work" that would be involved in developing the product as described. The director evaluates it creatively, contemplating the look of the characters, the sounds of their voices, the style of the background art, and the specific situations the user might encounter at the rescue sites. The writer anticipates the overall structure of the title. He or she begins to outline the functional specification. The lead engineer studies the technical ramifications of the design. When they pool their conclusions, a picture emerges about the level of effort needed to complete the product. Meanwhile, the client reads the-top level design to determine whether it accurately describes the product it wants to fund.

After the top-level design document for *Tonka Search and Rescue* was distributed and evaluated, Hasbro Interactive and Media Station signed an agreement to proceed with further design and development. Eventually, the product was developed over an eight-month period and released in the Fall of 1997. It became one of the top-selling children's products during that Christmas season.

Step 4: Perform a Cost/Benefit Analysis

Purpose of Cost/Benefit Analysis

A cost/benefit analysis is usually needed to reach a final consensus on the design of the product. It simply cannot be all things to all people, so something nearly always has to be pruned from the design concept. The analysis helps the design team look objectively at all of the content, features, functional control, look and feel, and overall structure and to *prioritize* these elements. A feature that will be experienced by the user only once and very briefly but will take weeks to implement and use 10 percent of the budget would have to be looked at very carefully. What might put it at the top of the priority list is that it breaks new ground, positions the product ahead of the head of all the competition, and is demanded by a large and loyal audience.

Modify the Design

The top-level design is often written with the idea that there will be additional modifications to the design. Modifications are usually driven by three things that occur after the design has been distributed and pitched to the client or company management.

1. *Feedback from the client or management or both.* If they are excited about the product, they will want to put a thumbprint on it, so count on modifications.
2. *Feedback from the team.* Suddenly, a technical glitch or incompatibility—something a colleague of mine used to call "mutually exclusive effects"—will be

discovered by the technical director, or the sound designer will determine that he cannot mix sound in real time.

3. *Sobering reality.* The bucket of cold water in the face can come from any direction. Legal may determine that rights for the Warner Bros. character you wanted to use are unavailable or extremely expensive. Engineering may determine that the flight simulation software you expected to license cannot be launched from the engine you expected to use for the rest of the product. Upon further examination, you may find that one disc isn't big enough for all the video and sound you had planned to use in the *Woodstock Retrospective* product you've designed.

Break Down the Design

After the top-level design has been socialized and modifications suggested or demanded, the producer should break down the design into its component parts for analysis. This procedure is very similar to the script breakdown completed by the production manager in film and video, but in this case it includes programming activities. Producers create a table that helps them evaluate the design on a node-by-node basis. In the example in Table 5.4, the hypothetical title *Flight Fanatic* is broken down only through a few nodes of the top layer of interactivity.

Obtain Estimates on Level of Effort

Each cell in Table 5.4 represents both an experience for the user and an expenditure of effort in terms of labor for asset creation or acquisition (video, art, animation, text, and sound), programming, software licensing, rights acquisition, management, testing, bug fixing, and so on. These individual tasks represent a level of effort to be expended by staff. The total development effort is called the scope of work. The scope of work determines the cost and time required to create the product. At this point in the process, the producer has only a general idea of what the cost of the product may be, because arriving at a real budget involves much deeper analysis of a much more refined design.

The producer researches the *possible* cost of each node and the components of it. The technical director or lead engineer provides an estimate for the level of effort involved in programming features. The art director estimates art and animation costs, and so on. Sometimes, the best they can do is say, "That's real hard," or, "That shouldn't take more than a day." The estimates they provide will be only as good as their understanding of the product, so the top-level design document, the breakdown table, and the verbal walk-through are critically important for communicating the product concept to them.

Is It Worth the Effort?

In every human endeavor, there is tension between what the creator wants to make and what the creator can afford to make. This tension is particularly acute in the

Table 5.4	A Node-by-Node Breakdown of a Top-Level Design				
Node	**Video**	**Art/ Animation**	**Sound**	**Engineering**	**Other Features**
Bumper	:20—archive footage	:10 animation 3-D logo	Original music	Quicktime	Click to skip
Title	:30—archive footage	:10 animation 3-D logo	Original music	Quicktime	Click to skip
Sign-on	None	Background Graphics Type font Buttons	Music Narration SFX	Keyboard input Display type Store name Compare to previous names Button rollovers and branching Determine next audio	If player has played before and saved game, have option to continue where left off.
Main menu	:20—misc. planes fly by	Background Graphics Icons Buttons :30 animated intro—P.W.	Music Sync V.O. SFX	Buttons and branching Quicktime Check user ID —play/don't play intro	If player has already seen intro, do not play again
Bloopers, etc.	15 minutes video—120 clips, half with sync sound	:20 animated intro Background Buttons and icons— VCR-type interface	Calliope music SFX Sync narration	Quicktime movies over BG Button branching Movie speed and direction controls	Player can control speed of video playback and run movies backward. Player selects movies from TV "channel" switcher.

commercial arts and in media production. Every multimedia development effort is, at best, a compromise between art, science, and business. Each must give ground to the others in order to arrive at the best possible product at the best possible cost.

Go through the breakdown item by item, and apply this simple formula:

$$Value = Effort$$

The team must ask itself, "Does the user care if we provide fifteen minutes of video bloopers? Are ten minutes enough?" "Do we really need the 'save game' option?" "Can we get away with less character animation?" "Is the cost of implementing such and such a feature worth it? Will the user ever notice it?"

Twice during my career I was involved in design and development efforts in which this step was skipped. Both times, the phenomenon known as "feature creep" was allowed to infect the design process. In both cases, the products became fat, lazy, and overblown. They were over budget and delivered late. Our company lost money and credibility. The client relationship broke down, employee morale suffered, and, as if that weren't enough, the products failed in retail. So please, do not be afraid to take very sharp pruning shears to the design to shape it into a reasonable product.

Edit the Top-Level Design

Edit the top-level design document into a final version that accurately describes the product the team, management, the client, the publisher, and the customer want. Importantly, describe a product that can actually be developed given the budget, schedule, and resources. Make success possible!

Step 5: Write the Functional Specification

The ultimate goal of the interactive design process is to create a document called the functional specification. It may also be called the design specification, the product design, or the game design. The functional specification describes in exhausting detail what the product consists of, how its contents are organized, how it behaves, what it looks and sounds like, and how the user controls it. The document also includes such things as the target platform (PC or Mac or both), minimum hardware requirements, memory "footprint," and other fairly technical details.

In film and television, the equivalent document is the screenplay or script. The audience for the written script is not the audience that sits in the theater, but rather the team of professionals who work on the picture. Every member of the cast and crew gets a copy of the script. The script describes the two components of the film— what is seen and what is heard. The order in which scenes are viewed in the theater is determined by the order in which they are written. In other words, the *structure* of the film is evident in the linear sequencing of the pages of the script. The producer, director, cinematographer, art director, talent, composer, and editor may interpret the script as the production proceeds, each adding his or her special creative or technical input to the visual and audio components. The "shooting" script contains all the information needed by the readers so they can make the finished film.

The functional specification is used in the same manner. However, it contains far more detail because it describes not only what is seen and heard, but also the complex structure of the multimedia product. The specification describes a system, not simply a linear sequence of events. The readership of the functional specification is more diverse than the readership of the screenplay because it includes programmers, who need to understand how the application behaves, not simply how it looks and sounds.

Audience for the Functional Specification

In multimedia, the audience for the functional specification is the team of professionals who will make the product. Again, every member of the development team gets a copy.

The team members include

Producer	Composer/arranger
Director	Musicians
Writer	Artists
Interactive designer	Animators
Game designer	Videographers
Instructional designer	Researchers
Subject matter expert	Software programmers
Art director	Quality assurance testers
Technical director	Marketing, sales, and public relations people
Sound designer	Focus group conductors
Voice and acting talent	Executive decisionmakers

Purpose of the Functional Specification

The functional specification serves three important purposes in multimedia development. First, it is the basis of agreement between the parties having a financial stake in the product. For example, publishers (the folks who pay for the product) and developers (the companies that create them) build their contractual arrangement around the product described in the functional specification. It is routinely attached to the contract and referred to within it. The second purpose is practical. The document serves as the development bible. From it all other development documents (such as asset lists and work orders, which we'll cover later) and creative and programming decisions derive. Finally, in the final step before manufacturing, the quality assurance testers use the functional specification to determine whether or not the product complies with the agreed-upon design. When a functional specification is written and used this way, a bevy of multimedia development headaches never have a chance to occur.

Legal Purpose. The functional specification is referred to in the contract between the developer and the publisher or client as the agreed-upon product. If the developer delivers a gold master (a CD-ROM from which all copies are made) that complies in every way with the product described in the functional specification, the developer has fulfilled its primary obligation. There may be other requirements in the contract, such as meeting intermittent milestones, obtaining periodic approvals and sign-offs, and providing screen shots for package design. The contract may also provide for modifying the functional specification during development with a procedure called "change orders." No matter, the developer is obligated to deliver a gold master that complies with the functional specification, along with any agreed-upon modifications.

Development Purpose. The functional specification has a critical development purpose. It is the development bible that instructs the work of all the people building the product. During development, the document comes to be called simply "the spec." From the spec the producer creates a number of other documents that initiate development. These include the development plan, budget, burn schedule, asset database, and work orders. The producer determines what voice, music, or acting talent to hire and prepares contracts for them. He or she determines, from the development plan, what freelancers or subcontractors are needed for art, animation, programming, or testing. The producer creates a detailed cash flow spreadsheet to track costs on a weekly basis and compares costs against actual progress. All of this flows from the functional specification.

The director reads the spec and interprets the art, animation, video, and sound needs. He or she articulates that vision to the art director, sound designer, and videographer, instructing them on what particular assets need to be created or acquired, how they will be incorporated into the product, and in some cases what technique to use to create or acquire them.

From the functional specification, the sound designer—usually under the direction of the director—casts the voice talent and music composer/arranger; searches for sound effects from sound libraries or creates Foley effects; and records, edits, mixes, and syncs narration. The spec even provides the sound designer with the file names under which to save every sound asset. The art director relies on the spec in the same way.

The software engineer—who may also be called the programmer or the "author," which refers to the fact he or she may be using an off-the-shelf "authoring tool"—reads the spec and devises a technical design or programming plan. The spec describes in detail all of the features and functionality of the product, indicating every instance when a button, slider, or hotspot must work properly if selected by the user. The spec doesn't tell the programmer what software to write, it tells him or her what effect the software must have. The programmer must then devise the software approach that will make the product behave as directed. Some features may require special-purpose software to be written that generates a random number, plays a certain animation, searches a database, displays text in a certain font, calculates a score, finds the value of a variable, or percipitates any of a thousand other events. The software engineer uses the spec to determine what features need to be programmed and then figures out how to pull it off.

During development, modifications to the spec occur. While recording dialogue, a voice talent turns a phrase better than it was written and the director chooses to keep the new version. A researcher finds a better piece of archival footage than the one called for, and it's less expensive. The producer OKs the change. The client asks for a new feature to be added and for the removal of another. It's a wash in terms of time and cost, so everyone agrees and a change order is executed. Changes are incorporated into the document and the revised spec distributed.

The quality assurance manager uses the spec to create a testing plan, and, just before the final release of the gold master, the testers use the final modified spec as their bible. They hammer away at the product on a number of different hardware configurations, trying hard either to break it or to find inconsistencies between how the product behaves and how the spec says it should behave. Anything other than perfect compliance is logged as a "bug."

A filmmaker can see how this use of the functional specification differs from the use of a screenplay in postproduction. Postproduction in video and film is still part of the creative process. Directors and creative editors can make significant changes to the film even at this late date. Nobody cares if the final cut matches the original screenplay, as long as the film is good, is the right length, and meets the desired MPAA ratings. In most multimedia development (less so for game development), the final burn must match the functional specification.

The Content of the Functional Specification

The functional specification has a large and diverse readership! Every individual team member scours it for the information he or she needs in order to contribute his or her piece to the puzzle. The functional specification must contain the following, all of which are described more fully in Chapter 6:

- An overview of the entire title—an executive summary.

- Global conventions to be used throughout the product. "Globals" are any characteristics of the product that are established early and then used throughout the product.

- File-naming conventions. All of the assets created for the product (pictures, sounds, animations, etc.) must be assigned names. A file-naming convention is a method for assigning names to individual assets so that they can be identified by purpose, place, type, and version number.

■ Minimum hardware requirements.

■ How the title is installed and uninstalled.

■ Starting, saving, loading, quitting.

■ A node map showing the entire title and all logical branching.

■ Rules and logic for games; goals, challenges, worlds, levels, scoring.

■ Visual descriptions of all backgrounds, graphics, props, buttons, characters, special effects, animations, and video clips.

■ How visual elements are laid out on the screen.

■ All dialogue and narration, sound effects, music, and ambient sound.

■ Transitions between pictures and between sounds—cuts, fades, dissolves.

■ Technical information about the color depth, palette, and resolution of still images; the size, frame rate, compression scheme, and format of the video; and the volume, mode (mono or stereo), and sampling rate for the sounds.

■ On a node-by-node basis, how the user interacts with the product.

■ An asset list for each node.

The design of the particular product may require more or less detail. The design of an educational application includes the learning objectives, teaching model, and evaluation methods. A game design has much more detail related to the game rules and logic. It may even include sample code. A product with a search engine and a database includes technical descriptions of both. The only rule about contents, really, is that the functional specification must include everything that anybody may need to know to build and test the product. If the writer leaves anything out, the team member building that particular component of the product will be forced to improvise: a very dangerous precedent. Chapter 6 covers the functional specification in detail.

Chapter Summary

In this chapter, we covered the five steps of the interactive design process. The design process leads to the functional specification, which is a document having profound legal and development importance.

The five steps begin with writing a concept document—a short two-page description of a proposed product. The second step is a competitive analysis to determine whether the proposed product has ever been attempted and, if it has, how the competitive products are performing in the marketplace. The competitive analysis often leads to modifications and further creative elaboration.

The third step is to write the top-level design—a more fully defined product description. Top-level design documents are sufficiently explicit to become the basis for initial contractual agreements between development partners such as a publisher and a developer. Top-level designs can be used for paper focus testing and are always used for budget estimates and preliminary development planning.

The fourth step is to perform an internal cost/benefit analysis of the top-level design. The producer breaks the design down into its component parts and determines the "scope of work." By studying the parts, the cost of the parts, and the contribution of the parts to the overall product, the producer, in consultation with key team members, can determine how to modify the design to arrive at the best product at the lowest cost.

The fifth and final step is to write the functional specification. The spec is a detailed design document that describes every node of the product. The functional specification becomes part of the contractual agreement between developers and publishers. A large and diverse development team relies on the functional specification to guide its work.

Recommended Reading

Korolenko, Michael. *Writing for Multimedia: A Guide and SourceBook for the Digital Writer.* Wadsworth: Belmont, CA, 1997.

Stansberry, Domenic. *Labyrinths: The Art of Interactive Writing and Design, Content Development for New Media.* Wadsworth: Belmont, CA, 1998.

The Functional

Specification

In this chapter, you will learn

- What the main parts of the functional specification are
- The step-by-step process of writing the functional specification
- The writing style and format of the functional specification
- What additional information to add if the document includes a game design

In this chapter, you are guided through the step-by-step process of writing the functional specification. Included is a sample functional specification with call-outs and comments to help you identify and understand the various parts of the document. By the end of this chapter, you should be able to write a functional specification for your own product. Game functional specifications require more detail than those for most other genres because of games' heavy reliance on interactivity and, therefore, complex software programming. For this reason, a special section dealing with the game design document is included at the end of the chapter.

Start with Structure

The writer should begin the process of writing the functional specification by creating, with the director (interactive designer), the node map of the product. The node map is a graphic representation of the logical organization of the product's content. It is the writer's most useful tool, acting as an outline for nearly all the elements the writer must include in the spec. The node map graphically reveals the following important characteristics of the product, which then direct the writer's thoughts:

- *How big the product is.* The node map reveals immediately how many chapters the writer will write. Unlike the screenplay writer, who knows that he or she must write 120 pages of action and dialogue, the multimedia writer does not know how massive the document will be until he or she sees its overall structure. Each node becomes a chapter in the spec.

■ *What video, animation, narration, or dialogue each node requires.* The node map reveals the audio/visual components of each node. The writer creates dialogue, narration, and scene descriptions in the manner of writing a screenplay.

■ *Which nodes are interactive and which are linear.*

■ *What interactivity to describe.* If a node has interactivity within it, the node map reveals this, and the writer must describe it.

■ *How the user navigates between nodes.* The node map reveals all branching between the nodes. The writer must describe the user's navigation between nodes.

■ *What buttons or other functional devices to describe.* Based on the interactivity, the writer can determine what real or virtual devices to describe for each node.

■ *What software events occur, as well as when and where.* Navigation between nodes, or other events that occur on screen, may be determined by software or program logic. The node map shows the writer the user or program actions that trigger these software events. The writer must describe them in the spec.

■ *What global conventions to describe.* The node map will reveal what features or capabilities are common to all or most nodes. The writer will include these as global conventions in the spec.

■ *What assets each node will include.* The node map reveals, by analysis of the previous elements, what individual pictures, videos, animations, and sounds make up each node. The writer includes the asset breakdown in the spec for each node.

Title Summary

The first chapter of the spec is the Title Summary. The best source material for the initial version of the summary is the top-level design. The Title Summary explains in five to seven pages the subject, genre, audience, content, features, functional controls, look and feel, and structure of the product. Many readers—particularly busy marketing executives—will read only this much. Even though this chapter appears first, it is often written last because it summarizes the rest of the document, which may take weeks or months to complete. (See page 120 for an example of a Title Summary.)

Sample Outline of Title Summary

1. Product Description
   a. Subject
   b. Genre
   c. General description or overview

2. Marketing Opportunities
   a. Branding
   b. Intellectual property
   c. Ancillary products
   d. Competition
3. Target Audience
   a. Age
   b. Sex
   c. Income, education, other demographics
4. Product Design
   a. Content
   b. Features
   c. Functional controls
   d. Look and feel
   e. Structure (general description)

Introduction

The Title Summary is followed by the Introduction. The Introduction provides a high-level overview of the structure of the whole product, global conventions, global software issues, equipment platform requirements, and any other topics that could be considered productwide, rather than node-specific. Although this chapter appears second in the spec, it too is written after the design of the product has been completed. Many of the productwide design issues will not have been devised until all of the nodes have been individually addressed.

The writer consults with the director and the technical lead while writing this chapter. The director has a clear idea of various global conventions he or she maintains throughout the title, such as what buttons appear on every screen to return the user to the main menu, to quit the title, or to open the Web browser. These may also include type specification for all text, how the mouse is used, how certain keys on the keyboard are used, how the user may interrupt the title, what the cursor looks like and when it may change, and how buttons may change "state" when the cursor moves over them. The technical lead has evaluated the design and knows more about the installation, memory requirements, hard drive requirements, compression schemes, and other technical issues that are driven by the design.

Sample Outline of Introduction

1. Structure
   a. Node map—detailed, for entire product
   b. Details of structural description

2. Conventions
    a. Global conventions
        i. Screen layouts
        ii. Recurrent buttons or features
        iii. Function keys
        iv. Button states
        v. Cursor states or behaviors
    b. Software or technical conventions
        i. Installation
        ii. Game saving and loading
        iii. Quitting the title
        iv. Palette(s)
        v. Video compression scheme
        vi. Video resolution size(s)
        vii. Audio sampling scheme
        viii. Event timing
        ix. Minimum hardware requirements

Node Descriptions

Following the Introduction, the writer fully describes each node in the title. Using the node map as a guide, the writer assigns a number to each node, which becomes the chapter number in the functional specification. The writer starts with an outline for each node and then relies on input from the director, art director, game designer, technical lead, sound designer, researchers, and content experts to provide much of the detail. (See page 130 for an example of a description of a node.) The writer's personal contribution is often the actual narration and dialogue and descriptions of animation, video, and graphics—not at all unlike the creative wordsmithing of the screenwriter.

Sample Outline of a Node Description

1. General node summary (brief paragraph)
    a. Type (linear, interactive, software event)
    b. If a game—brief description
    c. Screen or background description
    d. Characters, animation, video, or audio
    e. Buttons or other virtual devices
    f. Interactivity within node
2. Screen design (or, actual screen shot)
    a. Layout of screen showing location and size of all graphic elements

    i. Background
    ii. Buttons or other devices
    iii. Icons
    iv. Text
    v. Video or animation area
   b. Call-out boxes with descriptions of buttons, icons, and other elements
   c. Screen description—detailed and specific
  3. Game design
   a. Goal or objective of game
   b. Challenges or obstacles
   c. Enemies
   d. Success strategy
   e. Behaviors and attributes
   f. Scoring
  4. Music
  5. Ambient sounds
  6. Sound effects
  7. Animation or video
   a. Setting and location
   b. Characters or talent
   c. Action
   d. Dialogue
  8. Narration
  9. User interaction
 10. System response
 11. Assets

Sample Functional Specification

The following sample functional specification is for the product *Tonka Search and Rescue,* one of Hasbro Interactive's very successful products targeted at the children's edutainment market. The entire specification is over 240 pages long, so key parts of it were selected for illustrative purposes.

The Cover Page, which is not included here, contains simply the title, date, and version number. Version numbers are particularly important because changes are made regularly during development and all team members should be working from the identical, latest version.

The Cover Page is followed by the Table of Contents, which is also not included here.

Commentary that explains elements in the functional specification appears throughout the document.

1. TITLE SUMMARY

The paragraphs and bulleted lists below function as the *executive summary*. They are written in a "selling" style so that readers, including corporate officers, marketing managers, and sales reps, can get a quick glimpse of the product, without all the low-level details required for implementation. (See pp. 116–117 for a discussion and outline of Title Summaries.)

Tonka Search and Rescue is an exciting activity-based CD-ROM that gives kids the opportunity to role-play as adults—helping others by using trucks, boats, and helicopters in exciting search and rescue missions. In this title, you're in charge of the Emergency Dispatch Center, where incoming calls from all over town are reporting problems—and people who need help! It's your job to get there as soon as possible to search for folks in trouble and rescue them.

Seated at your Dispatch Center control monitor, you're confronted with three different emergencies. The Dispatch Center is a big plastic toy in itself, with colorful buttons, dials, and blinking lights. Like a 911 center for little kids! All of the emergencies involve people in trouble but not in life-threatening situations. There to help you is Tonka Joe, an emergency rescue expert who can tell you about every mission and how you can use every vehicle to save the day.

You can learn how to become a rescue worker at the Tonka Search and Rescue Academy, an activity center where you can learn how to drive, fly the rescue helicopter, or pilot the rescue boats and a myriad of other skills you may need at the sites.

Also from the console, you select the Tonka trucks from your motor pool of vehicles. You have a rescue Helicopter, a Rescue Boat, Fire Truck, 4×4, Tow Truck, Bulldozer, Dump Truck, Crane, Tractor Trailer, and other vehicles.

You can fix up, customize, and maintain the vehicles at the Tonka Rescue Garage, an activity center where you equip a fire truck, paint and decorate a boat, and repair a helicopter for your rescue missions.

When you see a rescue mission you're ready to tackle, you select it from the dispatch center.

Once you get to a rescue site, another character tells you what the problem is—what needs to be done to save the day. Interesting characters mentor you, helping you save the day in a step-by-step fashion with voice-over advice and encouragement.

When you're done with a rescue mission, the garage, or the academy, you can go to the Print Center. There, you can print a copy of a Special Edition of the newspaper that headlines the story of your daring rescue efforts, a diploma for graduating the academy, or a master mechanic license for working in the garage. When you complete all five activities, you receive a special commendation award that you can also print out.

You can also print out buildings from the missions on card stock and fold and tape them together. Or you can print out objects such as barrels and bricks that you can load into your real Tonka trucks. You can also create and print your own Tonka truck decals, iron-ons, badges, and even vanity license plates for your Tonka toys.

Target Audience
Boys and girls, ages three to eight. Target age is five.

Title Features
- Interactive play and noninteractive animated cinematics
- Three fun and exciting rescue missions with many variations
  - Put out fires with the Fire Truck
  - Run a maze with the Rescue Boat
  - Fly rescue missions with the Helicopter
- Tonka Search and Rescue Academy mission training center
- Tonka Garage activity center
  - Equip the Fire Truck
  - Decorate the Rescue Boat
  - Repair the Helicopter
- Tonka Print Center activity center
- Fourteen different vehicles
- Double-wide, scrollable backgrounds
- Intuitive user interface for controlling vehicles similar to Construction product
- Tonka Joe animated guide
- Five secondary animated characters—one at each site—the academy and the garage
- An animated dog character for comic relief
- Humorous animated vignettes
- Short-term rewards—newspaper articles after each mission, diploma after academy, mechanic's license after garage
- Print Tonka decals, iron-ons, and badges
- Create and print vanity license plates
- Print and construct buildings and other structures
- Print a commendation award for finishing all activities

Screen Structure
- Hasbro Bumper
- Media Station Bumper
- Title Screen
- Sign-on Screen
- Main Navigation Screen
- Print Center Screen
- Garage Activity Screen

- Rescue Academy Activity Screen
- Flood Rescue Site
- Zoo Rescue Site
- Warehouse Rescue Site
- Credits

A complete flow diagram of the title is included in this document (see Figure 6.1).

Characters
The following characters appear in this title:

- Tonka Joe (at the Navigation Screen and Print Center)
- Nate Cod (at the flood)
- Rudy Forest (at the zoo)
- Nick Park (at the warehouse fire)
- Coach (at the academy)
- Sparks (at the garage)
- Bernie the Dog—cameo appearance at all sites

Vehicles
- Front Loader
- Crane
- Tractor Trailer
- Bulldozer
- Helicopter
- Fire Truck
- Fire Boat
- Rescue Boat
- Rescue 4×4
- Backhoe
- Dump Truck
- Tow Truck
- Pickup Truck with boat hitch
- Wrecking Ball

The following sections lay the groundwork for more detailed descriptions of the features and functionality of the product. Artists, programmers, and testers begin to get a sense of what the product comprises, how it works, and what global conventions are used throughout the product.

Navigation and User Interface

Main Navigation Screen.   Players make high-level choices about what to do from the Emergency Dispatch Center. The Emergency Dispatch Center is the *Main Navigation Screen.* It depicts a 911-style console with a TV monitor and functional buttons. Functional buttons have small icon graphics on them to help nonreaders comprehend what to do. The Navigation Screen has the following buttons.

Site Button (3).   Plays a descriptive animation on the console monitor describing that particular rescue mission.

Garage Activity (1).   Displays a description of the Garage activity on the Dispatch Center. Clicking on the screen monitor branches the user to the garage.

Rescue Mission Academy (1).   Displays a description of the Academy activity on the Dispatch Center. Clicking on the screen monitor branches the user to the academy.

Selecting the Screen.   Branches the player to the rescue mission, garage, or academy as depicted on the monitor of the Dispatch Center.

Vehicle Buttons (14).   Plays 3-D turnaround of the selected vehicle on the console monitor and a voice-over description of the vehicle.

Sign-up Screen (1).   Branches to the Sign-on Screen by selecting the arrow at the lower left of the screen. The transition to the Sign-on Screen will appear to be a "scroll." At the Sign-on Screen, all saved games will be displayed next to small iconic screen shots. The screen shots are pictures of the last place the kid was when that particular game was saved. Selecting a saved game by selecting the icon will recall and load the following saved data:

- The name, age, and hometown of the player, if saved.
- The rescue missions completed during the saved game.

The player immediately returns to the Navigation Screen after the load function is complete. The Navigation Screen conditions revert to those of the loaded games.

Quit Game (1).   The player can quit the current game by selecting the "Quit the Game" button. "Thumbs up" and "thumbs down" icons will be displayed asking whether the player wants to quit or wants to return to the current game. "Yes" to quit returns the player to the desktop. "No" to quit returns the player to the Navigation Screen.

Note: "Yes" and "No" buttons will always look like "thumbs up" and "thumbs down" hands for all instances in which they are needed in the title.

Check Progress Button (1).   The "Check Progress" button appears in the lower lefthand area of the screen. Selecting this will display the six possible awards the player can win during the game—the three newspaper articles (one for each rescue site), the mechanic's certificate, the academy diploma, and the commendation award—all on the Dispatch Center monitor. Awards the player has won will be in color. Awards the player has not won are grayed out. This graphic remains until the player selects something else.

Print Center Activity Screen (1).   The player can branch to the Print Center Activity Screen by selecting the arrow button in the lower right of the screen. The transition to the Print Center screen will appear to be a scroll.

The following paragraphs are good examples of global conventions and how to describe them adequately. Global conventions are product-specific standards which, when established early by the designer, are used consistently in the product. Globals, as they are called, facilitate ease of use.

Options on All Rescue Site and Activity Screens. Within interactive Rescue Sites, the Tonka Garage, and the Academy, the player's options are represented by icons displayed over the background image. The available choices are shown in Table 6.1.

Table 6.1 Options		
Site/Activity Option	**Resource**	**Comments**
Return to the previous screen	U-turn road sign	Will generally be located on every background
Help	911	Will replay the last narrator instruction again
Return to Print Center	"Award" icon	The icon appears when the award has been "earned" at the activity site
Print current screen	"Print" icon	The icon appears if site is customized and at the end of individual garage activities

Tables such as these present technical information clearly and concisely to the reader. Artists, programmers, and quality assurance testers appreciate that information is not buried in prose.

Text. This title has no on-screen story text. Text appears on the Sign-on Screen as keyboard response. Text appears on the Print Center screen when customizing license plates.

Button and Icon States. All buttons and icons have three graphic states, which are displayed in Table 6.2.

Table 6.2 Button States	
State	**Graphic Appearance**
Steady state (enabled, selectable)	Normal appearance with graphic
Cursor present	Highlighted
Selected	Depressed

All navigational icons are enabled at all times. Clicking an icon at any point interrupts any action in progress and closes the screen immediately.

Sound Effects.   There will always be a sound effect to accompany a button or icon select. Other sound effects are used as appropriate throughout the title.

Cursor Appearance and Functionality.   The cursor will have two states when being used for Navigation purposes, a third state when the cursor is being used to control a vehicle during a rescue mission, and a fourth state in the "click and drag" mode in the rescue sites, garage, and academy (see Table 6.3).

Table 6.3 Cursor States	
State	**Graphic Appearance**
Normal state, not over selectable area	A "Tonka" arrow
Over a selectable button, icon, or vehicle	A hand with pointing finger
When controlling a vehicle at rescue sites, the garage, or academy	Cursor disappears and becomes the vehicle
When selected and controlling and dragging items at rescue sites and garage	A grasping hand over the item

Keyboard Commands.   The keyboard commands displayed in Table 6.4 are active in this title.

Table 6.4 Keyboard Use		
Key	**Function**	**Notes**
Spacebar	Return to Dispatch Center	
Right arrow	Plans right on wide screen	No effect on single screen
Hit 911 on keyboard	Plays last narrator instruction	Useful when player has vehicle/cursor during mission and cannot hit 911 icon. Will play telephone "tones"
Command-Q (Mac)	Quits the title	Immediately returns player to the operating system
Alt+F4 (Windows)	Quits the title	Immediately returns player to the operating system
Crtl + V (Windows)	Displays software version	Displays a dialog box with information about the current software version

Screen Transitions. When progressing from one screen to another, one of the following screen transitions will be used:

- Cut
- Fade to black and then up

Screen transition is noted in each screen's individual specification.

Player Inactivity. If the player does not move the mouse for an extended period of time, the background music or ambient sound assigned to that screen continues to loop until the player moves the mouse. In some cases, characters or the background will have recurrent animations. These are described for each screen.

Saved Games. The engine will automatically save the current game often and periodically during play. The game will be saved under the name the child "signed in." If the child did not sign in, the game will be saved under "Recruit1" through "Recruit9." The exact time when auto-saving will occur will be determined during early prototyping to discover when it will have the least effect on performance. In general, the engine will save the current game whenever the user has completed a specific activity within a rescue site, the academy, or the garage. The saved information will enable the player to return to approximately the same conditions if he or she quits the game and returns later.

Mission Presentation. Each rescue mission begins with a noninteractive, animated introduction by a main character (see "Characters" above). The character appears in the lower part of the screen. This character

1. Tells the user what the trouble is.
2. Tells the user how to exit the screen and how to get help.

The animated intro is followed by the interactive state, in which the user may select vehicles and use them in the proper way at that particular site. Rescue sites are double-wide backgrounds viewed from a third-person perspective from above. Each site presents a different goal and objective and requires different vehicles for success.

During a mission or activity, the main character will be a voice-over and will

1. Tell the user what vehicles are needed and how to use them.
2. Encourage the user to get going and have fun.

During the mission, while the user is controlling vehicles, small humorous animations featuring dweebles—"rescue guys and gals" and "rescuees"—will occur on the screen.

At the end of a rescue mission, the user is congratulated by the main character (voice-over) while a truck drives onto the site with "click and drag" decorations for the site. Upon completion of the mission, the character tells the user that there is an award waiting for him at the Print Center. The main character tells the user that he can customize the site or choose to get the award at the Print Center. The user may then customize the site with new trees, benches, and other site-specific decorations or branch to the Print Center to get the award. The "Award" icon remains on screen during customization.

After customizing, a "Print" icon appears and the main character tells the user he can print a view of the current screen. The user may then select the "Award" icon, the "Print" icon, or the "Go-Back" button. Selecting the "Award" branches the user to the Print Center. Selecting the "Print" icon will immediately print the screen to the user's printer.

Garage Presentation.   The Garage activity begins with a noninteractive, animated introduction by a main character. The character appears in the lower right of the screen.

The Garage is an activity center where the child may do the following:

1. Attach equipment to the Fire Truck (and print a picture of it).
2. Paint and decorate the Rescue Boat (and print a picture of it).
3. Repair and tune up the Rescue Helicopter (and print a picture of it).

When the user completes individual activities, such as equipping the Fire Truck, a "Print" icon appears. The user may print the current screen by selecting this icon.

If the user completes all activities at the garage, the main character congratulates the user while the "Award" icon appears. The character tells the user that he may select the "award" icon to branch to the Print Center and see (and print) the award. Conditions for "completing" the garage are described in the functional specification for the garage.

Search and Rescue Academy Presentation.   The Search and Rescue Academy activity begins with a noninteractive, animated introduction by a main character. The character appears in the lower right of the screen.

The Search and Rescue Academy is an activity center where the child may do the following:

1. Aim the water cannon from the Fire Truck at fire leaping from different windows.
2. Pilot the Rescue Boat around obstacles in a maze course, rescue people and animals, and return them to the dock.
3. Fly the Helicopter over various locations and use rescue baskets suspended from the chopper to pick up people and animals and move them to a safe location.

If the user completes all activities at the academy, the main character congratulates the user while the "Award" icon appears. The character tells the user that he may select the "Award" icon to branch to the Print Center and see (and print) the award. If the user completes at least one event in each of the three activities, the game will consider the activity "complete" for award purposes. For example, if the user brings back at least one dweeble with the rescue helicopter, that particular activity will be considered "complete." The user may rescue as many dweebles as he wants.

Print Center. The Print Center activity begins with a noninteractive, animated introduction by Tonka Joe.

The Print Center is an activity center where the child may do the following:

1. Print out an issue of a Newspaper that tells about the rescue mission just completed. The child's name—available through the Sign-On screen or at the time of printing—is inserted in the headlines of the newspaper.
2. Print out a Master Mechanic Certificate upon completing the activity at the garage.
3. Print out a Diploma for completing the academy training.
4. Print out a Commendation award for completing all the missions. The child's name, available through the Sign-On Screen or at the time of printing, is inserted in the commendation.
5. Print out stored art which can be cut out and assembled by gluing or pasting tabs together.
6. Customize and print vanity license plates that can be attached to the child's Tonka Trucks.
7. Print out stored decals, badges, and iron-ons that can be attached to the child's Tonka Trucks or clothing or used for room decorations.

The Hardware Requirements section details the minimum hardware requirements for the product. When completed, the product must test well on these platforms. If the product performs well on these platforms, it will generally perform exceptionally well on more robust platforms—PCs equipped with the Pentium processor or Power Macintosh G3s, for example. This information will appear on the product packaging, so the importance of getting it right cannot be overstated.

Minimum Hardware Requirements

Windows
- Intel 80486SX processor, 66 MHz or faster
- DOS version 5.0 or later

- Microsoft Windows version 3.1 or later (or Windows for Workgroups version 3.1 or 3.11) *OR* Windows 95
- 8 MB RAM (8 MB recommended)
- 10 MB free disk space
- Microsoft-compatible mouse
- Standard AT-101 keyboard
- SVGA 256-color video display and driver, with 640×480 resolution
- Sound Blaster-compatible sound card (8-bit or 16-bit sound)
- Double-speed (2X) CD-ROM drive (or better)—minimum 300 KB transfer rate

Macintosh
- Motorola 68030 33MHz or better *OR* 68040 25MHz or better *OR* any PowerPC Macintosh processor
- System 7.1 or higher
- 8 MB with 4000 KB free contiguous memory recommended
- 10 MB free disk space
- Standard keyboard and mouse
- 256-color video display, 640×480 resolution
- Double-speed (2X) CD-ROM drive (or better)—minimum 300 KB transfer rate

The second section of this functional specification, Screen Assets, is not included in this sample. The third section, Node Map—Top Level, follows. This section is the top-level node map of the entire product. The programmers and testers are primarily interested in seeing this graphic illustration of the structure of the title (see Figure 6.1). At a glance, they can see how various nodes are accessed and exited and which are interactive and which are linear. If navigation is determined by system or application software, they see where special-purpose programming is required. Each rectangle represents a node. Most interactive nodes, in turn, have another node map associated with them.

3. NODE MAP—TOP LEVEL

The fourth and fifth sections of this functional specification, Bumper and Title Screen, are not included in this sample. The sixth section, Sign-On Screen (P1), follows. This section is typical of an interactive node. This node is the Sign-In Screen that invites the child to type his or her name, age, and hometown. Describe the node briefly with a few sentences, as follows. (See p. 118 for a discussion of node descriptions.)

FIGURE 6.1   Node Map

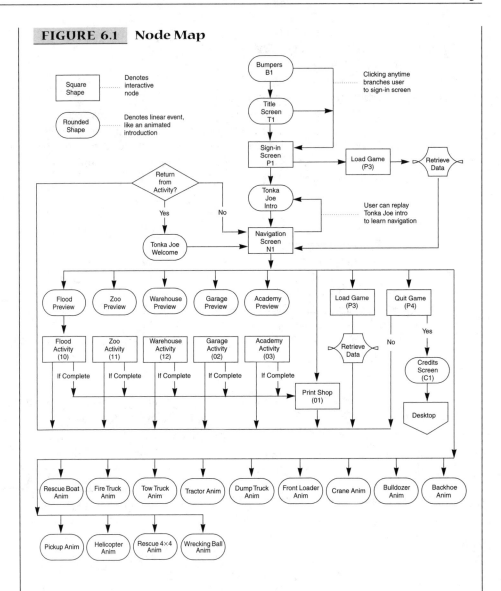

6. SIGN-ON SCREEN (P1)

Sign-On Screen Overview

The Sign-on Screen is used to obtain the user's name, age, and hometown (see Figure 6.2). This information is used by the game engine to customize newspaper articles (at the end of rescue missions), the diploma (Rescue Academy), the mechanic's certificate (garage), and the Commendation Award (all sites and activities).

FIGURE 6.2   **Sign-On Screen**

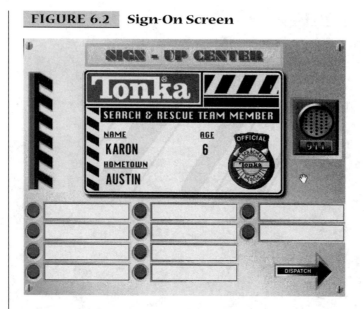

     The user may decline to provide this information and can click his mouse anywhere at any time to branch to the Main Navigation Screen.

The artist who creates the picture for the Dispatch Center knows to save it under this file name.

Background #1

7T N1 GB001 ALL.PIC

Establishing shot of Dispatch Center and Print Center showing how they are interconnected (see Figure 6.3).

The sound designer who creates the ambient sound that plays continuously in the background will save the sound under this file name.

Ambient Sound

7T N1 SA001 ALL.AIF

911 police station sounds—phones ringing, teletypes and typewriters pounding away, crackling radios.

Music

7T N1 SM002 ALL.AIF

This is the Tonka Joe theme.

FIGURE 6.3 **Dispatch Center**

Animated Greeting

7T P1 AP001 USA.MOV

Tonka Joe is standing in front of the console, an empty chair in front of him.
He gestures toward the console as he talks:

> TONKA JOE
>
> Hello there! Glad you could make it to the Dispatch
> Center! I'm Tonka Joe, your partner today. We have
> plenty of search and rescue missions that need your
> help, but first, how about signin' in. Or you can continue
> with a game you already started.

Dialogue is written in the style of the screenplay—character's name in caps, dialogue indented left and right below. Various characters and their dialogue will be scattered throughout the functional specification depending on when and where they appear. Because it is not necessary or desirable for the voice talent to carry the entire spec into the recording booth, it is useful to create another set of documents—a dialogue script for each character—which include only the dialogue and the file name for each sound bite.

Background #2

7T P1 GB001 USA.PIC

Special sign-on background screen. This screen will have space on it for 12 saved games plus space for the user to type in the name he wants to play the current game with. Saved games will be displayed with the name the user used during the game as well as a small graphic icon showing where the user was when the game ended. A red button, small icon, and the name next to it is the hot spot. The user may select a saved game, or he may type in his name. If the user does not input a name, the game will be saved as "Recruit 1." Subsequent games will be saved as Recruit 2, 3, and so on.

It is a very good idea to include drawings in the functional specification and, later, full-color images from the product as they are completed. These graphics help the testers. It is typical to subcontract some, if not all, quality assurance testing, and these strangers to your product need all the help they can get to understand what is intended.

Table 6.5 is a list of the individual screen assets and their file names, which are not specifically identified elsewhere. Such a list is very important to the artists or sound designers who create the assets and the programmers who use them. It is typical that an asset needs to be recreated, sized differently, or otherwise modified before a programmer can use it. When both the programmer and artist can refer to it by file name, fixing problems becomes trivial.

Table 6.5 Asset List	
Name	**Description**
7T P1 GG001 All.PIC	Coach icon
7T P1 GG002 All.PIC	Sparks icon
7T P1 GG003 All.PIC	Nick Park icon
7T P1 GG004 All.PIC	Rudy Forest icon
7T P1 GG005 All.PIC	Nate Cod icon
7T P1 GG008 All.PIC	Red button highlight
7T P1 GG009 All.PIC	Highlight around button & name plate
7T P1 GG006b All.PIC	911 cursor present
7T P1 GG006c All.PIC	911 selected
7T P1 GG007b All.PIC	Return to Dispatch Center cursor present
7T P1 GG007c All.PIC	Return to Dispatch Center selected

All companies have their own file-naming systems or conventions. File-naming conventions make it possible to have a unique name for each of thousands of individual assets. At Media Station, the company that developed *Tonka Search and Rescue* under contract with Hasbro, the file-naming system not only serves the individual project, but also allows the company to have several different projects in development at the same time without any confusion about what product an asset belongs to. For more information about file-naming conventions, see Chapter 9.

Audio Prompt

If there are no saved games, the following audio plays:

7T P1 SV001 USA.AIF

TONKA JOE (OFF CAMERA)
Just type your name first, then hit that return key.

If there is at least one previous game saved, the following audio plays:

7T P1 SV01A USA.AIF

TONKA JOE (OFF CAMERA)
Just type your name first, then hit that return key. Or, click on a game you already started and continue with that one.

Table 6.6 is a very clear and concise way to tell the programmer what the user may do and how the application should respond. The tester reading this section and playing with the product can determine whether the system is responding to the user's actions as designed.

User Interaction

The following instruction is directed to the programmer. When the game begins, the user types a name on the Sign-on Screen. This name is stored immediately in a database of saved names. The programmer (or software engineer) knows to check the name typed in by the user and to compare it to names already stored in a database of stored names. If the new name matches a saved name, the following sound file must play.

Table 6.6 System Function			
User Action	System Response	Animation or Sound	Assets
Click on previous game.	Branch to Navigation Screen with all conditions as they were when the selected game was quit.	Cursor present icon. Highlight icon. Icon selected.	TBD
Type in name.	Display text on card.	Display text.	
Type in name—if name matches a previous game.	911 cursor present.	Display text.	
	Play audio cue V.O.	"You've been here before . . ."	7T P1 SV01C USA.AIF
	Display graphics.	Highlight previous game.	TBD
Hit return.	Play audio cue V.O.	Instruct to type in age.	7T P1 SV002 USA.AIF
Type in age.	Display text on card.	Display text.	
Hit return.	Play audio cue V.O.	Instruct to type in hometown.	7T P1 SV003 USA.AIF
Type in hometown.	Display text on card.	Display text.	
Hit return.	Play audio cue V.O.	Move on to work . . .	7T P1 SV004 USA.AIF

Audio V.O.

Conditional—if name typed in matches name in saved game:

7T P1 SV01C USA.AIF

TONKA JOE (OFF CAMERA)

You've been here before. Do you want to start over, or continue from where you left off? If you want to start over, just hit the return key. If you want to continue where you left off before, click on the other game that's lit up.

7T P1 SV002 USA.AIF

> TONKA JOE (OFF CAMERA)
> OK, now, how about your age. Same thing. Hit that
> return key when you're done.

7T P1 SV003 USA.AIF

> TONKA JOE (OFF CAMERA)
> Fantastic! Now type in your hometown. Hit that return
> key and we're all done.

7T P1 SV004 USA.AIF

> TONKA JOE (OFF CAMERA)
> Let's go to work!

Here are more instructions directed at the programmer. The programmer knows he or she must start a timer, and when the clock hits certain times, certain sound files must play.

User Inactivity

If the user does not respond to the first of the prompts above within 10 seconds, the prompt is repeated once:

7T P1 SV001 USA.AIF

If the user does not respond within 10 seconds of the repeated prompt, the system plays:

7T P1 SV004 USA.AIF

The system then immediately branches to the Navigation Screen. The user will be saved as "Recruit X," where *X* is the next numerical saved game.

Note: After 10 saved games, the system replaces games beginning with the first saved game.

The Game Design Document

As for the functional specification, the audience for the game design document is the team that creates the art, sound, and software and tests the final product. The document must have sufficient detail that nothing is left to the interpretation of the development staff. Games have much more interactivity—more features—than other genres of multimedia products, so the dialogue between computer and player is richer. The programming is more complex. In the game design document, the specifics of interactivity are described in greater detail than in a functional specification for, let's say, a reference product.

Contents of the Design Document

The game design itself, including the many programming decisions, logic trees, and algorithms (which we won't get into), is the responsibility of the game designer and the lead programmer. *The game design document, however, is written by the writer in consultation with the designer.* Game designers often rely on the writer to flesh out the design and add the details. Experienced writers develop strong characters, describe worlds, write dialogue, and juice up action sequences.

The game design document is very similar to the functional specification. It contains the following:

1. *Executive Summary*—A two-page description of the game which includes the genre, audience, target platform, and features, marketing hooks, or other competitive pluses. It contains a *brief* description of the goals, challenges, rewards, characters, backstory, and characters.
2. *Detailed Game Description*—Describes the goal of the game and what the success strategy is. If the game is competitive, it describes how players win or lose. It describes the game world and environment, the levels within it, the game rules, global conventions (see previous chapter), the challenges, and how players overcome them.
3. *Story and Characters*—If the game features a story and characters of any kind, the document describes them in detail. It details the attributes and behaviors of all characters.
4. *Functionality*—It describes how players control the game—what real and virtual controls they use to manage their experience. This section includes a description of the interface—that part of functionality which is displayed on the screen.
5. *Look and Feel*—This describes the art and sound direction of the game.
6. *Drawings*—The document often provides layouts (blueprints) of the game world and turn-arounds (multiple views) and color mark-ups of characters. The document may provide storyboards of any animated or video scenes that will be produced and "canned"—shown as movies in the game.

7. *Node Map*—The flow diagram of the game, similar to the node map of the functional specification, showing how players get from one level to another.

8. *Node-by-Node Breakdown*—The document includes a breakdown of every node (or level) in the game, as in the functional spec. Each breakdown includes detailed descriptions and drawings, when appropriate, of all assets (art, video, animation, and sound) and all interactivity (what the user does and how the game responds and vice versa):

- Goal or objective of this level
- Challenges of this level—what enemies, obstacles, puzzles, or problems players must overcome
- Rules for this level—how players overcome the challenges
- Description and drawing (could be line art) of the level, background, or environment. Need to indicate location and purpose of all buttons, icons, hotspots, and other key game elements.
- Description of characters in this level—describe who are they and what powers or weaknesses they have and when and under what circumstances they appear. Describe how they behave and what circumstances may cause their behavior to change.
- Description and storyboard for any canned (preproduced, as opposed to real-time) animation or video
- Dialogue or voice-over—who speaks, what they say, and under what conditions
- Music and sound effects—what they are and when they are heard
- Asset (file) names for all picture and sound elements
- Interactivity of the player—describe what players can and cannot do in this level
- Response of the game to the player—when players do x, what does the game do?
- Describe what happens if players are successful and what happens if they fail
- Transitions—describe the visual effect of entering and exiting this level

The game designer will provide many more details the programmers will need having to do with timing, pacing, frequency of events, and so forth. These, too, must be written into the node-by-node breakdown. Some of this information will lead to the inclusion of another node—perhaps a software event of some kind that determines the next graphical occurrence in the game.

Level of Detail of Game Design Document

More so than for other genres of multimedia, there is a critical link between the assets—the pictures and sounds that appear on the screen—and the software programming of a game. This is a direct result of the high level of interactivity. In previous chapters, we talked about turning over control of the multimedia experience to the user. This is especially important when designing a game. Games employ more hotspots, buttons, and other virtual controls and may require mouse, keypad, joystick, and other real controls. More of what happens on the screen is a direct result of some action taken by the player. The action and reaction of the player and the game must be instantaneous and seamless. This requirement puts pressure on the design and development team to design the interactive experience very carefully and to identify the assets needed to realize the design.

Asset Descriptions.   Assets, you remember, are all of the art and sound elements that make up the player's audio/visual experience. Game play is the interactive experience itself—what the player can do and how the game responds. Game play drives asset development. During development, you must create the assets that enable the game play.

The producer, director, writer, and game designer in consultation with the art director, sound designer, and lead programmer must determine, on a node-by-node basis, what assets are required to display the game experience. These sessions are called "database meetings" because the list of assets that results from these meetings is put into a database, usually by the producer or an assistant.

For all assets, the group must determine

- Whether the asset will play off the CD-ROM or be put into memory and played from there
- File format (html, pict, aif, wav, jpeg, rtf, etc.)
- File name

For all graphic assets, the group must determine

- Resolution or size (exactly, in pixels)
- Color palette
- Position on screen (exactly, in the form of X,Y position from the upper left corner)
- Whether the asset moves and, if it does, when, where, and how fast

For text assets, the group must determine

- Font, size, and style
- Color, shading, highlighting
- Alignment, justification

For video and animation assets, the group must determine

- Frame rate (frames per second)
- Length in seconds and frames
- Compression scheme

For sound assets, the group must determine

- Sampling
- Duration in seconds and frames
- Volume
- Mono or stereo

Chapter Summary

This chapter describes the principal document created during the design of an interactive multimedia product, the functional specification. It may also be called the design specification, the design document, or the game design. It describes, in exhaustive detail, the product the developer and its client intend to develop so that it can be used as the basis for their agreement with each other and as the blueprint that guides the activities of the development team.

Because it serves so many purposes for a large and diverse reading audience, the functional specification is an unusual document. It is part screenplay and part software specification. It contains diagrams, drawings, tables, figures, screen shots, and photographs. It features long lists of assets which have mysterious-looking file names attached to them for the use of the production staff. Elsewhere, the spec pitches the possibilities of ancillary products and licensing opportunities for the benefit of the product managers.

The functional specification is the design document around which the entire product development effort orbits. It makes possible the development process, which is described in the next part of this book.

Recommended Reading

See the functional specification written by two multimedia students in Appendix A and visit the web site to see the downloadable functional specification.

Development

The Development

Process Overview

In this chapter, you will learn about

- The importance of the phased approach to development
- The meaning of the terms *prize, deliverable, task, milestone, the critical path, and resource*
- Who the client is:
    - Internal
    - External
- What the phases of development are:
    - Discovery
    - Design
    - Prototype
    - Development
- What the prize of each phase is
- What deliverables compose each prize

The objective of this chapter is to give you a broad overview of the development process, which begins when a developer and publisher first decide to work together and ends when the gold master, or final product, is complete. We cover the development process from a fairly high altitude. In subsequent chapters, we look more closely at each of the concepts covered in this chapter.

The Importance of Phases

Developing a multimedia product, just like building a bridge, publishing a book, or making a film, is a step-by-step process. The four steps in the development process are called *phases*. This term is borrowed from management and engineering practices in systems analysis and from the instructional development process, regimens that require formative evaluations periodically during the development of a system. Formative evaluations enable systems designers to modify and fine-tune their design before moving on to the next, usually more costly, step. Depending on its core business or product focus, a company may recognize more than four phases in its development cycle. Educational and instructional products, for example, may go through as many as nine phases because they require more formative evaluations during development and very rigorous summative evaluations after completion (Johnson & Foa, 1989). Additional phases are subsets of the four phases covered in this book.

In multimedia development, the phases are

- The discovery phase
- The design phase
- The prototype phase
- The production phase

The interactive design process, which you learned in Part 1, takes place during the discovery phase and the design phase. Typically, the concept document, competitive analysis, top-level design, and cost/benefit analysis are completed during the discovery phase. The functional specification is written during the design phase.

Phases must be completed in the proper order, and each should be completed before the next one starts. Nearly all projects involving the construction of a product mirror this step-by-step method.

In home building, for example, an architect would never spend time designing a home until she had interviewed her clients and discovered what their lifestyle is like, what their preferences are, and how much they intend to spend. Construction doesn't begin until the blueprints are complete and all of the necessary approvals have been obtained. If the building incorporates some new and daring engineering approach, the contractor will test the concept in some small and harmless manner before using the technique throughout the house. This common sense approach to inching forward with development is used in multimedia as well. That is, when multimedia is done properly.

Each of the phases of development is characterized by having a unique goal or *prize.* Each prize is made up of specific deliverables, which are tangible items that the team produces. The team must complete a series of tasks to create the deliverables. And in order to complete the tasks, the producer must use certain resources.

The Prize and Deliverables

Each phase has a "prize," an overarching goal, that must be completed and approved before the next phase can be started. The prize of each phase is reached by creating predetermined deliverables and completing certain milestones. The sum and substance of the deliverables make up the prize or make the prize possible. The approval of the prize (usually by the client) signals the end of the phase and leads to the "kick-off" of the next phase.

Deliverables and Tasks

Deliverables are created by the successful completion of specific tasks. A deliverable of the design phase, for example, may be *casting voices for animated characters*. Tasks performed to complete that deliverable include the following:

1. Design characters (draw them)
2. Write backstory (create a life) for each character
3. Write sample dialogue
4. Listen to audition tapes of prospective talent
5. Select best talent
6. Record sample of talent performing specific character

Milestones

A milestone celebrates the approval of a deliverable by the client or the completion of a formal evaluation of the deliverable. In the example above, the deliverable is the recorded voice sample, which is delivered to the client for approval. When the client has approved the voice sample for use in the product, that event is called a milestone. Milestones are often used for billing purposes. The producer identifies a number of milestones, which represent the successful completion of major deliverables, and lists those milestones in the contract as triggering a progress payment from the client. The amount of the payment covers the costs accrued to complete the deliverable. Because the contract, with progress payments itemized, is drawn up before work actually starts, the producer must estimate what those costs are likely to be. This requires a great deal of estimating skill, usually based on experience.

Serial and Parallel Tasks

Many tasks are performed serially, meaning one after the other. There is usually some dependency between serial tasks. For example, the sound designer cannot record narration until the writer has written the dialogue and the director has cast the talent. Some tasks can be completed in parallel, meaning that because there is no dependency between them, they can be worked on independently and simultaneously. The narration can be recorded by the sound designer and backgrounds painted in the art department at the same time.

The Critical Path

On every development project, there is some interdependency between tasks that begin on the first day of development and end with the delivery of the final product.

An interruption of any task along this string of serial events causes the intended completion date of the development to be delayed. *Slippage* is a term used for a delay in progress. The dependent string of tasks is known as the critical path. The critical path must be identified by the producer very early in development and followed—or "tracked"—closely in order to keep development on schedule and on budget.

Resources

This brings us to resources. Each task requires the expertise and labor contribution of certain staff using certain equipment. People on the development team and the equipment or supplies they use to complete each task are collectively called resources. The sum of all the costs associated with employing all the resources during the course of development, together with certain other costs, is the development budget.

Who Is the Client?

Throughout the following chapters on development, you will see reference to the client. It is important for you to know who the client is and to be aware that in multimedia, just as in retail, manufacturing, and every other business, there is always a client.

Multimedia products are developed in studios. In multimedia parlance, these studios are called developers. Developers are full-service studios that provide design, writing, animation, audio, video, and software services to create a finished multimedia product. Developers may be independent companies of almost any size—from very small, two-person boutiques to fairly large (100+ employee) organizations. Some publishers, such as Broderbund Software of Novato, California, own their own in-house development studios. Kids Studio created the *Arthur* series of children's CD-ROM products for its parent company, Broderbund. Broderbund, in turn, is owned by the publisher The Learning Company, which itself is owned by Mattel, Inc.

Developers make money by being paid to provide product development services. The client for the services may be an *external* client, such as a software publisher or even another developer.

The Publisher in Search of a Developer

The developer may be engaged by an outside entity to develop a product under a "work-for-hire" arrangement. Usually, this scenario begins when a product concept originates at a publisher and the publisher must find a developer whose core competency, track record, availability, and other attributes match the product. The developer and the publisher agree on a product design, a cost, a schedule, and other terms covered in Chapter 10, on the development agreement. The publisher pays the developer an agreed-upon amount for the product, and the developer relinquishes all rights to the product in exchange for a fixed fee. There may be other terms of their agreement which make the arrangement a bit more complex, but the general idea is that the developer is a hired hand and the company paying for the development services is the client.

The Developer in Search of a Publisher

Frequently, a developer designs and partly develops a product on its own and then approaches a publisher with the product idea. If the publisher agrees that the product concept is a revenue opportunity, the developer and publisher enter into a different kind of agreement. The developer does not work on a work-for-hire basis. Instead, it is paid a royalty, a percentage of gross or net sales, rather than a fixed fee, and does not relinquish all rights in the product to the publisher. Royalties are paid after the product is completed and is sold in stores or over the Internet. Because many developers lack the financial resources to develop the product and then wait for royalty payments, which can take over a year, publishers pay the developer an advance against royalties. For example, a publisher may pay a developer $500,000 to cover the direct costs of development. When the product is complete and selling to the public, the publisher recoups, or earns back, the advance paid to the developer. After recouping its advance, the publisher begins paying the developer royalty payments on sales. Under these agreements, the developer may retain some or all of the copyright in the product.

Approvals and Ownership

In both these arrangements, the publisher carries the greater financial risk and behaves like a client, often exercising final approval of all creative and technical work that goes into the product. The client approves the art, animation, voice talent, music, video, interactive features, and functionality. When the product features branded or copyrighted characters, stories, music, or situations, the approval process can be grueling and time-consuming—a fact that future producers should be aware of. Unless agreed upon otherwise, any new characters or other intellectual property created by the developer for the client while working for a fee under a work-for-hire arrangement become the property of the client.

Media Station, Inc., of Ann Arbor, Michigan, is a highly respected developer of children's products. The company has produced a number of products for Hasbro Interactive, a publisher. *Tonka Search and Rescue, Tonka Garage,* and *Tonka Speedway* were developed by Media Station for Hasbro under a work-for-hire arrangement. In the process, Media Station designers and writers created a number of new characters, which are now the wholly owned intellectual property of Hasbro.

Internal Clients

Even when the developer is owned by the client, the relationship between developer and client is the same. In this instance, the client is an *internal* client, but nonetheless the entity with ultimate authority to approve the product and own all rights.

Many companies that begin in the work-for-hire business aspire to develop their own, wholly owned products and to make their money not as service providers, but rather through the net profits of product sales. These companies invest their own money, time, and effort and develop a product. One would think that in such a situation, there is no client. Quite the opposite. The internal client in such a situation is the CEO, the president, the owner, the marketing director, or a committee of all of them. The producer, director, and writer move the development forward on approvals from the internal client.

The Development Phases

The treatment of product development in this part of the book focuses on the work-for-hire relationship. In this scenario, the publisher usually seeks out a developer to provide full design and development services for a multimedia product or application. There is seldom a complete design. There is often a licensed intellectual property. The publisher/client usually has a fixed budget and timeframe in mind. These parameters make the phased approach to design and development absolutely essential.

There are four phases in product development:

1. *The discovery phase.* In this initial phase, the developer establishes a relationship and understanding with the client and reaches an initial contractual agreement based on a top-level design and a preliminary budget and schedule. In educational and instructional product development, the needs analysis takes place during this phase.
2. *The design phase.* In the next phase, the developer writes the functional specification and creates a final budget and development schedule based on the design.
3. *The prototype phase.* During this phase, a small working version of the product is developed and tested for overall design, new technology, and development processes.
4. *The production phase.* In this final phase, all audio/video assets and computer software engineering is completed leading to the "gold master," the final CD-ROM which is sent to the manufacturer.

The phases share these characteristics:

- They are completed in a fixed amount of time.
- They have clearly defined goals, deliverables, and milestones.
- They are completed sequentially.

Failure to develop a product in this manner usually results in one or more disasters. Among the typical problems is failure to meet client expectations. One of the most common phrases heard in a producer's worst nightmare begins with the words "I thought it would be like this . . . " This problem usually originates during the discovery or design phases. It happens if a product design is not well documented or if the client does not read and approve a product design before the developer begins developing it.

A second common disaster is an overdesigned product—one that is too big or includes mutually exclusive features. This usually occurs when the producer, who must keep the product's size and shape consistent with the budget, does not exercise sufficient oversight of the development process.

If managed properly, each phase results in deliverables and approvals that move the development forward with little or no negative impact on the budget, the schedule, or the quality of the product. Spread over time, the phases with their respective prizes look like the chart in Figure 7.1.

FIGURE 7.1   **The development phases**

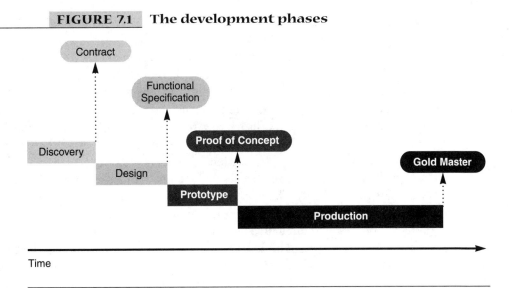

Note that the phases do not overlap in time and that the production phase is as long as the others combined. Ideally, the developer does not begin work on the next phase until the current phase is complete. The temptation to jump the gun and get a head start on work required of the next phase is very strong and should be avoided.

For example, the first phase, the discovery phase, is nearly always undertaken without a formal agreement or contract between the developer and the client. It is the phase during which the decision to have a contract and proceed with development is made. The temptation to act as though a contract exists and to put certain resources to work on the design, or research, or other costly activities is great, especially if the client is sending strong signals that the decision is made and the contract is merely a formality.

The contract is more than a formality. Without a contract, the client can end the relationship for any reason and owe the developer nothing. In the Spring of 1996, I had just become the general manager of a development studio which had several products in the discovery phase. The company had, on the promise of quickly reaching agreement with the various clients, begun work on all of them. Artists, animators, writers, and others were already hard at work on products for which we did not have contracts. As our prospective clients watched their Fourth Quarter (Christmas, 1995) results come in and saw that their previous products had not done well, they ceased negotiations with us and pulled out to regroup. We were left with nothing and had no recourse. It took months to recover from the losses.

The Discovery Phase

As the name suggests, the discovery phase permits the developer and client to learn about each other, develop a working relationship, and agree on a product design, cost, and schedule. When two parties already enjoy a working relationship, they must still agree on the rest. There is no escaping the discovery phase.

In order to generate work-for-hire business, developers employ sales and marketing tactics to reach potential clients with news of their existence and skills. Advertising, word of mouth, cold calls by sales reps, previous relationships, and referrals often enable developers to find potential clients. Likewise, publishers and other clients are always on the hunt for better, faster, and budget-conscious developers.

The discovery phase begins when a developer and a client join together to discuss a potential product. The *prize* of the discovery phase is a signed *contract* or *letter of intent*. Although it is preferable, it is unlikely that either party will be prepared to sign a contract without a final design, budget, and schedule, which are developed during the design phase. Think about it. The two parties want to work together but don't have anything substantive to agree on. The letter of intent, which may also be called a deal memo, breaks the logjam. The letter of intent is an instrument that enables the parties to move into the costly and time-consuming design phase and to negotiate a contract simultaneously. In order to reach the point where the parties can craft and sign a letter of intent, the following items must be discussed and agreed upon:

- *What the product is.* This is usually defined, at this juncture, in the form of a top-level design, as described in Chapter 5.
- *How much the product will cost.* Although it is too early to create a detailed budget, the product design must be do-able within an agreed-upon figure.

■ *When the product will be complete.* This is the "gold master" date when the product must be final. The producer must put together an initial or preliminary development plan.

■ *Roles and responsibilities of the two parties.* If the client must provide certain rights or assets, this must be spelled out.

■ *Other terms and conditions,* which may include copyright ownership, warrantees, or royalty payments to the developer in addition to the development fee.

The contract is discussed in more detail in Chapter 10, where a sample agreement is presented and commented on. There are links on the web site to Ladera Press, publisher of *Multimedia Law and Business Handbook,* one of the best resources for a clear explanation of this subject.

The Proposal and Bid. The deliverables of the discovery phase are the top-level design, a preliminary budget, and a preliminary development plan. These items are bundled together in the form of a proposal and bid to the client. When the client accepts the proposal, the parties have an agreement to proceed.

The developer and client reach agreement on these items during a process of meetings, discussions, brainstorming, and corporate courtship. During this mating ritual, it is the job of the producer to lead the business effort and to establish a relationship of mutual trust and understanding with the client. It is essential for the client to perceive the producer as the manager, leader, and point of contact for all issues related to the product development. The producer must get the client to appoint one person on the client side to serve the same purpose.

The producer is responsible for analyzing the top-level design as it is being written and for determining the resources that will be required to create the assets and write the software. The producer must create a "straw man" budget and development plan based on the careful evaluation of the top-level design. This preliminary budget includes estimated costs for completing each of the three subsequent phases.

The director is responsible for listening carefully to the creative needs of the client and translating them into a coherent and exciting interpretation. The director must be perceived as the creative driver of the product, the one who will direct the artists, animators, videographers, and sound designers to realize the shared vision.

The writer must contribute creative ideas during this phase and bring everyone's creative notions together in the form of the top-level design. The top-level design becomes the basis for the shared creative vision as well as the basis of a legal agreement between the parties.

The Design Phase

The design phase begins when the two parties have reached an agreement to proceed with development. The top-level design, the preliminary budget, and the preliminary development plan form the jumping-off point for all of the work done during the design phase.

The *prize* of the design phase is *client approval of the functional specification*. As you know from Chapter 6, the functional specification is both the development bible and the basis of the final budget, the development plan, and the contract with the client.

In many instances, the parties sign a definitive agreement, or contract, after completion of the design phase. All of the substantive elements are available at that time: a detailed design, a detailed development plan, and a budget based on the design and plan. In the best of worlds, the business affairs people representing both parties have worked through the other contractual issues congruent with the design phase. They have agreed on such issues as copyright ownership, royalties, payment schedules, approval stages, and so forth. However, this is not always the case, and many projects are completed with a letter of intent or deal memo standing in as the only legal agreement right through to delivery of the gold master. This is not advisable, but it's sometimes unavoidable. The producer must decide if the good faith relationship established with the client will sustain development.

Deliverables necessary to complete the design phase include

1. The complete functional specification, which includes

    a. A node map of the entire product
    b. A node-by-node description of the product
    c. Screen layouts and designs
    d. Button and icon designs
    e. Font specifications
    f. Character designs
    g. Storyboards
    h. Dialogue and narration
    i. Game designs

2. Approval of voice talent and, in some cases, music
3. Rights clearances for any copyrighted material
4. Agreements with subcontractors
5. Asset list
6. Final development plan
7. Final development budget

During the design phase, the producer, director, and writer work very closely together to coordinate their activities.

 The Producer's Job. The producer must manage the design process to ensure that all of the deliverables are created within the budget and timeframe for the phase. The producer brings in the art director, the sound designer, an arranger/composer, voice talent, and various artists to create the art and sound deliverables. The producer brings in a technical director—usually the lead engineer who will write all the software—and has him or her evaluate the design and identify programming issues.

At the same time, the producer must watch the design itself very carefully, as it is developed by the writer and director (and other contributors), to be certain it can be produced within the target budget and schedule. In other words, while the functional specification is being written and the ancillary art, designs, and storyboards are being created, the producer must evaluate the work from the point of view of what it will take to produce it. It is the producer's responsibility to prevent the product from becoming too big or complex for the budget.

The producer must also anticipate what subcontractors and vendors may be needed during development and obtain bids from them for their work on the project in the future. The producer must include these future costs in the development budget.

As the functional specification is written, the producer begins the process of creating a development plan and, from it, a development budget. These are described in more depth in Chapter 9.

As if this isn't enough, the producer must make certain that the contract negotiations between the legal representatives of the parties continue and that there are no insurmountable obstacles. Ideally, the only thing preventing a contract from being signed at any time during the design phase is the absence of the functional specification, development plan, and final budget.

The Director's Job.　The director instructs the activities of the writer, the artists, and the sound designer to assure design quality and consistency throughout. It is the director's responsibility to have a broad, high-level vision of the entire product and to give each design team member clear instructions on what each needs to create in order to contribute his or her piece to the whole. This is exactly the same responsibility that the film director has.

John Lucas, who directed *Tonka Search and Rescue* at Media Station, Inc., directed the work of artists who drew layouts of all the backgrounds, designed characters, thumbnailed storyboards, and constructed 3-D computer-generated vehicles. John knew how all these elements would come together in the end and gave the artists clear instructions on how to create these elements so they all fit together properly.

The Writer's Job.　The writer writes the functional specification. As described in Chapter 6, the functional specification is a massive and extremely detailed document. The top-level design acts as the rough outline for the functional specification, and the writer fleshes out every single detail of the product on a node-by-node basis. During the writing activity, the writer is in nearly constant consultation with the producer, director, art director, sound designer, and technical director.

Remember, the writer is writing a document that will be used by these people to direct their activities during development. By discussing with them the content, look and feel, structure, features, and functional control of the product, the writer can be certain there is a consensus and buy-in by the entire team. Equally important, the writer can be certain that the document is, in fact, usable by the team.

The Prototype Phase

At this point, the developer and the client should have a contract. The contract identifies the product described in the functional specification as the product the developer will produce. The contract stipulates that the final development plan and final budget are based on the functional specification.

After the functional specification is approved, production of assets and development of software for the final product begin in earnest. The prototype phase is an interim step in the development of the final product during which the *prize—a working mini-version of the final product*—is produced and tested. Although this phase is called the prototype phase, the small working version of the product may not necessarily be, in the strictest sense, a prototype. It may be called, more appropriately, a "proof of concept."

What's the difference? To be a prototype, the product utilizes or showcases the actual, underlying technology that will be used in the final product. For example, if the final product is designed to be driven by a new game engine or to have a seamless and transparent link to a web site during operation, the prototype is driven by the game engine or actually has a seamless link to a web site during testing.

However, if the game engine or the software that makes the Web link possible cannot be programmed during the prototype phase because of time or cost issues, the small working version may be merely smoke and mirrors. It may only *look* like it is behaving properly, and it will only prove that the *concept* works, not the technology. It cannot be called a prototype.

The prototype is produced to test the following:

- The overall design, in terms of content, features, functional control, look and feel, and structure
- Development processes
- New or special purpose software or other technology

 Because the prototype, or proof of concept, is a subset of the final product, the producer determines what part—what selection of nodes from the overall design—provides the best test of the above items. The producer moves the prototype nodes to the front of the development pipeline. The producer and director then manage the development of assets and the programming of software to create those nodes, which the programmers integrate to create the prototype.

The deliverables during the prototype phase include

1. Final-quality assets
   a. Background art
   b. Animation
   c. Narration
   d. Video
   e. Buttons, icons and text

2. As well as
   a. Software programming of the prototype
   b. Quality assurance testing
   c. Focus testing of the product with the target audience
   d. Modifications to the design (formative evaluation)
   e. Revised plan, budget, and possibly a revised development agreement

If the product is well designed, and the prototype well executed, all of the testing will confirm that the development should continue as planned. Most of the work that went into the prototype is not wasted. The art and sound assets can be used in the final product. If the programming is coded as it would be for the final product, it is also salvageable.

However, it is not unusual that testing the prototype points to problems. The product may have to be redesigned, development processes reassessed, or technology reconsidered. That is the purpose of the prototype—to unmask problems with the product before the commitment of time and money to final development.

During the prototype phase, the producer manages the budget and development plan and tracks the progress of asset production and software development. The director supervises the creative talent, artists, and sound designers on a daily basis to ensure that they are producing the right elements in the proper manner. The writer is in a maintenance mode. He or she keeps the functional specification updated with any minor changes or fixes that come up. After the prototype has been tested, the producer, director, and writer may have to readjust the design of the product, the budget, and the development plan and even rewrite portions of the functional specification before continuing with the fourth and final phase.

The Production Phase

Unless the product is a complete flop during testing, the prototype phase generally results in some modifications to the product, which do not completely interrupt continued development of assets and software development. The production phase is the continuation of these activities leading to the *prize*—the *gold master*.

The three main activities during the production phase are asset development, software engineering, and product testing. Artists, animators, videographers, and sound designers produce assets, while software engineers or programmers develop software (code). Versions of the product are burned on disc and tested by quality assurance. Generally, the producer manages the flow so that the three groups work on nodes in the same order, with software engineering trailing behind asset production slightly, since programmers need assets for final integration with software. As graphics and sounds are created and approved, they are turned over to the software engineers, who write the software and incorporate the assets into the product.

As time goes on, more and more of the product takes shape. When about 80 percent of the assets and software are complete and it is possible to play with the product, it is considered an Alpha version. An Alpha disc is burned, and the quality assurance testers inspect it for bugs. As they discover problems, bugs are "logged" and reported to the producer, who relays bug-fixing instructions to the appropriate department. A piece of art may be the wrong size, a sound may be recorded incorrectly, or a button may branch a user to the wrong node. While development continues on unfinished nodes, Alpha nodes are fixed. This process continues until 100 percent of the product is complete, but not bug-free. At this point, the product is considered a Beta version. Beta discs are burned, tested, and fixed until there are no known bugs. The last bug-free Beta is considered "gold."

The gold master is the final, thoroughly tested master disc, which is sent to the manufacturer. From it, thousands of replications are made, labeled, packaged, shrink-wrapped, and sent to the distributor.

During production, the following deliverables are produced:

1. All final art and sound assets
2. All software development and integration
3. Various pre-final discs (Alpha, Beta)
4. Exhaustive quality assurance testing and bug reports
5. Package design
6. Release notes and manuals
7. The gold master

If the developer has taken the product through the first three phases of development and has achieved the prize at the end of each before proceeding to the next, the production phase will go very smoothly. Still, many things can go wrong, or cause the otherwise smooth development process to stall. The two things that producers must count on are changes requested by the client and changes necessary to "tweak" an application.

The producer manages the budget and time line, tracks progress daily, and weekly compares progress against expenditures. During the production phase, it is the producer's job to keep the product on budget and on schedule. The producer does this by moving resources in and out of the development pipeline as necessary.

The producer also maintains a steady flow of status reports to the client and to upper management.

The director supervises the staff, directing the development of art, audio, video, and the development of software.

The writer continues to keep the functional specification updated. During development, various small modifications are made to the product almost every day. The functional specification must be made completely compliant with what the product now looks, sounds, and behaves like. During the testing phase—when the product undergoes rigorous testing by people whose job it is to try and break the product—the testers will have the functional specification on their laps and the disc in the computer. The two must match or the testers will believe they have found a bug.

Chapter Summary

The multimedia development process consists of four phases: discovery, design, prototype, and production. The successful completion of a phase signals the beginning of the next. Each phase has a major goal, or "prize," which makes it possible for the developer to undertake the next phase safely and confidently. Earning the prize in each phase is a matter of creating certain deliverables. Deliverables require the successful completion of various tasks. Tasks require the labor contributions of certain staff using certain equipment. Together, these are called resources.

The producer, director, and writer each play key roles during all four phases. The producer must interface with the client, establish the budget and schedule, and manage the entire development effort. The director must have a clear overview of the creative and technical requirements and must direct the team so that each individual member creates each piece of the whole in the correct manner. All the pieces must fit. The writer must write and maintain the functional specification—an extremely important document that acts as both the development bible and the legal agreement between the developer and the client.

Recommended Reading

England, E., and Finney, A. *Managing Multimedia.* Addison-Wesley: Harlow, England, 1999.
Goldberg, Ron *Multimedia Producer's Bible.* IDG Books: Foster City, CA, 1996.

The Discovery Phase

In this chapter, you will learn that

- The prize of the discovery phase is the development agreement
- The developer must qualify the client
- The client qualifies the developer
- Some clients need an education in multimedia
- Developers must learn about the client and its needs
- Developers and clients must negotiate certain deal points for their agreement
- Developers create the following discovery phase deliverables:
    - The top-level design
    - The preliminary development plan and budget
    - The proposal and bid

In previous chapters, we established that developers (multimedia studios) produce multimedia products and web sites for clients. Clients for CD-ROM products are usually software publishers, but on occasion a client may be another developer that needs additional art or programming services. Clients may also be from outside the multimedia community. A major accounting firm may hire a developer to create a multimedia training application. A pharmaceutical company may hire a developer to develop sales and promotional materials. An advertising agency may hire a developer to create a media-rich Web advertisement for one of *its* clients. Sometimes clients are external—approaching the developer from outside the company—and sometimes internal—from within the company. In all cases, the developer and client must establish a relationship of trust, understanding, and collaboration and reach agreement on the product, development schedule, and price. The discovery phase is for this purpose.

The Prize of the Discovery Phase

The prize of the discovery phase is a legal agreement that enables the parties to begin work. Ideally, the agreement is a fully executed development agreement, or contract. A fully executed contract binds the parties together to design and develop a specific product, over a period of time, for some cost. The contract specifies such things as production milestones, deliverables, procedures for modifying the design, copyright ownership, royalty payment schedules, termination clauses, and other terms and conditions discussed in Chapter 10. If there is an existing design document or product prototype when the discovery phase begins and both parties agree that it accurately represents the product the developer will create, then a development agreement can be reached during the discovery phase.

However, if there is no design or prototype when the discovery phase begins, there is insufficient information for the parties to reach such a detailed agreement. If an accounting firm approaches a developer with a training need but no idea what the multimedia solution may consist of, neither party has the basis for a contractual agreement. If a software publisher wants to hire a developer to design and develop a new game but does not have a design document, the parties don't have anything substantive to agree on. In such a scenario, the developer and the potential client use the discovery phase to write a top-level design (described in Chapter 5), and they derive from it a preliminary schedule and a preliminary budget. If the parties agree on these items, they can reach an agreement—often an interim agreement known as the letter of intent—to move forward with a more complete product design (a process described in Chapter 9) and to derive from it a final schedule and a final budget.

Why Discovery Is Necessary

Very often, a client approaches a developer to provide development services for a multimedia application for which it has a concept, but no design. Depending on the client, the concept may be one sentence long, a concept document, or the results of a needs analysis that suggests a multimedia solution to an instructional problem. It is impossible for the two parties to reach a definitive agreement—a contract—unless and until there is a well-defined product. When no design exists, the parties must begin work on a product design with an interim agreement in place. In order to reach the initial agreement—that nonbinding letter of intent—the two parties try to arrive at a top-level design and a preliminary schedule and budget in the discovery phase. Even when a design does exist, the parties must agree on cost, schedule, milestones, development process, ownership issues, royalty payments, and other terms.

Clients that are not part of the multimedia industry rarely have a finished design for a product, but rather a subject or a general idea of what they would like. Such clients have approached developers to create multimedia products based on existing magazines, books, cartoon characters, toys, automobiles, animals, music, and various educational subjects such as math, science, reading, and medicine. Corporate clients approach developers to create instructional multimedia products that are components of more elaborate, multitiered training programs. Most of the time, the client has only a vague and sometimes incorrect notion of what is involved in multimedia development. In such cases, the developer must educate the client about multimedia.

There are times when clients have very well-defined product designs. Some software publishers have strong in-house creative teams that propel product design to a fairly well-defined state before approaching a developer. Disney Interactive, for example, usually completed the functional specification and produced the bulk of the assets in-house, and then hired a developer to perform the software engineering and quality assurance work. Disney Interactive published CD-ROMs based on such feature films as *The Lion King, The Little Mermaid, Pocahontas, The Hunchback of Notre Dame,* and *101 Dalmatians* using this procedure.

Other publishers own or license the rights to brands from other media, which have strong characters, story, game play, or ancillary products. There are many examples of brands from linear media—print, TV/film, and even toys—that gave birth to derivative multimedia products. From Mattel, there are a number of *Barbie* and *Hot Wheels* products. From Hasbro, there are products based on its line of Parker Brothers board games. There are products based on the children's TV series *Rugrats* and the *Arthur* book series released by the publisher Broderbund Software.

Whether a potential client calls on a developer with a vague concept or a finished design for a multimedia product, the developer must orchestrate the discovery phase so the parties can reach an agreement to develop it. The developer and client must qualify and educate each other, develop a relationship of trust and collaboration, and work out a design, cost, and schedule.

The Developer Qualifies the Client

Most multimedia publishers are experienced and professional. Reputable publishers have been publishing multimedia products for some time and fully understand the development process. Publishers work hard to study the market, identify consumer buying trends, select potential product ideas that sell, acquire the rights to branded properties, or develop new properties. These potential clients know what a quality product costs, know how long it takes to produce one, and understand the design and development process. Visit the web site, where there are links to major multimedia publishers.

Many potential clients are inexperienced and require a great deal of care and nurturing. Some clients are on fishing expeditions. They have a vague concept for a CD-ROM product and visit developers to scour for creative concepts, which they cheerfully include in their product concept. Some clients look for the best price. Some have insufficient funds and are shocked to find out they do not have a fraction of what's needed to create the product they had in mind. As in every business, a very, very few are unscrupulous.

Before taking a meeting with any potential client, qualify it. In a word, the developer must determine whether the client is genuine. There are four tests the client must pass.

1. The client must have a budget to develop a multimedia product, it must know what its budget is, and it must tell the developer what it is. Even reputable clients are often unwilling to reveal the precise amount they have earmarked for the product. It is customary to talk about ranges: "High six figures," "Less than we spent on such and such." The client must have a realistic budget.

2. The client must have a distribution plan. This is rarely, if ever, a problem for reputable multimedia publishers. Many novice clients do not realize that it is pointless to produce a multimedia product unless there is some way to recoup the costs. Without distribution, there is no way to do so. Determine that the client has a strategy for selling the product. This, of course, is not an issue at all if the client will utilize the product for its own purposes, such as for employee training.

3. Determine whether the client is "shopping." The client may be talking to a number of developers. If the client has provided you with a request for proposal, or RFP, then there is a strong probability the client is asking for bids from a number of developers. There is nothing wrong with that, but it is necessary to know what its criteria are for selecting one. Is it price? Creative ideas? Technology? The developer needs to know.

4. The client must be reasonable. Multimedia development is a collaborative endeavor that often lasts over a year. Do not engage in a project with a client that is intractable, unyielding, and unreasonable.

Clearly, the first few questions can be simply asked. There is no need to beat around the bush. Just ask the client if it has a budget and how much it is. Ask about distribution. Ask about competition for the project award. On the fourth test, use best judgment. If the client has ever created a multimedia product before, inquire about its experience. It would be reasonable to inquire about previous developers, in the manner of checking references.

If the client scores high on these four criteria, then the relationship is worth pursuing. The developer should arrange to meet with the client as soon as possible. If the client has any material it can send to you, arrange for that as soon as possible.

The Client Qualifies the Developer

Guess what? The client is busy checking the developer's credentials, as well. What is the client looking for? Consider its point of view. A publisher has invested a great deal of time and money building an organization, analyzing the market, acquiring properties, developing new properties, developing relationships with distributors and retailers, building a reputation for itself, and generally getting to the point where it is profitable in an extremely competitive business. The publisher is very cautious about the developer it chooses to hire or partner with.

Assume that a publisher has approached you. It has a concept, but not a design, for a CD-ROM. It's the first in what will become a line of products that the publisher hopes will generate $6 million in revenue during the Christmas buying season. There is a budget of $500,000 to develop the product from design through gold master. The product, an educational CD-ROM to teach children Spanish, is built around a branded character owned by another company. The publisher has invested $50,000 to acquire the interactive rights to the property. It's now late January, and the publisher needs the product to be complete in late August so it can be shipped by October, at the latest, to the stores. One more thing: This particular product concept involves the use of some new and as-yet untested technology that will allow the user to control the game with voice commands. The publisher will provide the license for the voice recognition software from yet another company.

The publisher knows that this is a tall order. A big project, a moderate budget, not a lot of time. What are they looking for in a developer? What will instill confidence and a desire to move forward? Based on a panel discussion involving leading publishers at the Electronic Entertainment Expo in April 1999, the answer is and always has been a strong, experienced *team* with a track record of success. The ideal team consists of strong management, strong creative, and strong technical direction.

A Strong Producer

The client looks for a producer who is strong, professional, and organized. The publisher knows that to make the deadline, the project must be well managed. The developer must demonstrate a sound, foolproof development process. There is no time in a seven-month schedule for any kind of slippage.

The Initial Contact

The initial contact is vitally important. The adage that there's no second chance at a first impression is true. The client's first indication that the producer is organized occurs at their first meeting when the producer distributes a detailed agenda. The agenda includes the following, as the major topics:

- A discussion of the schedule, with the seven months broken down into probable/possible design, prototype, and production phases. This preliminary schedule may also include dates when certain milestones have to be met and leads to a discussion of client approval dates.

- A discussion of the budget, with examples of how complex or extensive the product can be given the proposed development budget and schedule. A very worthwhile document to prepare is a chart or graph showing how many characters, levels, screens, nodes, or other quantitative measures are possible within the proposed budget, based on experience with other products. This is a very important tack that controls the client's expectations at the outset.

- A discussion of the intellectual property and whether or not the rights holder will be involved in creative decisions or approvals.

- A discussion of what assets the rights holder or the client will provide. It may be able to provide character designs, video, photographs, music, or voice talent. These items can reduce the workload, sometimes dramatically. If the client does provide content for the product, this has copyright implications that are explained in Chapter 10. Be sure to know what they are.

- A discussion of the licensed voice-recognition software—what it is, what programming language it is written in, how well tested it is, and when it will be available for evaluation by the developer's engineers.

- A backup plan if the licensed software does not work as expected.

- A discussion of the roles and responsibilities of the two parties. It's always a good idea to list the various major tasks and then to indicate who does what. In this instance, it must be determined who will provide translations for that part of the narration, dialogue, and text in the foreign language.

- A pitch of the creative approach to the product, followed by a brainstorming session.

- Action steps.

Following is some advice about the kickoff meeting.

Kickoff Meeting

Usually, a meeting is arranged between the client and the developer. Ideally, the meeting takes place at the developer's studio, where the client has an opportunity to evaluate the workplace and meet the staff. The client invests a great deal of money, time, and energy in product development and seeks a trustworthy developer.

The producer, director, and writer represent the developer at the initial meeting. Available for consultation during the meeting is a technical expert—usually a software engineer—and the art director and sound designer. If the product is a game, the game designer should be present. If it is an instructional or educational product, the instructional designer should be present.

The producer should chair the meeting, distribute an agenda, and set a tone of professionalism and organization. Following is a sample agenda for a meeting held between Media Station, a developer, and Hasbro Interactive, the potential client for a product called *Tonka Search and Rescue.* This meeting occurred after several phone calls between the parties and after Media Station had the opportunity to review a product Hasbro had already released, which was similar to the one it wanted Media Station to develop.

Before this meeting, Hasbro had already indicated to Media Station what kind of product it wanted to develop, how much it was prepared to spend, and when it wanted the product complete. Media Station was able to prepare a creative pitch for a product that met all of Hasbro's criteria. Not all clients are as clear about their objectives as Hasbro Interactive, and often the kickoff meeting needs to be choreographed to extract all of the necessary information from the client. On the following pages are examples of kickoff meeting agendas.

Tonka Search and Rescue CD-ROM Kickoff Meeting

February 3, 1997

Attendees:
John Sutyak, Creative Director, Hasbro; Joe Gammal, Marketing Manager, Hasbro; Larry Elin, Producer/Writer; John Lucas, Director; James Eschman, Lead Engineer

Objectives:
- Reach early agreement on creative direction of *Tonka Search and Rescue* title
- Benchmark development plan and milestones
- Action steps for design phase

12:00–12:30	Tour of Media Station	All
12:30–1:00	Lunch, Intros—Go over agenda	All

1:00–2:00	Hasbro presents Tonka Branding concepts and focus test results from previous product	Sutyak, Gammal
2:00–2:30	Current design pitch Basic navigation, Dispatch Center, Print Shop, Motor Pool, Rescue Sites, Characters, Gags	Elin, Lucas
2:30–3:00	Design review, modify	All
3:00–3:30	Present, adjust development plan and milestones	Elin
3:30–3:40	Break	All
3:40–4:00	Action Steps	All
4:15	Leave for airport	Sutyak, Gammal

Reality Check Memo

Immediately following the kickoff meeting, the producer must fire off a memo to the client outlining everything they covered and agreed on during the meeting. This is essential. Included here is the follow-up letter sent to Hasbro. It indicates how detailed the follow-up memo should be. Err on the side of information overkill during contact with the client at this and every other stage. After the client has received, evaluated, and responded to the follow-up memo, which details exactly what was decided at the meeting, the design of the product can proceed with a high level of confidence. Absent this reality check, the two parties could be miles apart on their understanding of the product's basic design.

Date: February 3, 1997
To: John Sutyak, Joe Gammal
cc: Kevin Gillespie, Jim Maslyn, John Lucas, Jim Eschman
From: Larry Elin
Subject: Reality Check of Brainstorming Meeting—*Tonka Search and Rescue*

It was a pleasure for all of us here to meet with you and brainstorm the *Tonka Search and Rescue* CD-ROM product. The marketing data, focus group test results, the free interchange of ideas, and creativity was energizing!

The following is a list of decisions that came out of the meeting. That is followed by the action steps. Please look this over and let me know ASAP if we have left out or misunderstood anything. These decisions will provide us with direction for the next body of work—fine-tuning the designs, characters, story, narrative, vehicle controls, etc.

Desired Improvements from Construction *CD-ROM*
- Improve the truck maneuverability
- Improve the truck selection process
- Make "tweaking" of game play and vehicle control possible
- Improve the "help" and "instruction" part of the game—make it context sensitive or occur in a step-by-step fashion
- Improve the sound mixing, use to enhance the fantasy

Got to Have in This New Product (big hits in previous one)
- Blow stuff up
- Fix things in the garage
- Decorate sites after missions
- Short-term rewards
- Print stuff out
- Characters with good race and gender mix
- Right level of complexity for the target age
- Humorous little dweeble animation

Screens
- Bumpers (Hasbro and MSI)
- Title screen (to be designed)
- Sign-on screen
- Dispatch Center
- Print Shop
- Tonka Garage
- Tonka Rescue Academy
- Bridge/Flood rescue mission
- Burning warehouse at the docks rescue mission
- Loose zoo animals rescue mission
- Credits

The bumpers and title screen will be designed later. We will want an interesting and content-specific title animation—something to do with emergency search and rescues.

The sign-on screen will enable the kids to input their names, hometowns, and ages. Later, this information will be used for

- Putting their names, ages, and hometowns on "Newspaper" articles
- Putting their names, ages, and hometowns on award certificates or "commendations"
- Saving and loading games

The Dispatch Center is the main navigation screen and allows the kids to access the following:

- Garage
- Academy
- Print shop
- Bridge/Flood rescue mission
- Burning warehouse at the docks rescue mission
- Loose zoo animals rescue mission
- Vehicles (exact number to be determined)
- Quit
- Save game
- Load game

Note: There is an alternative rescue mission called "Lost Expedition." This we would have in the title instead of any of the three other rescue missions or the academy.

The Tonka Garage is not designed yet but will consist of the following:

- Three rescue vehicles—Fire Truck, Helicopter on the roof, Rescue Boat
- "Cool tools" brand incorporated into the things that are done in the garage
- Ability to paint vehicles
- Ability to equip the vehicles with rescue stuff
- A little maintenance done on the vehicles (change tires)

The Tonka Rescue Academy is not designed yet but will consist of the following:

- An activity center
- Activities to learn rescue techniques
- Could include driving, flying, boating drills
- Demolition by explosion, wrecking ball, and Godzilla

The Print Shop will be able to

- Print newspaper articles with kids' names, hometowns, and ages
- Print objects that can be constructed
- Print decals
- Print license plates (all 50 states plus UK)
- Allow kids to customize their license plates
- Print driver's license
- Print medal of honor
- Print other "iron-ons"

The Bridge/Flood rescue mission has

- Double-wide screen
- Bridge is washed out

- Burning tree in roadway
- Another tree in roadway
- People trapped on roof top
- Dog trapped on dog-house top
- Car in ditch
- Rescue vehicles all drive up from different directions, sirens blaring, wheels screeching
- Need *fire truck* for fire
- *Crane* and *tractor trailer* bring bridge components
- *Bulldozer* moves trees
- *Tow truck* moves car in ditch
- *Pickup truck* tows boat to water
- Launch *rescue boat*
- Rescue folks from roof top
- Rescue dog from roof top
- Cart off rescued people in ambulance or *"rescue 5" vehicle*
- Customize the site with: danger signs at bridge, saw horses with yellow flashing lights at roadway into water

The Burning Warehouse at the Docks rescue mission has

- Double-wide screen
- Freighter near dock
- Sailors up on deck
- Warehouse on fire
- Burning oil drums floating in water
- Vehicles come into view from different locations
- *Fire truck* on dock—use to put out warehouse fire
- Need to pump water from sea
- *Fire boat* on water—use to put out oil drum fires
- Rescue *tug boat*—tow the freighter away from dock
- Sailors slide down rope to *tug boat*
- Use *fork lift* to move piles of lumber from dock
- Use *wrecking ball* to demolish what's left of warehouse
- Blow up floating oil drums
- Use *front loader* to scoop up debris from warehouse
- Cart away debris in *dump truck*
- Customize site as follows: Turn dock into amusement park—*tractor trailer* drives up with ferris wheel, roller coaster, and merry-go-round. Park benches and ticket booth. Click and drag to build new park.

The Loose Zoo Animals rescue mission has

- Double-wide screen
- All of the zoo homes have been wrecked by a big wind storm
- Cages are split open

- Seal pool is empty
- Bear is trapped in the moat around his "mountain"
- Souvenir shop is on its side
- Trees are knocked over
- Zoo animals are wandering around
- Rescue vehicles come screeching in—sirens blaring, lights flashing
- Use *bulldozer* to clear trees
- Use *dump truck* to haul away trees
- Bring in new cages with *tractor trailer*
- Use *crane* to repair brick wall
- Use *helicopter* to lift and position new cages—have to match cage shape to foundation
- Have to drop cage when animal is in the right spot
- Use *helicopter* to rescue bear—drop ladder down to him
- Use *helicopter* to straighten up the souvenir shop
- Use *fire truck "pumper"* to fill seal pool with water
- Customize as follows: *tractor trailer* brings in new trees, benches, signs, fences. Click and drag to customize the zoo.

Lost Expedition.   This alternative rescue mission would be the title instead of Rescue Academy.

- Double-wide screen
- Volcano, jungle, ruined pyramid
- River running through background
- Expedition is lost in jungle somewhere
- Got to find them and bring them out with their "discovery" before volcano blows
- Bring up rescue vehicles on barges towed by *tug boat*
- Fly *helicopter* over jungle to search for party
- Party fires off flare from jungle when *helicopter* is near it
- *Helicopter* parachutes down supplies
- *Bulldozer* clears foliage and boulders—makes road to party
- *Front loader* loads stuff on dump truck
- *Truck* hauls away stuff
- Reach the lost expedition and make clearing with *bulldozer*
- "Discovery" is giant, stone, ancient Groucho Marx statue
- Load statue on flatbed *tractor trailer* with *crane*
- Take to barge
- Bring people out with *4x4 rescue truck*
- Customize: bring in trees and foliage—replant jungle. Very Greenpeace friendly.

Vehicles Information.   All the vehicle information is available at the Dispatch Center. A "3-D" rotating version of the vehicle will appear on the screen with voice-over describing its features.

- Quit—same as all games. Screen will ask if you really want to quit. Yes—to desktop.
- No—back to dispatch screen.
- Save Game—players can save the game they are playing.
- Load Game—players can load any saved games.

Vehicles.   Based on the above mission descriptions, these are the probable vehicles:

• Fire truck	• Rescue 5 vehicle
• Crane	• Fire boat
• Tractor trailer	• Tug boat
• Bulldozer	• Dump truck
• Tow truck	• Front loader
• Pickup truck	• Helicopter
• Rescue boat	• Wrecking ball

Characters

- *Tonka Joe* will appear at the Dispatch Center (either on the monitor or in the room with kids). He will describe how to use the center. He will also appear at the Print Shop to describe how it is used. At other times, his voice-over will tell the kids how to use the vehicles at rescue missions and at the academy. This will be context-sensitive help, or guidance, at the sites. This replaces the long, on-camera explanations of secondary characters in the *Construction* product.
- *One main character* will appear at the beginning introduction sequence of the three rescue sites, the academy, and the garage. A different character at each screen. They will each spend 10 to 20 seconds explaining what the situation is—what the problem is and what needs to be done.
- *Dweebles* are tiny characters who do humorous things at the sites. They can be rescue workers, people needing rescue, bystanders, or animals. Most of their antics will be short, 5- to 10-second gags.

Action Steps.   At the end of our meeting, we agreed to the following action steps:

1. Hasbro will try to get character designs and other source material from the original developer of the *Construction Project* CD-ROM.
2. Hasbro will try to get 3-D models (computer graphics database) of Tonka Trucks from previous developer.
3. Hasbro will track down the music from the previous developer.
4. Joe Gammal will put us in touch with Avery Labels so we can begin to talk printing with them.

5. Joe and John Sutyak will respond to this memo with changes, clarifications, additions, or subtractions.
6. This memo will become a guide for future development of the design.

The next steps to be taken by MSI (assuming approval of this memo) are these:

7. Polish new background designs of the three rescue missions.
8. Develop concept for Garage activity center.
9. Develop initial concepts for the Rescue Academy activity center.
10. Polish character designs for each site, academy, and garage.
11. Make comprehensive list of all printable graphics for the Print Shop activity center.
12. Make list of all vehicles needed for the sites, academy, and garage.
13. Develop ideas for dweeble animations for sites.
14. MSI will have the above ready for Hasbro review and feedback February 14.
15. Meanwhile, development of the functional spec will continue.

Note: We are aiming for March 1 as the first completion date of the functional specification. This will be followed by a Hasbro/MSI Design review, then time to complete the document and art design samples by March 10.

Follow up the reality check with a phone call, and encourage the client to respond to the memo as soon as possible. Distribute the memo, along with any changes or clarifications provided by the client, to the design team. The memo provides clear guidance to the interactive designer and writer in the writing of the design document.

A Creative Director

The client arrives with a concept, but no design, for an educational product featuring a branded character and some new and untested technology, both of which it has licensed at some cost. The client wants a fresh and exciting idea, one that convinces it that the product will generate a return on investment. The director should present a scintillating creative approach that indicates that the developer can add value to the licensed property. A few pieces of full-color conceptual art add a great deal to conceptual presentations.

The Creative Process

The director begins the creative process by logically determining, and then assessing, the target user. The licensed character is popular with children aged 8 to 12. The director uses market research to develop a demographic profile of this user, with special attention to needs, desires, educational background, and buying trends. Because this is an educational product, the director must consider *what* the target user has already learned (based on both probable academic work and popular culture) and *how* the target user learns (based on research in this area). In this case, research shows that the target user has probably taken no language lessons, but has picked up a smattering of Spanish from television, radio, and other popular media. Other research shows that this age group learns well in collaborative, exploratory, self-directed environments, especially when some discretionary help or guidance is available.

The director considers what the learning objective of the product should be. Should the focus be on reading and writing or on listening and speaking? The voice recognition software suggests that learning how to interpret and speak the language is a natural approach. Grammar, vocabulary, diction, and conversational proficiency are possibilities.

The director's thoughts turn to the general scope of the product. Based on the user profile and the learning objective, what is the content? How large is the database of material? Based on the user and how the user learns, what is the appropriate genre and features of the product?

The director formulates a theme, or overarching creative approach. For this product, the director envisions an adventure game—a mystery—in which the user must gather clues and locate a long-lost city in the mountains and jungles in South America. The player's companion is the branded character. Together, they learn to speak Spanish, using the speech recognition software to communicate to the local population. As their skills grow, the level of difficulty increases—locals use phrases with more complex vocabulary and sentence structure.

The director has a starting point to proceed to design and pitch a strong concept. It makes good use of the licensed property to create a compelling and educational product for the target user. More and more features are added, based primarily on the genre chosen and an analysis of the competition in the market.

Finally, the director considers the possibilities for follow-on products in other languages and ancillary products in other media.

Appropriate Technology

At a minimum, the developer must demonstrate that it has the technology to develop the product pitched by the director.

In this particular scenario, the client has licensed new software that the developer is required to launch from its own, proprietary software. The voice recognition software needs to drive other events on the screen. The developer needs to demonstrate to the client that it knows that this is the overriding technological constraint and that it has already considered the potential problems and how to overcome them.

The director and the technical director should evaluate the design and make certain they are pitching a product the technical staff can, in fact, program. They should talk through all of the technical issues as they relate to the creative approach.

A Track Record

The developer must demonstrate that it has already successfully developed products of a high quality on short schedules and that past clients are satisfied with the results. As important as the final product is the *process*. All experienced publishers and developers have been involved in development that resulted in a successful product but that was also extremely unpleasant for the participants.

If the developer is perceived as professional, creative, technologically competent, and experienced, the client will be eager to reach an agreement to move forward with design and development.

Educate the Client

In the process of qualifying the client, the developer determines the client's expertise in multimedia development. If the client has never before produced a multimedia product, the developer must educate the client. If the client is a multimedia veteran but has had a bad experience (and this is more common than you might think), the developer may have to provide a remedial education.

The three areas in which a client may need education are, not surprisingly, related to the business issues, the creative possibilities, and the technology of multimedia. The education process begins with the first conversation with the client and continues to the wrap party a year later.

The Business Issues

Even clients who are experienced business people may lack specific knowledge of the following multimedia development issues:

1. *The phases of development, as described in these chapters.* As you are learning now, the development of a multimedia product is divided into bite-sized chunks of activity, each with very specific prizes, deliverables, milestones, tasks, and resources. Some of the responsibility for the tasks belongs to the developer and some to the client. If the client is new to the process, *it doesn't know what it's responsible for and when.* Nor does it know how critical its contribution may be to the smooth completion of the product. The developer should provide an overview of the development process at the beginning of the relationship and provide the client with weekly updates.

2. *When and how to make modifications to the design of the product after development has begun.* It isn't at all unusual for an inexperienced client to expect to make any design change at any time. This is because some clients do not understand the development process and how difficult and costly even a minor change can be if requested at the wrong time. The developer should make it clear that any change requested after development has begun may involve additional cost, additional time, or both.

3. *When and how to make approvals of deliverables.* The typical development agreement calls for the client to review and approve various deliverables during development. For example, the client must review and approve such things as character designs, layouts, color schemes, music, voice talent, text, content, and so forth. Because many deliverables are part of the critical path, which means development cannot proceed until they have been approved, any delay in approval causes the entire development effort to grind to a halt. Not only should the developer hammer home this point, but also the developer should insist that the client appoint one person responsible for making or obtaining all approvals.

4. *The importance of copyright clearance.* Because multimedia is so new, older licensing agreements may not include the interactive rights. Developers should warn prospective clients of this and encourage them to have their attorneys check all existing agreements.

5. *Related to the copyright issue, how much control does the original rights holder maintain?* It is not unusual for the original rights holder to maintain some if not a great deal of control over the use of its intellectual property. Broderbund Software licensed the *Rugrats* characters from Nickelodeon for a series of CD-ROM products. Kid Studio, the in-house developer at Broderbund Software, was required by the licensor, Nickelodeon, to send animated drawings of the *Rugrats* characters to Klasky Csupo, the TV animation studio, for approval. The developer should make sure the client is aware of these restrictions and the impact they could have on the budget or the schedule.

6. *Ownership issues after development is complete.* Even when a developer works for a client in a work-for-hire arrangement, ownership of certain components of the final product may not be with the client. Ownership of original music, art, and software do not automatically revert to the client when the final product is completed and paid for. All are negotiable. Many multimedia developers have their own, proprietary software, which they use to create products for many different clients. Developers protect the ownership of this software and generally grant each client a non-exclusive license to use the software for the proper display of its product.

The Creative Possibilities

Clients who have never before developed an interactive multimedia product do not often understand the creative possibilities of the medium. The most common assumption is that multimedia is a new way to display old media. These individuals labor under the misconception that CD-ROM and the Internet are to books, magazines, or TV programs what CD audio was to vinyl records. In their minds, then, adapting an existing story, situation, character, or property to interactive multimedia is simply a technical problem.

Everybody already knows that a multimedia product includes text, sound, animation, graphics, video, and computer software. However, not every collection of such material representing some subject will make a compelling product.

The biggest creative hurdle to overcome while conceptualizing an interactive multimedia product is determining why a particular subject is best expressed interactively. As a developer, educate the client with the following concepts:

1. *Relinquish control of the experience to users.* This, of course, is the most difficult conceptual hurdle for linear storytellers: "What? You mean they get to go wherever they want?" Of course, but even this is not enough. For instance, you have control of *this* book, but that does not make it an *interactive* experience. Creating a multimedia product in which the user can "click around" the way you can skip around in this book still falls well short of the creative possibilities.

2. *Allow users to customize their experience.* This is getting warmer. When provided with the ability to specify a preference for the kind of experience they want, users begin to feel intimacy with the product—to feel as though the product is listening and responding to them. Good examples of this are games that allow each player to set a level of difficulty and Web browsers that allow each user to customize a search.

3. *Give the product a mind of its own.* Now it's getting hot. Artificial intelligence is a feature that allows the product to compete with users in a game or work for users as an "agent" in a search engine. Computer chess games, which have been around for decades, have not always been the best examples of multimedia but are in some ways still the best examples of interactivity. Users can carry on a *dialogue* with the game.

4. *Give the product a personality.* Bingo! The greatest creative challenge of interactive design is to arrive at just the right combination of content, features, functional control, look and feel, and structure so that the product actually has a personality. Now, cars, houses, and restaurants are sometimes credited with having personality, and in their own ways, they do. What gives a multimedia product personality is the degree to which users can carry on a rewarding dialogue with it.

The Technology Issues

The third critical area in which a novice client may need guidance is the technology of multimedia. This, of course, could require a book all by itself—volumes of books, in fact. Clients don't need to know, nor do they want to know, all of the technology that goes into the product. What they should know are those technology issues that directly affect design and marketing decisions. Developers and their clients must cover all of these issues early in the relationship. Among the more important technology issues are the following:

1. *Make certain to identify the target platform.* As far as CD-ROM products are concerned, there are two home-based platforms: the PC and the Macintosh. As of this writing, the PC market is by far the largest, and getting bigger, while the population of Macintosh computers is remaining comparatively flat, at least in the consumer market. Many multimedia products are no longer targeted at the Macintosh market, especially if the product relies on technology that is optimized for the PC. Whether the product is a "hybrid" CD-ROM—one that runs on both the PC and the Macintosh—depends on the target user and the additional expense of creating a hybrid disc. Many schools, for example, still have Macintosh computer clusters, and if the target market is schools, the product should be a hybrid product.

2. *Identify the minimum system requirements.* This refers to various components of the target platform that are needed for the product to run properly. The features of the product, and the software that enables those features to behave properly, often require such things as fast processor speed, math coprocessing, 3-D accelerator cards, sound cards, and other hardware or software embellishments. The content and features included in a product can dictate the minimum requirements. The inverse is also true. If the developer decides on the minimum system requirements (perhaps based on market size), this will certainly determine the content and features that can be included in the product. Look at any package for a multimedia product. Somewhere on the box, the minimum system requirements are printed. Among the minimum system requirements are the following:

- *Processor speed.* In the PC market, the low end (slow processor) is Pentium I and the high end is Pentium III. If a product is capable of running on the lowest end of the processor spectrum, the potential market will be large but the product may not be as rich and rewarding as it would be if it took full advantage of fast processing on the higher-end machines.
- *Operating system.* In the PC market, most products now require the user to have Windows 95. On the Macintosh side, a PowerPC is often required.
- *Memory.* CD-ROM products nearly always require a certain amount of system memory that will be used by the product during play. This is sometimes referred to as the "footprint." Products may require from as little as 1 MB to as much as 16 MB of RAM.
- *Hard Drive Space.* CD-ROM products require hard drive space for both permanent and temporary storage of data and files. The product's installation program and other libraries will be permanently stored on the user's drive. A typical product may require 10 MB to 20 MB of space.
- *Color display.* The display resolution is usually 640 × 480, which refers to the number of pixels across and the number of lines of pixels down, and 256 colors.

- *CD-ROM drive.* CD-ROM drives capable of 4X speed are a typical minimum speed. This means that the drive can read about 600 K of data from the CD-ROM per second.
- *Sound card.* All multimedia CD-ROMs require some sound card.
- *Mouse and keyboard.*

3. *A CD-ROM holds a finite amount of data.* A conventional CD-ROM holds 650 MB of data, while a DVD-ROM holds about 17 GB. The point, of course, is that the product is finite in size. Most of the available space on the disc can be used for text, pictures, sound, animation, and video. Other space is reserved for the application software. The quantity of multimedia content that can fit on the disc depends on color depth, compression schemes, sound quality, size and frame rate of video, and the software that makes the whole product behave.

4. *There are certain trade-offs when including video.* Although video compression schemes are good and getting better and DVD technology allows for full-screen, full-motion video, the typical multimedia product still uses video compression schemes that are limiting. This is especially true when the target platform is a slower machine. Designers decide between a fast frame rate, a large screen size, or color depth, but cannot have all three.

5. *There will almost always be bugs.* Bugs are problems with the product that occur after it has been released. Even though all products undergo exhaustive testing on almost every conceivable home computer configuration, somebody, somewhere, will have a problem. Many products are released with known bugs—bugs that are so insignificant or occur with such irregularity that it isn't worth the effort or it isn't possible to fix them.

Learn from the Client

In the process of discovery, the developer must learn from the client the criteria for success. It varies from one client to the next. Is the client building a new brand or exploiting an old one? Is it developing an intellectual property that it can exploit in ancillary markets? Is it just testing the multimedia waters so that it does not want to invest much time or money now? Is it investing in an "A" product that will hit the top 10? This is just the beginning.

When Media Station produced animated storybooks for Disney Interactive, the team learned early that Disney's philosophy is quality, above all else. Every animated feature film became another gem in the company's crown, and Disney Interactive was intent on maintaining a high level of animation, sound, and music and on adding a very high level of interactivity in its CD-ROM products. Each CD-ROM product pushed the envelope a little farther than the last. Subsequent products became bigger, more complex, and more demanding on the development staff.

Because the developer knew this about its client, Media Station could serve Disney's needs on project after project.

There are six things the developer must know and understand about the project. The developer must gain this understanding from the client.

1. *The client's intellectual property (or content or subject or brand).* If the product is an educational product, the developer must understand the product's learning objective and the intended instructional method.
2. *The client's market, or customer base*
3. *The client's time line* and the date the product has to get into the distribution channels
4. *The client's mid-development milestones* such as conventions, sales conferences, focus tests, and magazine reviews
5. *The client's competition*
6. *What content or other material the client can provide*

As you learned in Chapter 3, when the product is educational or instructional, client and developer engage in a formal needs analysis during which these issues and many others are brought to light.

Understand the Property

All clients approach developers with something in mind. On one end of the spectrum, it may be just a general subject: cars, planes, zoo animals, sharks, the environment, astrology. It may be more specific: the history of racing cars, military aircraft, animals at the San Diego Zoo, great white sharks off Australia. Perhaps the client owns video, photographs, or a museum full of "content." Maybe it owns the intellectual property rights to "007" and wants to create a 3-D real-time game featuring the characters and situations of the spy film thrillers. Or, as in the case of Hasbro Interactive and its Tonka brand, maybe it owns a well-known brand and wants to further exploit it in the multimedia market.

The developer must devote the time to understand the subject, content, and intellectual property or the brand and to become, to the extent possible, content experts. When Media Station was approached by Hasbro Interactive about producing the second of what would become a line of multimedia products based on Tonka toys, it researched the concept. Hasbro sent Media Station a copy of the first product and boxes of Tonka toys. Media Station focus-tested the product and the toys with the children of its employees. This primary research gave the design team a sense of the products' appeal. The Hasbro marketing team gave Media Station its own focus group results and described the play pattern generally associated with toy trucks. This background gave Media Station the necessary understanding to draft a creative pitch *that the client was already prepared to accept!*

Understand the Target Market

The client knows its target market. It is the job of the developer to understand the client's customer as well as the client does.

Hasbro Interactive developed a character, Tonka Joe, and a group of friends who use Tonka trucks and vehicles in various ways within their own virtual community. The development team studied Hasbro's research on the target users for the product—young boys between 4 and 6 who are developing an awareness of

1. *Roles*—Young boys watch and imitate their male role models, usually their fathers.
2. *Place*—Children at this age begin to notice the world around them, especially their immediate neighborhood and town. They travel with their parents to shop, eat at restaurants, or attend religious services or school. The idea of a larger, more complex world is setting in.
3. *Accomplishment*—They learn new skills every day, perhaps in school or in organized sports, music, or dance lessons. Every day brings with it some new accomplishment, some new learned skill.
4. *Reward*—Children in this age bracket are often rewarded for their accomplishments. Short-term rewards include verbal encouragement from parents and teachers.
5. *Friendship*—Children in this age bracket socialize and make friends.
6. *Family (or community)*—Children at this age begin to look beyond themselves and notice the family unit—parents, siblings, grandparents, aunts and uncles, and cousins. They see the extended community, perhaps through a combination of school and new friendships.

By analyzing the young user of Hasbro products, Media Station and Hasbro collaborated on a design that embraces all six concepts. The design adopts and expands the role of Tonka Joe and his friends, who become the users' mentor and companions. The design includes a community called Tonka Town, which includes familiar architectural landmarks. The activities involve the child in solving mildly dramatic problems that foster the learning of new skills. The user is richly rewarded with encouragement and prizes.

Know the Time Line

The multimedia business is seasonal. Most products are completed by the late summer and are on the store shelves by Thanksgiving, at the latest. However, some products are released in concert with some other event, such as the national elections, the World Series, the Super Bowl, the Olympic Games, the release of a feature film, the opening of a new park or resort, or some other major, but off-season, occurrence.

It's up to the developer to know when the product must reach gold master status and to create a development plan that ensures completion by that date. Don't assume anything about the completion date—verify it with the client.

Identify Milestones

 Even after establishing the gold master date with the client, there may be other milestones along the way when some interim version of the product must be usable. The client may need a working version of the product—"It doesn't have to be complete, just reliable"—for various marketing purposes. These include

- In-house conferences and meetings to show upper management or other divisions of the company what the product is going to be like
- Focus testing with target users to determine whether the product is going to sell well
- Focus testing with target users to determine whether educational objectives are being met
- Providing magazine reviewers with "demo" versions of the product so they can review the product favorably and create a prerelease buzz
- Providing a downloadable demo version of the product so customers can try it out before buying it
- Demonstrations of the product for prospective distributors and retailers

These milestones put pressure on the development pipeline, and must be identified and planned for early.

The Electronic Entertainment Expo, or E3 as it is known, is a conference and convention of multimedia products and games. It is held every year in the spring. The typical multimedia development effort is in full swing at that time, but seasonal products are not complete until late August or September. Unless the product created during the prototype phase is adequate, the developer may have to create another, more robust version of the product specifically for use at the conference. Such an effort requires careful planning. It is important to create the E3 version without adversely affecting the overall development schedule and budget.

Know the Competition

Every multimedia product, no matter how new and innovative, is targeted at a specific market and fits into one or more of the established genres. We talked about this in previous chapters. There are existing products the target users will compare the new product to. New products must be better than the competition in a majority of the five components described in Chapter 2. A new product must have more or better content, features, functional controls, look and feel, and structure. Sometimes, a new product can establish a market foothold based on brand loyalty or star quality, but those products tend to fade as the reality sinks in (among buyers) that the product just doesn't compare to the competition. The developer must study the competition and design a product that beats the competition.

Determine Client-Provided Content

Disney provided the bulk of the animation, backgrounds, voice-overs, and music for the animated storybooks developed for them by Media Station. Hasbro was able to provide a few assets, including the music and the voice talent, for their Tonka products. They also sent about twenty actual Tonka toys, which 3-D computer animators used to create the computer models. Whenever a product is based on an existing intellectual property, the client provides specifications, drawings, original music, and sometimes the actual voice talent.

It is important to determine what the client can bring to the development process and to establish whether or not it can be used. It is also important to determine when the assets are available and to make certain the timing is right, given the development plan. It does no good if the client can provide animation for the CD-ROM product, but not until the feature film is complete. This may be months too late for the development cycle.

Establish Deal Points with the Client

During the discovery phase, the developer must establish the ground rules for reaching the definitive agreement—the final contract. In addition to the three most important issues—what the product is, how much it will cost to produce, and when it must be completed—there are many other specific terms, which the two parties must agree on. These are called "deal points." The developer must know what kind of deal it is looking for and must find out early what kind of deal the client is anticipating. Among the deal points are

1. *The nature of the relationship.* In many cases, the client hires the developer on a work-for-hire basis. There are many legal ramifications related to this arrangement having particular impact on rights ownership. However, two parties may agree to copublish a product. In this relationship, one party may actually take on the role of the developer, responsible for creating the product, and the other may publish it, responsible for marketing it. However, they share the costs of the entire effort and reach an agreement to share the revenue.

2. *Payment for services.* When the client hires the developer to perform the development services, the two parties may agree on a lump sum for the work. This is often called a development fee. The developer evaluates the scope of work and bids

a price to complete the work. The client either agrees that the price is fair or doesn't. Another arrangement is on a time-and-materials basis. The two parties agree that the developer will perform various development services and invoice the client for the work at agreed-upon hourly, weekly, or monthly rates.

3. *Royalty payments.* Another payment method is royalty. Royalty payments are paid to the developer by the client based on various formulas related to the sales of the product. For example, royalty payments are often a percentage of net revenue. When royalty payments are made, the development fee is often regarded as an advance against royalty. The client does not pay the developer a royalty on net revenue until the client has recouped, or earned back, the development fee.

4. *Roles and responsibilities.* Many tasks are performed during development, and both parties have roles and responsibilities related to those tasks. Since these have to be itemized in a contract, reach agreement on them early. Table 8.1 parcels out tasks between the developer and the publisher.

5. *Object code.* Developers often depend on their own, in-house, proprietary software to create multimedia products. In some cases, developers have invested a great deal of time and money to write this code, and the code may be one of their selling points. When this software is used to create a multimedia product in a work-for-hire arrangement for a client, the question invariably comes up, "Who owns the software?" Typically, the parties agree that the underlying, preexisting, and compiled object code belongs to the developer, and the use of that code to fashion the product is then licensed to the client. In the agreement the parties draw up, the developer grants a nonexclusive license to the client to use the object code in its product.

6. *Other rights.* Developers typically grant all other rights in the product to the client. This includes art, new characters, video, sounds, and all materials used in the development of the product. However, on occasion, especially with regard to original music, the parties may agree that original music belongs to the composer/arranger, who grants a nonexclusive license to use the music in the product.

7. *Changes and modifications.* During development, the client (or the developer) may want to change or modify the design of the product. Sometimes, these changes do not substantively affect anything. The development continues as though nothing happened. The budget and the schedule are unaffected. However, with uncomfortable regularity, changes and modifications that do affect the budget, the schedule, or both are requested. The parties must agree on a process that makes it possible for changes and modifications to be made without penalizing either party.

There are many other terms and conditions that the parties must agree to in a final contract. The terms above are those that, if not agreed on in principle early on, can prevent a definitive agreement from being reached later. These are the most contentious issues, so they are often referred to as potential deal killers.

Table 8.1	Roles and Responsibilities	
Task	**Resource**	**Comments**
Executive produce	Client	
Rights, clearances	Client	
Provide character designs	Client	for existing
Provide color mark-ups	Client	for existing
Access to voice talent	Client	for existing, if necessary
Approve all design and work	Client	
Functional spec	Developer	
Graphic design	Developer	
Interactive design	Developer	
Script	Developer	series writer possible
Character design	Developer	for other characters
Storyboards	Developer	
Layouts	Developer	
Key animation	Developer	
Animation	Developer or sub	
Scan, ink, paint	Developer or sub	
Backgrounds	Developer	
Scene compositing	Developer	
Casting	Developer	
Audio recording, mixing, editing	Developer	
Sound EFX, music	Developer	
Special-purpose software	Developer	
Title engineering	Developer	
Quality assurance	Developer	
Customer technical service	Client	
Package design	Client	
Package art	Developer	
Package inserts and manuals	Client	

Creating Discovery Phase Deliverables

Three items are generated during the discovery phase that make the development agreement (contract or the letter of intent) possible. They are appended to the development agreement, becoming an integral part of the initial agreement between the client and the developer. These deliverables are the top-level design, the preliminary budget, and the preliminary schedule. It is the producer, director, and writer who create the top-level design (with input from key team members, as discussed in Chapter 5). The producer and director collaborate on the preliminary schedule, and the producer calculates the preliminary budget.

In Chapter 5, we covered the process and form of the top-level design. Refer back to that chapter, paying particular attention to the document itself and to the breakdown chart assembled by the producer.

Determine the Scope of Work

The producer uses a breakdown chart (see Table 8.2) to arrive at the scope of work. The scope of work is the amount of effort—measured by labor hours and equipment use, plus other activities—needed to develop the product described in the top-level design. Because about half of the effort involves creating content, the producer determines how much content the design calls for. Content is composed of assets, such as art, animation, video, text, graphics, buttons, icons, music, voice-over, and sound effects. The producer determines the assets to be created and acquired.

The other half of the effort is programming. The producer determines what software is required to drive the product's features. Some of the required software may already exist, perhaps even off-the-shelf authoring tools such as Macromedia Director. Other software may have to be written by programmers. Still other software may have to be licensed.

In filmmaking, the producer breaks down the script, which results in various lists of scenes, locations, settings, props, set dressings, effects, cast, and so forth. From this breakdown, the producer is able to generate a production plan, a shooting schedule, and a budget.

The multimedia producer must do essentially the same thing. At this point in product design, there is not enough detail in the design itself to generate a detailed breakdown. However, the producer makes a stab at it based on the top-level design and in doing so, actually creates certain parameters which will be used during the design phase to keep the more detailed design from growing too big.

Quantify and Qualify

From a breakdown like Table 8.2, on a node-by-node basis, the producer totals up the assets. The producer looks at the engineering effort and, after consultation with

Table 8.2	Asset Quantification						
Nodes	Back-ground	Main Character Animation	Dweeble Animation	3-D Vehicle Animation	Other Animation or Art	Sound	Software
Bumper screen (B1)	2	None	None	Helicopter flies over	Company logos	Music	MSI Engine
Title screen (T1)	1	None	None	None	Title graphic	Music	MSI Engine
Sign-on screen (P1)	Special sign-on screen	Tonka Joe —10 seconds	None	None	Text	Music narration	MSI Engine Keyboard input Store data
Main navigation screen (N1)	Dispatch Center	Tonka Joe —60 seconds	None	14 vehicles	2 minutes	Music Narration Ambient SFX	MSI Engine
Quit game screen (P4)	Dispatch Center	None	None	None	Text	Narration Ambient SFX	MSI Engine
Print center activity screen	Print Center	Tonka Joe —60 seconds	None	None	90+ graphics and text	Narration Ambient SFX	MSI Engine Keyboard input Store data
Garage activity screen (02)	Garage Exterior	Sparks and Bernie— 30 seconds	None	3 vehicles	Recurrent animation	Music Narration Ambient SFX	MSI Engine Click & drag
Fire Truck activity (03)	Garage interior	None	Dog dweeble— 10 seconds	1 vehicle	Equip-ment, clickables, props	Music Narration Ambient SFX	MSI Engine Click & drag
Rescue Boat activity (04)	Garage interior	None	Dog dweeble— 10 seconds	1 vehicle	Paint, flags and de-cals, clickables, props	Music Narration Ambient SFX	MSI Engine Click & drag Vehicle control

(continued)

Table 8.2 (continued)							
Nodes	Back-ground	Main Character Animation	Dweeble Animation	3D Vehicle Animation	Other Animation or Art	Sound	Software
Helicopter activity (05)	Garage roof screen	None	Guy dweeble—10 seconds	1 vehicle	Tools, clickables, props	Music Narration Ambient SFX	MSI Engine Click & drag Vehicle control
Rescue Academy screen (06)	Academy exterior	COACH—30 seconds	30 seconds	3 vehicles	Recurrent anima-tion, props	Music Narration Ambient SFX	MSI Engine Click & drag Vehicle control
Fire Truck academy activity (07)	Burning building	None	30 seconds	1 vehicle	Smoke, water, fire, props	Music Narration Ambient SFX	MSI Engine Click & drag Vehicle control
Rescue Boat academy activity (08)	Large lake	None	45 seconds	1 vehicle	Water, sharks, fire, props	Narration Ambient SFX	MSI Engine Click & drag Vehicle control
Helicopter academy activity (09)	Canyon/ gorge	None	45 seconds	1 vehicle	Water, props	Narration Ambient SFX	MSI Engine Click & drag Vehicle control
Rescue site #1—the flood (10)	2x flood site	Nate Cod and Bernie—30 seconds	45 seconds	10 vehicles	Water, fire, props, explosions	Music Narration Ambient SFX	MSI Engine Click & drag Vehicle control

the lead engineer or programmer on the job, determines the level of effort needed to create the software for the product. The producer derives a quantitative sense of the scope of work. However, it is also necessary to *qualify* the scope of work. The quantification of the work is objective, but the qualification is subjective and relies on interpretation. To the extent possible, the producer and writer must describe the assets in sufficient detail that all concerned have a shared and measurable sense of the quality of the work. Table 8.3 qualifies the assets.

Table 8.3	Asset Types and Qualification
Type	**Qualification**
Background art	Hand-painted backgrounds and/or 3-D computer-generated art. These will look similar to the background art in the Tonka *Construction* product.
Main character animation	Hand-drawn character animation of a TV broadcast quality—similar to the level of animation in a Saturday morning cartoon.
Dweeble animation	Hand-drawn character animation of very small characters equivalent in quality to the dweeble animation in the Tonka *Construction* product.
Vehicle animation	3-D computer-generated vehicles which will look similar to the vehicles in the Tonka *Construction* product.
Other animation	Special effects animation and recurrent animation, such as water, fire, smoke, flapping flags.
Still art, icons, and buttons	Hand-drawn and/or 3-D computer-generated still graphics of a quality similar to the Tonka *Construction* product.
Voice-over	Professionally narrated voice-overs for the main characters—each with its own unique personality. Voice-overs will be TV-broadcast quality.
Sound effects	Event-specific sound effects to accompany all major events, including vehicle start-ups, driving, and shut downs.
Ambient sound	Background sounds that add to the feeling and sense of the background environment.
Ambient sound	Musical accompaniments and interludes. These will be specially arranged and created by staff composer.

Using Metrics

The producer consults with the responsible team members and uses experience, research, and metrics to measure the breakdown and arrive at the scope of work. *Metrics* refers to the accumulated history of past performance on similar projects or tasks. Metrics may show, for example, that it takes an artist 8 hours to paint a background of the quality wanted or that it takes a programmer 32 hours to engineer the type of activity called for in a particular node. Although the actual time will depend, eventually, on who the artist or programmer actually is, metrics help the producer begin to calibrate the project.

Sample Scope of Work

Based on the breakdown of the design, the producer may arrive at a scope of work like the one in Table 8.4 for the product. This table represents the producer's initial view of the labor demands of the product and is the first indication to the producer that the project can be developed within the target budget and by the target delivery date.

Create a Preliminary Development Plan

Once the producer has a breakdown of the amount and type of assets to produce and has evaluated the software engineering effort, he or she can plan how to create

Table 8.4 Scope of Work		
Resource	Comments	Labor Hours
Management		
Producer/director	Full time, 6 months	1,000
Creative		
Writer	Functional spec, 200 pages	240
Graphic designer	Design 12 backgrounds, buttons, new font	240
Interactive designer	Design game, write design document	160
Assets and Engineering		
Backgrounds	16 pieces	160
Animation	10 minutes, no characters	400
3-D animation	5 minutes, no characters	240
Other graphics	150 pieces	200
Sound recording	25 minutes, 3 narrators	400
Video	-0-	
Photographs	-0-	
Programming	12 nodes, existing engine	1,200
Testing and Other		
Testers	2 testers for 3 weeks	240
Research, focus tests	Intern, video crew	140
Total		4,600

the assets and code the software. The producer makes a list of the specific tasks that will create assets and software and puts those tasks in chronological order. Each task will take a certain amount of time and effort, and some tasks are dependent on the completion of others, as discussed in Chapter 7. Keep in mind that the producer must also factor in the interim step of creating a prototype and of other milestones he or she may have discovered while working with the client. For instance, there may be a demo needed in early June for E3.

Eventually, the producer creates a detailed development plan based on the actual design. However, at this stage, the plan is a one-page document, made with *Microsoft Project* or *MacProject,* or some other management tool. Figure 8.1 shows an example of a preliminary development plan. It lists the major development tasks on the left in the order they must be accomplished. If any tasks are dependent upon the completion of any others, those tasks are graphically connected to show the dependency. The producer allocates resources and time requirements, and attempts to place the time when the tasks will be tackled along a timeline, which stretches from left to right. The plan graphically demonstrates that the scope of work can be accomplished in the allotted time, assuming that the resources are available.

Create the Preliminary Budget

The preliminary budget is a confidential document used by the developer to estimate the cost of developing the product. The budget includes hourly rates, overhead, administrative costs, and other proprietary information the producer does not want to share with the client. The conservative producer adds at least a 10 percent contingency to the cost estimate. The contingency is there to cover unexpected costs or estimates that are off. If the bottom line is within the client's target cost parameters, then the producer can bid on the project with a degree of confidence.

There are three things necessary to create a preliminary budget:

1. *The development plan*—which must be based on a careful evaluation of the top-level design
2. *Accurate rates* (hourly, daily, or weekly) for in-house and subcontracted resources
3. *Good estimates* of out-of-pocket and miscellaneous expenses

The development plan provides the number of hours, days, or weeks of labor for asset development and programming, which are the two largest expenses associated with product development. Other labor costs are for the producer, director, writer, talent, and quality assurance testing. Miscellaneous costs include supplies, travel, shipping, legal costs, and equipment rental or lease. There may also be costs for video or film production, which would include crew, cameras, lights, microphones, talent, sets, costumes, props, and expendables.

FIGURE 8.1   **Preliminary Development Plan**

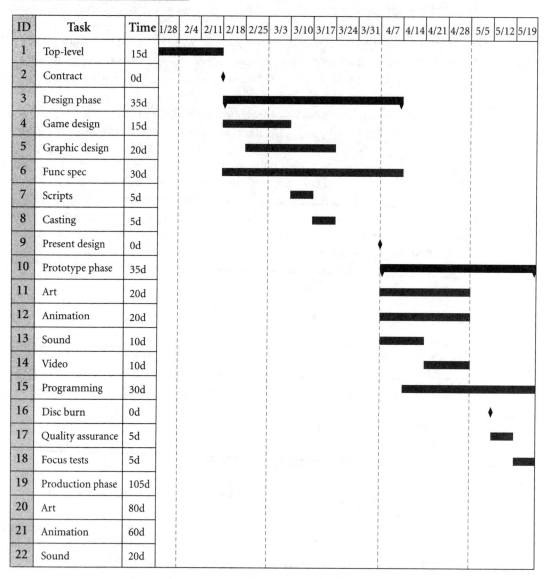

ID	Task	Time	1/28	2/4	2/11	2/18	2/25	3/3	3/10	3/17	3/24	3/31	4/7	4/14	4/21	4/28	5/5	5/12	5/19
1	Top-level	15d																	
2	Contract	0d																	
3	Design phase	35d																	
4	Game design	15d																	
5	Graphic design	20d																	
6	Func spec	30d																	
7	Scripts	5d																	
8	Casting	5d																	
9	Present design	0d																	
10	Prototype phase	35d																	
11	Art	20d																	
12	Animation	20d																	
13	Sound	10d																	
14	Video	10d																	
15	Programming	30d																	
16	Disc burn	0d																	
17	Quality assurance	5d																	
18	Focus tests	5d																	
19	Production phase	105d																	
20	Art	80d																	
21	Animation	60d																	
22	Sound	20d																	

Sample preliminary development plan. The producer makes an educated guess about the length of time each task will take and uses experience to schedule the tasks in the proper order and to determine any dependencies. Later, when the product is fully designed, the producer develops a very detailed and comprehensive plan, with tasks broken down into many subtasks.

The beauty of the development plan is that the budget derived from it can be laid out as a spreadsheet, showing costs and expenses on a weekly basis. By creating a budget using Microsoft Excel, for example, the producer can determine with a high degree of accuracy how much it should cost to complete every task on the development plan. It is possible to calculate how much it will cost to reach every milestone, such as the prototype or the E3 demo. This is very important when negotiating a payment schedule with the client. Reaching a milestone usually triggers a payment. The agreed-upon amount of the payment from the client should cover the cost of reaching that milestone. The developer should not find itself financing the development of the client's CD-ROM by spending more than it is invoicing. Such a practice causes serious cash-flow problems. It can drive a developer out of business.

Look at the preliminary budget in Table 8.5. Each labor category—producer, creative, art department, engineering, etc.—has a labor rate associated with it. The fully burdened labor rate is the average salary of the people in the category, plus payroll taxes, benefits, overhead, and general and administrative costs. A good accountant or financial officer should establish these rates for the developer. Certain kinds of development agreements do not allow the developer to be paid an advance that covers overhead. Be certain the labor rate includes only allowable components.

The producer should estimate the miscellaneous costs and, when appropriate, research others. If the developer is located in New York and the client is in Atlanta, find out what the round trip airfare is. Use the worst case scenario—a last-minute walk-up price. Assume overnight packages will be sent to the client at least once a week. If the client has never before created a multimedia product and, worst of all, is using an inexperienced law firm to negotiate the contract, count on lengthy negotiations and costly legal fees.

The Proposal and Bid

When the producer has completed the analysis of the top-level design and is satisfied with the preliminary development plan and preliminary budget, he or she writes a formal proposal to the client with the three documents attached. It is usually not necessary, nor advisable, to provide the client with the actual hours and hourly rates used to arrive at the budget. Because every bid is based on a large number of assumptions, the producer predicates the bid on the assumptions made and stated in the proposal. The producer includes in the proposal any and all terms and conditions the parties discussed and agreed on. These terms may include deal points discussed earlier, payment milestones, change procedures, copyright issues, and so forth. When the client accepts a proposal and bid, that can be construed as a

Table 8.5	Preliminary Budget			
		Hours	Rate	Total
Producer	Budgeted	700	$125	$87,500
	Actual			
	Variance			
Art	Budgeted	1,600	$80	$128,000
	Actual			
	Variance			
Engineering	Budgeted	1,200	$120	$144,000
	Actual			
	Variance			
Eng support	Budgeted	0	$50	$ – 0 –
	Actual			
	Variance			
Sound	Budgeted	600	$60	$36,000
	Actual			
	Variance			
Writer	Budgeted	240	$120	$28,000
	Actual			
	Variance			
QA super	Budgeted	200	$80	$16,000
	Actual			
	Variance			
Test support	Budgeted	440	$40	$17,600
	Actual			
	Variance			
Miscellaneous	Budgeted			$50,000
	Actual			
	Variance			
Weekly totals	Budgeted	4,889		$507,900
	Actual			
	Variance			

contract. To protect himself or herself from being bound by a vague and incomplete proposal, the producer should include statements that

- The bid is based on the top-level design, pending a more detailed design
- The bid is based on an analysis of the scope of work represented by the top-level design. Include the breakdown. It must be made clear that the bid may change if the design and, therefore, the scope of work change.
- The bid is based on the availability of certain talent, video, imagery, music, software, equipment, locations, etc.
- The bid is based on the following discussions (state what was understood):
  - Roles and responsibilities of the parties
  - Various deal points (ownership, payment schedule, royalties, etc.)
  - Content provided by the client
  - The technology that can be used, such as existing engines or other software that can be licensed
- The bid is based on starting and ending by certain dates
- The bid is based on timely approvals of materials by the client

The proposal and bid, if accepted by the client, clear the way to the letter of intent, deal memo, or development contract. If not carefully crafted, the proposal and bid can lead to serious problems. Be absolutely certain to include every item, every consideration, and every assumption which led to the bid.

Chapter Summary

In this chapter, we covered the discovery phase of multimedia development. Full service studios, called developers, create multimedia products for their clients, which may be external or internal. External clients include software publishers, developers, and other entities. The discovery phase is a period of time when a developer and a client develop a relationship with the objective of producing a multimedia product. The prize, or goal, of the discovery phase is the development agreement. However, many projects begin with the execution of a letter of intent, which is also called a deal memo. The letter of intent is an interim agreement between the developer and the client, which launches the design process. It engages the developer to create a complete design document and a final budget and development plan which can become the basis for a definitive agreement. Both are covered in detail in Chapter 10.

The first step in the discovery phase is for the two parties to qualify each other. The developer determines whether the client is committed to producing a product, can pay for it, understands the process, and is reasonable. The client determines whether the developer is professional, is creatively and technically competent, and has a proven track record. The two parties educate each other. The developer lays out the development process, a creative approach, and technically relevant issues for the client. The client educates the developer concerning the subject, the property, the target market, milestones, delivery dates, and other critical issues.

During the discovery phase, the developer creates a top-level design, based on input from the client. The top-level design describes the intended product in sufficient detail that the producer can create a preliminary budget and development plan. These three documents are presented to the client and form a proposal and bid. If the client accepts the proposal and bid, this may constitute a legal agreement between the parties to move on and design and develop the product. The parties eventually sign a development agreement, the fully executed contract.

Recommended Reading

Fisher, Roger. *Getting to Yes: Negotiating Agreement without Giving In.* Penguin: New York, 1991.

Gotbaum, Victor. *Negotiating in the Real World: Getting the Deal You Want.* Simon & Schuster: New York, 1999.

9

The Design Phase

In this chapter, you will learn about

- The prize of the design phase—the functional specification
- Graphic design deliverables
- Sound deliverables
- Technical deliverables
- Role of the producer during the design phase
- Final development plan and budget
- Role of the director during design phase
- Role of the writer during design phase

The design phase begins when the developer and client sign the letter of intent or a development agreement. The agreement makes it possible for the writer to begin the detailed design document called the functional specification, discussed in Chapter 6. In addition to the functional specification, many other design elements and business documents are created during the design phase. Certain team members create graphic, sound, and technical deliverables, while the producer creates an asset database, a final plan, and a final budget.

The parties agree in the letter of intent or contract how long the design phase lasts and what the deliverables and milestones are. If the client engages the developer by a letter of intent or deal memo, the client usually pays the developer a fee for the completion of the design phase and the approval of the deliverables. As a rule of thumb, the design fee averages around 10 to 15 percent of the total targeted budget for the product.

In this chapter, you will learn what the deliverables and milestones of the design phase are and what resources are used to create them. You will also learn what the producer, director, and writer do during this phase to ensure the timely and correct creation of those deliverables.

In several ways, the design phase is the linchpin of the entire development process. The design determines the exact specification for the product to be built; upon it is based the final development plan, the final budget, and the definitive contractual agreement between the parties. The design is the catalyst for everything that follows. A well-executed design phase can almost guarantee that the development of the product and the relationship with the client will be successful. Once again, the producer, director, and writer have critically important roles during this phase. It is their responsibility to manage the design process and to ensure that the product defined therein is of a high quality and can be produced for the budget and within the timeframe agreed upon with the client.

The Design Phase Prize

The prize at the end of the design phase is the functional specification (spec). The art director, the sound designer, and the technical director (lead engineer or programmer) contribute to the spec. If the product is an educational or instructional product, an instructional designer and a subject matter expert are major collaborators during this phase. If it is a game, a game designer plays a pivotal role.

You may wonder why the functional specification is the prize and not the contract that the spec makes possible. It's simply because development can continue without the contract, but not without the spec. In fact, if the development agreement is not signed during the discovery phase (but a letter of intent is), contract negotiations can often drag on well into subsequent phases. The parties very often rely on the letter of intent and various side agreements to keep the development moving while negotiating the contract.

The deliverables include graphics such as screen layouts, icon and button designs, font specifications, character designs, and storyboards. The sound designer's deliverables include casting voices and selecting music and sound effects. Technical deliverables include a software evaluation of the design, an implementation plan and schedule, game and database designs, tool and engine specifications, and special-purpose software specifications.

There may be a great deal of content research, particularly if the product is educational or scientific. Students in a multimedia course at the S. I. Newhouse School of Public Communications at Syracuse University design and produce CD-ROM products. They often rely on professors and students from other colleges and departments to collaborate as content experts. In a product they produced during the Spring of 1999, students from the College of Nursing provided data, demographics, and research methods for a CD-ROM designed to instruct and track women at high risk of contracting HIV. This type of collaboration is not only typical, but also essential when dealing with products whose effectiveness depends on scientific accuracy or on effective teaching and learning.

While the writer writes the functional specification, the producer and director constantly and diligently evaluate the spec. The producer must break down the spec to determine the precise and accurate scope of work. This exercise leads to the creation of an asset database, which provides the producer a view of the mountain of work the team must produce. It also provides a means of measuring, or tracking, work progress during development. The director looks at the scope of work from a slightly different point of view. He or she evaluates the work to determine the development process, to determine the picture and sound formats, and to come up with innovative development methods. The director can then direct the activities of the staff on a daily basis, ensuring that every moment of its time is spent producing images or sounds or writing software that fits right into the product.

The functional specification gives birth to a number of other documents and plans, which are illustrated in Figure 9.1. The most important of these are the final budget and the final development plan. Along with the spec, they become part of the final contract with the client.

FIGURE 9.1

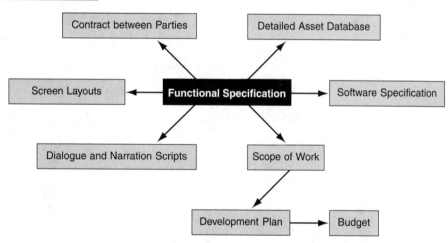

The functional specification drives the creation of many other documents.

Review of the Functional Specification

The functional specification, you recall, is an exhaustive design document. It serves three purposes. First, it is the basis of the agreement between the client and the developer. It is specifically referred to in the contract the two parties sign as the product they agree to produce. Second, it is the development bible that directs the activities of every member of the development team. It is the product's blueprint. Third, the quality assurance testers use it to determine whether the final product conforms to the functional spec agreed on in the contract. For these reasons, the spec must be extremely detailed. Whatever is not explained or described in detail will be made up or interpreted by somebody during development. Whenever that occurs, anarchy reigns. Whatever must be interpreted will almost certainly be interpreted differently by the client and the developer. This can lead to disagreements and ugly moments between the parties.

The audience for the spec, when used as the development bible, is the team that produces the product. The team includes the producer, director, and writer, as well as researchers, content experts, artists, animators, videographers, sound designers, composer/arranger, voice talent, software programmers, and quality assurance testers. Because the spec is used as a component of the contract, the audience includes top management, marketing executives, product managers, and the business affairs people who write the contract.

In order for a document that must speak equally well to a large and diverse audience to be written, deliverables from many sources are required to ensure completeness and correctness. Figure 9.2 shows graphically how many design team members contribute to the spec.

FIGURE 9.2

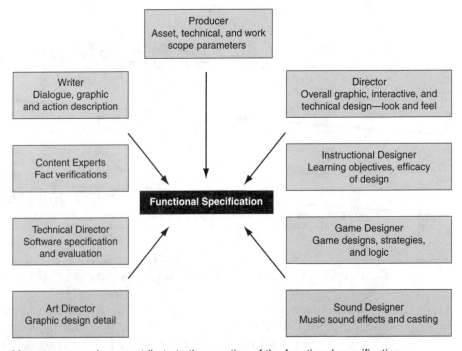

Many team members contribute to the creation of the functional specification.

Design Phase Deliverables

During the design phase, the producer must manage a process in which various team members contribute design elements, which the writer then incorporates into the overall design. The director ensures that the contributions actually comply with the intended creative concept of the product. Table 9.1 shows the design phase deliverables.

Table 9.1 List of Design Phase Deliverables	
Deliverable	Responsible Party
Screen designs and layouts	Art director
Icon and button design	Art director
Font specifications	Art director
Character designs	Character designer
Cast talent	Director
Storyboards	Artists
Palettes	Art director
Cast voices	Sound designer
Select music	Sound designer
Select sound effects	Sound designer
Technical estimate/schedule	Lead programmer
Tools and engines	Lead programmer
Technical parameters	Lead programmer
S/W, database design	Lead programmer
Game design	Game designer
Functional specification	Writer

Graphic Deliverables

The team has the top-level design to get started with. The director (or the interactive designer) creates a node map with the writer from the top-level design. You recall from Chapter 2 that a node map graphically represents the structure of the application. It is a visual aid that enables the producer to create an asset breakdown: a list of graphic elements to be designed on a node-by-node basis. It is the director who provides the creative approach—the look and feel—for these designs. The director collaborates with the art director, whose team of artists creates the work.

The graphic deliverables include

- Screen designs and layouts
- Icon and button designs
- Font specifications
- Character designs
- Cast talent (on-camera video talent)
- Storyboards
- Palettes

Some of these elements are placed directly in the spec as pieces of art, while other elements are simply submitted to the client for approval along with the spec. Later, during the production phase, the design elements are given to the appropriate development team members, who follow the designs to create the assets.

Screen Designs and Layouts

One of the tenets of design covered in Chapter 2 is that the user interface should be designed so that it is consistent and intuitive. Graphic and functional elements should be located geographically where the user would most likely look for them, and they should be designed so the user understands their functional purpose. The director can determine the makeup of each screen now that there is a top-level design and a node map to work from.

The screen layout is a simple graphical representation of the screen. It carves up the real estate and specifies what is needed on the screen, where it goes, and what its dimensions are.

Figure 9.3 is an example of a rough screen layout. The designer often includes the intended sizes of the elements on the screen in pixels. Typically, the maximum screen size is 640 pixels across by 480 pixels down. Other references on the screen may include the "X,Y location" of the graphic elements. X,Y location refers to the position of the upper left-hand corner of the graphic element, as measured from the upper left-hand corner of the screen. Again, this measurement is made in pixels.

Screen layouts such as these are completed for every node. The screen layout serves as the blueprint for the development of the graphic elements, which will occupy the reserved space on the screen. The layout also provides the director with a graphic device to make certain that each screen has room for the required graphic elements before a lot of time has been invested in an artistic interpretation. The director can make sure that each screen serves its functional purpose. In the example in Figure 9.3, the director can see that there is room for the five buttons, a title, an icon, and a button so the user can toggle between two languages.

FIGURE 9.3 The Screen Layout

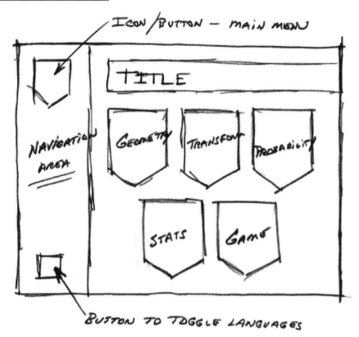

This drawing is an early attempt by the designer to carve up the available screen real estate and to allocate space for the necessary buttons, icons, text, and other elements.

The screen design takes the layout to the next level. The screen design incorporates the graphical look and feel of the product. The director may communicate to the art director that he or she is looking for a clean, uncluttered look with a receding background. Based on the director's vision and the screen layout, the art director might come up with something like the picture in Figure 9.4.

The director may then give the art director further direction, and the iterative design process continues until a final, attractive, and functional graphic design is reached.

Figure 9.5(a) is a concept drawing for a scene from *The Journeyman Project 3: Legacy of Time*, developed by Presto Studios and published by Broderbund Software. Computer artists used this drawing to build and render the 3-D scene in Figure 9.5(b).

Icon Design

Icons serve two purposes: practical and aesthetic. The practical purpose is communicative. Icons are used in all cultures as images that convey meaning. Their

FIGURE 9.4   The Screen Design

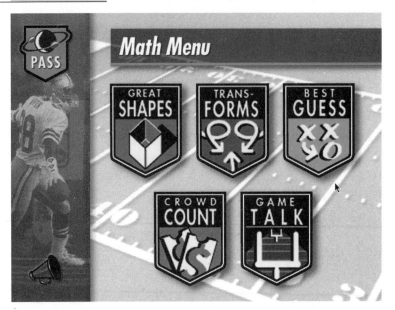

This is the main menu screen for *Project Pass*, an educational CD-ROM jointly published by GTE and the National Football League.

practicality is enhanced by the fact that icons can be cross-cultural and have universal meaning. The aesthetic purpose is to make an artistic statement. Because icons are images, they can be drawn in many different ways, and each rendition carries with it yet another meaning. Figure 9.6 shows two examples of icons used to label men's room doors. Each says, "men's room," but each has a slightly different "voice."

As you drive into the Dallas/Fort Worth Airport, you notice they have gigantic signs that tell you what gates the flights are leaving from. Now, this is important. If you stop and park at the wrong terminal, it can take forever to get to the right one. If you're carrying a lot of luggage, it can be a real hassle. The trouble with the signage at DFW is there aren't any graphical icons. Just text. Identical text. There are no visual cues to direct your eyes to the United flights, or the American, or the Continental. No familiar logos. So, while you are busy trying to read the icons of the practical realm—words—and process the information, you almost always wind up in the wrong lane and you park in the wrong lot anyway.

I don't know why the airport authorities think everyone driving in is a speed-reader. Icons work so much better at communicating specific information in a

FIGURE 9.5

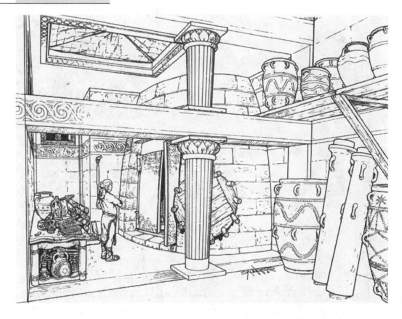

(a)

(b)

(a) An artist draws a conceptual sketch to resolve graphic art challenges early and to create the look and feel of the multimedia product. (b) A 3-D computer-generated scene is created based on the drawing.

FIGURE 9.6   **Two Examples of Icons Used
to Label Men's Room**

fraction of the time. Icons work even better when they are the icons we are already familiar with as a result of exposure through advertising or common use.

In his wonderful book, *Understanding Comics, the Invisible Art*, Scott McCloud calls icons "any image used to represent a person, place, thing, or idea." "Symbols," he says, "are one category of icon we use to represent concepts, ideas, and philosophies" (p. 27). He goes on to explain how some icons have fixed and certain meanings, no matter how they are represented (or drawn), because they represent invisible ideas. Peace symbols, for example, come in countless shapes and sizes, are hand drawn, stamped in silver, or printed on tee shirts. But the peace symbol always means the same thing.

According to McCloud, icons have the effect of amplifying meaning almost as a result of their simplicity. This should be the mantra of the icon designer. Design simple, effective icons that communicate unambiguous information quickly.

Icons in multimedia design are extremely important because of the role they play in promoting the dialogue between user and product. Graphical icons in multimedia, just as they would at the Dallas/Fort Worth airport, do a better job of communicating information quickly and accurately than text does. Icons can be used to tell users where they are, how they got there, and how to get back. Icons can be used to indicate the purpose and function of buttons and screens. Icons may be the best and only way to communicate this information in products aimed at very young children (nonreaders) or in products that have non-English-speaking users—the users you may find at the international terminal of the Dallas/Fort Worth Airport.

During the design phase, the art director designs icons to be used in the product. The graphical appearance of the icons is driven by the practical and aesthetic purpose of the icons. These purposes will be driven by the profile of the typical user, by the functional controls, and by the look and feel of the product.

Font Specification

Type fonts also serve two functions. There is the practical purpose of forming words and the aesthetic purpose of conveying mood and emotion through artistic representation. The type font chosen for this book, for example, was carefully selected to create a mood, or ambiance, for the text. Whether you're aware of it or not, another font would have you feeling a little different about this book.

So, too, in multimedia. The art director carefully selects type fonts, which are used for the screen titles, buttons, text boxes, message windows, and even the credits. In addition to selecting the type, the art director has a great deal of latitude about how type is rendered. PhotoShop, Illustrator, and other computer graphics programs afford the artist the ability to create many artistic interpretations of all the various font styles. Fonts can be treated like any other art element, once they have been selected and placed on a screen. Besides appearing in any color, type can be made to look 3-D, embossed, outlined, underlined, italicized, skewed, scaled, and rotated. There are limitless combinations.

Type font specification is driven by considerations that include the nature of the product, the user, and the look and feel of the product. Some fonts, for example, are dignified. Some are whimsical, others romantic, and still others scholarly. Some are old fashioned, others modern or even futuristic.

Character Designs

Animation isn't just for kids, anymore. Animation is routinely used in all multimedia genres, including children's products, informational products, kiosks, games of all kinds, and many educational titles. During the design phase, characters that will appear in the product are designed. The purpose of character design is to nail down the physical appearance and the movement style of the animated characters. The appearance of the character determines for the user what the character is like, because animated characters, like icons, communicate a lot by their appearance.

There are two kinds of animated characters. Two-dimensional characters, such as Mickey Mouse and Popeye, are still, by and large, drawn by hand, one frame at a time. Characters such as Woody, from the animated feature film *Toy Story*, are generated by computer and appear to be 3-D. Both types of characters are designed from scratch, unless, of course, the characters already exist in another medium. When character designers create new characters, they focus on what the character looks like and how it moves.

If the characters already exist but are not ordinarily animated, as in the case of comic book characters, the character design task may involve determining how an existing character moves. When an animator looks at an existing character, one of the first questions that crosses his or her mind is, Where are his knees? Animators always wonder how a character moves and, when it does, what the character looks like from various angles.

Developer Media Station, Inc., developed an animated storybook for Mattel, Inc., featuring the Barbie character. Everybody knows what Barbie looks like as a doll, but how does she move? What does she *act* like? Nobody knew, for sure, and the process of designing and redesigning the animated Barbie took an enormously long time.

The *Tonka Speedway* product produced for Hasbro Interactive required a number of new characters. Tonka Joe, the main character, had already appeared in previous products. However, he needed to be put into a new costume because the subject of the new product was racing while the earlier products were about construction and rescues. Darrin Brege, a talented character designer, went to work and arrived at the new Tonka Joe—the pit crew boss—pictured in Figure 9.7.

FIGURE 9.7   **Design of Tonka Joe in Racing Costume**

For each character, the animators need the following:

■ *Full-body turn-arounds.* These are a series of drawings showing the character from the front, from ¾, from the side, and from the back.

■ *Poses.* These are key poses showing the character in various positions. They show an animator how the character bends at the waist, crosses his legs, slouches in a chair.

■ *Expressions.* These are close-ups of the character's face, showing laughter, anger, or no emotion.

■ *Mouth positions.* These are close-ups of the character's face, showing how the character forms certain vowels and consonants when speaking. Generally, there are five key mouth positions, and synchronized speech can be created by accurately lining up the correct mouth with the spoken syllable or phoneme. Really inexpensive lip sync can be accomplished with only three mouth positions. It looks cheap, too.

- *Color mark-ups.* These are drawings of the character with colors filled in. The "ink and paint" people who add color to drawn characters use color mark-ups as visual aids. Color mark-ups have to be chosen carefully so every possible drawing can be properly colored. It isn't unusual for the art director to get a call in the middle of the night from ink and paint artists who want to know what color the inside of a character's mouth is supposed to be.

Because a character often speaks, the director must match the sound of the character's voice with his or her appearance. The director may wait until the character is designed before casting an appropriate voice, or may cast just the right voice and then provide that voice to the character designer who will come up with the matching look.

Cast Talent

The product may include video. If the video already exists, the producer will have to license the rights to it and, as an added precaution, make certain the talent appearing in the video are not entitled to further compensation for the use of their performances in a multimedia product. A proper licensing agreement with the copyright owner should warrant that no other rights are infringed by the use of the video.

If the design calls for original video, and if the video includes talent, the director must cast the talent during the design phase. The top-level design usually describes in sufficient detail the talent that appears in the multimedia product. It may call for two middle-aged males with southern accents or a youthful female with a French accent. The producer and director should be certain that as the design develops, new talent is not added without good reason, especially as this adds significant cost to the product.

Talent agencies provide the best resource for acting talent of all kinds on short notice. Simply provide the agency with the characteristics the design calls for, as in Figure 9.8(a), and they will send over a picture portfolio of potential actors and actresses, as in Figure 9.8(b). Some have these available over the Internet. Select those best suited, and hold a casting session, during which each candidate reads for the director. It'll be necessary for the writer to provide at least a sample of probable dialogue in the form of a script. Videotape these sessions, and provide the tape to the client for either selection or approval of the director's choices.

The web site features links to the various unions and guilds that represent talent and other craft persons who work on multimedia products. These web sites have sample contracts.

FIGURE 9.8

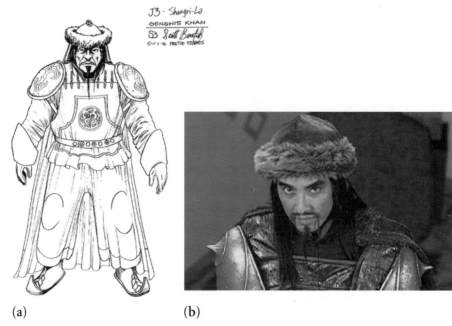

(a)   (b)

(a) Concept sketch of the character Genghis Khan and (b) the actual talent cast for the part in Presto Studio's *The Journeyman Project 3: Legacy of Time,* published by Broderbund Software.

If the developer is a signatory of a collective bargaining agreement with the Screen Actors Guild (SAG) or with the American Federation of Television and Radio Artists (AFTRA), it will be able to hire almost any actor for the multimedia product. If not, union members are not permitted to work. The unions are willing to work with small companies and those that do not ordinarily shoot live action. The unions are willing to sign one-time contracts, which enable the developer to use union talent.

Besides casting the talent, the producer must resolve the cost of the talent. Union minimum rates are set, so the producer must figure out how many different actors he or she needs and for how long. If the talent is nonunion, day rates will be somewhat lower, though in my experience the higher rates for union talent are warranted by their professionalism. The producer must include these costs in the budget.

Storyboards

A storyboard is a series of still images—usually drawings—that convey action, shot composition, and transitions between shots. It resembles a comic strip, but without the dialogue and thought balloons. Storyboards depict a scene of video or animation in a small number of drawings. The director supervises the drawing of storyboards by working with an artist who is sometimes called a "wrist." The storyboard artist works very quickly, drawing a tight sequence of frames that animators and videographers use as a guide to stage and time their shots. Besides showing action, storyboards may also reveal location, setting, costuming, props, and other visual elements the producer and director must account for in their planning and budgeting.

FIGURE 9.9

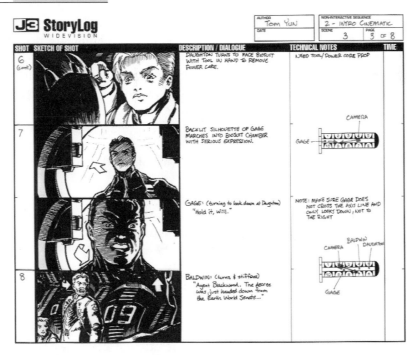

Storyboard panel for scene from *The Journeyman Project 3: Legacy of Time*, developed by Presto Studios and published by Broderbund Software.

Palettes

The word *palette* has two meanings to the multimedia designer. It refers to the family of colors that the director and art director choose for the product, based on its specific design requirements. From the millions of colors available, the art director chooses those that best fit the mood, ambiance, and overall look and feel of the product. Children's multimedia products—just like their TV programs and toys—typically use a palette of bright, primary, cartoon colors. One needs only to look at the packaging on the store shelves to see how true this is. Mysterious, moody, dramatic products, such as most of the war strategy games, have a palette of darker blues, greens, and grays. These are often called doom and gloom colors. In the design phase, the director must see a number of color treatments of backgrounds and other art and direct the development of the product's palette to the appropriate range on the color spectrum.

The other meaning of the word refers to the specific colors—256 in all—that may make up the allowable colors in the product itself. The consumer world is still populated with computers that are incapable of displaying more than 8 bits of color. Technically, this limits the total number of individual colors on the screen at any one time to 256. There isn't anything wrong with the display monitors. It has to do with something called video random access memory, or VRAM. Older computers have limited VRAM. The percentage of computers that cannot display more than 256 colors is decreasing rapidly in this country, and it is unlikely that this will be an issue for multimedia developers in the year 2000. However, if the product will be distributed internationally or to schools, which adopt new technology more slowly than the consumer segment, then the art director must develop a 256-color palette that can be used in the product. Even if all computers could display thousands or millions of colors, images made up of more than 256 colors take up more space. The space available on the CD-ROM then becomes the limiting factor.

It is the producer's job to know when this is an issue to be addressed during the design phase. He or she must know how the product will be marketed and to whom and should know the computer platform most prevalent in that market.

Sound Deliverables

The sound designer, like the art director, works under the direction of the director to develop certain deliverables during the design phase. The sound designer finds voice talent, music, and sound effects that fit the look and feel of the product, as determined by the director. These choices are then presented to the client for approval, usually in the form of sample audio tapes or computer sound files the client can review.

Casting Voices

Sound designers at most studios have a library of audio demo tapes from voice talent or agents. Most sound designers know many talented actors and have used them before. The director tells the sound designer what he or she is looking for—what kind of voice is appropriate for the product—and the sound designer puts together a selection of three or four good possibilities. Sometimes a particular accent or regionalism is needed. Sometimes the director looks for a certain quirkiness, or cartoon voice. Other times he or she may want a deep, dignified, resonant voice. The sound designer finds the talent capable of producing the desired effect and calls them in for an audition.

During this time, the writer writes dialogue or narration for the product. There may be a lot of dialogue to write, but the writer tries to write at least a little dialogue for each character early on. He or she then gives sample narration scripts—one for each character—to the sound designer.

In a recording session, the director and sound designer direct the talent to perform the correct voice for the character. They repeat this for each candidate and choose the best to present to the client for approval. During this exercise, the director visualizes and hears how the character design and the voice work together to create a convincing and engaging new personality.

When talent has been selected and approved, the producer must execute the proper agreement with the talent or the talent's agent. It isn't likely the talent will work during the design phase. After all, the complete design doesn't exist yet. However, the producer must determine how much the talent will cost the project, and he or she must include that cost in the development budget. If the developer has signed a collective bargaining agreement with the Screen Actors Guild (SAG) or with the American Federation of Television and Radio Artists (AFTRA), the cost is already determined.

Selecting Music

Music is used to create mood, so music is selected based on the look and feel desired by the director. The sound designer can obtain music for the product by selecting it from a music library, hiring a composer/arranger to create original music, acquiring the rights to use already existing music, or using music in the public domain. The client must approve the music during the design phase, and the producer must calculate the cost and include the cost in the budget.

There are many music libraries available to multimedia studios. A Web search will result in a few hundred hits on music libraries. The financial arrangements for acquiring the rights to library music vary. In some cases, the developer may pay a fee and acquire unlimited rights to all the music in the library. Or the developer may pay no fee for the library but pay a small royalty every time it uses music from it. The use of library music is the most painless (fast and inexpensive), though not necessarily the most creative, way to get music for a product. It is particularly efficacious for student projects.

The developer may also hire a composer/arranger to create original music for the product. There are many talented composer/arrangers who provide music services on a freelance or subcontract basis. Digital music technology has made it possible for a single musician to create almost any sound and style in a short period of time and at reasonable cost. If the developer is a signatory with the American Federation of Musicians (AFM), the financial and contractual arrangements with the composer are already determined. If not, almost anything can be negotiated. The producer must be certain to determine that the composer/arranger will compose, arrange, and produce the music and provide the master recording. The producer must also make certain the developer will own the copyright in the music when it is complete.

The product may require already existing music. Already existing music includes anything that was composed, performed, and placed in some permanent media. It is copyrighted material, and the producer may have to acquire two or even three licenses to use the music in the product. Whoever wrote the music owns the composition rights, unless he or she assigned those rights to another entity, such as a publishing company. Another party may own the master recording rights. The London Festival Orchestra, for example, may own the master recording rights to its rendition of a Cole Porter composition. The producer may need to obtain a license from both the London Festival Orchestra and Porter's estate, or whatever entity currently holds the composition rights to his work. If the producer obtains the rights to a particular song for the product, the developer still does not have the right to change or modify the song in any way unless he or she obtains another kind of license. The producer must be certain to clear all applicable rights issues and to determine the exact cost of obtaining the rights; these costs must be included in the budget. Visit the web site, and link to Ladera Press, which has published a comprehensive book on the subject of copyrights for multimedia products.

Some music is in the public domain. This means that the work is not protected under copyright law. Either its copyright has lapsed and was not renewed or it never had a copyright because no law was in effect when it was composed. Almost any composition older than 75 years is in the public domain. A developer may use the composition freely but would still have to license the actual recording of it if the recording is recent. For example, the tune "Happy Birthday" is in the public domain, and the developer may use it. But the recording of Marilyn Monroe singing it to John F. Kennedy is not in the public domain. The developer must acquire the license to use the recording in its multimedia product.

However the developer chooses and acquires music, there will be costs and other complications involved. The producer must be cognizant of these costs and any other liabilities during the design phase and build them into the budget and development plan. Samples of the music should be provided to the client for its approval as a deliverable of the design phase.

Selecting Sound Effects

Sound effects in multimedia, just as in film and television, are used to add realism to a live or animated scene. However, multimedia has another requirement for sound effects. The interactive designer uses sound effects to add audio reinforcement to the dialogue carried on between users and the product. Sound effects should accompany almost every user interaction to communicate back to users that what they have just done has "registered" with the product. For example, whenever users click on a button, the action should be accompanied by some appropriate sound effect. Typically, the sound is of a button push. It may be a chime, a bell, a click, or a musical note. The design of the sound effect is as important as the design of the graphic representation of the button.

Sound designers choose the sound effects for the user interface based on the look of the graphics the sound is synchronized with and the theme of the product. A children's product, for example, with large, clunky, colorful buttons, may call for the sound of a bicycle horn when selected. Small radial buttons on a reference product may call for a simple sharp click.

Another sound effect that may be needed is ambient sound, also known as room tone. This is the sound that adds depth and perspective to a graphic or background scene. If you stop your reading right now and listen carefully, you will hear the ambient sounds of the space you are in. What you may suddenly hear is the sound of the air conditioner, a radio off in the distance, a dog barking, and traffic on the freeway three blocks away. You must be in Encino! Sometimes, ambient sound is barely audible; other times, it dominates the track. It always, quite clearly, plays a major role in establishing location.

Whether for adding realism to a video or animation—such as car doors slamming, wheels screeching, gun shots, or screams—or for accompanying interactions by the user, sound designers find their sound effects in two ways. There are sound effects libraries, just as there are music libraries. The best of them have thousands and thousands of sound effects. They even have search engines that enable the sound designer to type in a keyword to obtain a list of all the sounds available in the library matching the description. The financial arrangement is simple—the developer may license the library royalty-free for one fee or may license the sound effects on a case-by-case basis.

The other method is to create the sound effects. This is called Foley sound, named after the Hollywood sound person who first developed the art of creating believable sound effects from things he had at hand. Bashing a sheet of metal creates the sound of thunder. Thumping around in a sandbox creates footsteps on the front walk. With enough imagination, a good sound designer can create sound effects for any occasion.

The sound designer should prepare a representative sample of sound effects during the design phase, matching them properly with the graphic art they will synchronize with. The sample should be presented to the client for approval.

Technical Deliverables

As we learned way back in Chapter 2, features—the product's interactive playthings—are one of the five basic components of a multimedia product, and features have to be programmed. During the design phase, the writer thoroughly fleshes out and describes the features of the product in the functional specification. Once a feature is described in terms of its outward appearance—or how the user experiences it—the technical leader of the design team has to figure out how to make it happen. Ideally, the two events—the description of the feature and determining how to make it happen—are iterative. Software engineers get annoyed when the creative folks come up with some kind of harebrained interactive megaevent and then tell them—the "technical" folks—to go and figure out how to do it. The technical director should be consulted constantly during the design process to determine whether the product's interactive promises can, in fact, be programmed. Many times, technical experts can arrive at even more elegant creative solutions if they are included in the discussions early on.

In any case, once the technical director understands the features of the product, he or she can generate a number of documents or, as is more often the case, contribute information, which the writer includes in the functional specification and the producer includes in the budget and development plan.

Implementation Estimate and Schedule

The most important feedback the technical director provides about the product design is its feasibility. Only the programmer can estimate how much time and effort will be involved in implementing the design and whether the product will actually behave the way it is described in the functional specification. The programmer must also create an implementation schedule—a list of the programming chores in the order they will be completed. It must correspond to the completion schedule of the product and in particular to any prerelease deliverables, such as downloadable demos or samples for conventions. With proper planning, the programmer's implementation schedule and the overall development schedule—which is often governed by the needs of the client—are in accord.

Tools and Engines

The programmer must specify the programming tools and engines needed to implement the design. A well-established developer probably already has the necessary software tools, libraries, and engines, which are simply existing programs that were written to make further programming easier or unnecessary. However, the design may require something more, and the programmer must evaluate the design to determine what is needed and to recommend how to get it. The solution for missing software is either to write it or to license it. Real-time 3-D game engines, for example, can be licensed. If the developer plans on creating only one product that includes that feature, it makes sense to license the engine for the product rather than invest hundreds or thousands of labor hours creating a new one. The visual and behavioral effects of these tools and engines are important information for the director; the cost and time are important to the producer.

Technical Parameters

The design may make demands on the programming, which in turn may create parameters for other development elements, such as art and sound. Art, animation, sound, and video may have to be created in a certain manner because of the technology used. For example, it may be necessary to shoot, digitize, and compress the video at a certain size and frame rate so it plays back at a reasonable speed. All of the art may have to be indexed to a certain palette. There may be issues with sound—whether it can be played back in stereo or mixed in real time. The technical director must identify any parameters caused by the technology and communicate them to the writer, producer, and director so allowances can be made in the functional specification, the budget, and the plan.

Software and Database Designs

If more than one programmer will work on the product, the technical lead must write a document that details the software and database designs and the whole software development approach. By the time the design phase is complete, the budget, development plan, and functional specification will have been based on programming assumptions and advice provided by the technical lead. The software must be developed according to the same set of assumptions.

The Producer during the Design Phase

Design begins when the client and the developer agree, in a letter of intent, deal memo, or development contract, to proceed with the product. The agreement includes both a schedule and a budget for completion of each phase, starting with the design phase. The producer's first responsibility, then, is to manage the activities of the design team and to make certain that each component, or deliverable, that goes into the functional specification is completed on time and according to budget. The design team typically consists of the producer, writer, director, art director, sound designer, and technical lead. It may also include an interactive designer, game designer, instructional technologist, content expert, researcher, and assistants. While managing the design phase, the producer is also busy preparing those plans and documents that make the prototype and production phases possible. More about that later in this chapter.

Marching Orders

The producer provides each member of the team with a list of the tasks to be completed during the design phase, with the specific tasks each is responsible for highlighted. The task list includes start dates, end dates, and dependencies—instructions on how the tasks of one member depend on the successful completion of work by another. If it isn't clear exactly what each task is, a complete description of the task is written and attached. These task lists are called marching orders, and team members usually appreciate them for providing clear, unambiguous direction.

		Tasks	Owner	Start	End	Comments
3/4/00 to 4/26/00	1	Research	Intern	3/4	3/21	Give to Smith (3)
	2	Node map	Riley	3/4	3/12	Give to Bowers (6)
	3	Write spec	Smith	3/4	4/20	
	4	Sample dialogue	Smith		3/12	Give to James, Riley (11)
	5	Game design	Farnsworth	3/4	3/21	Give to Smith
	6	BG layouts	Bowers	3/13	3/21	Give to Cooke
	7	Screen design	Bowers	3/22	4/15	
	8	Other graphics	Bowers		4/15	
	9	Character design	Cooke	3/13	3/21	Give to James, Riley (11)
	10	Storyboards	Cooke	3/21	4/20	
	11	Cast voices	Riley, James	3/12	3/21	
	12	Audition actors	Riley, James	3/12	3/21	
	13	Select music	James	3/21	4/15	
	14	Select SFX	James	3/21	4/15	
	15	Technical evaluation	Farnsworth	3/21	4/15	
	16	Asset database	Subricki, intern	3/21	4/26	
	17	Plan	Subricki	3/4	4/20	
	18	Budget	Subricki		4/20	
	19	Review session	All		4/21	
	20	Modify	All	4/21	4/25	
	21	Client pitch	All		4/26	Business attire

Table 9.2   Design Phase Marching Orders

Weekly Meetings

The producer should hold formal weekly status meetings with the team and should expect each team member to relate briefly but accurately the current status of his or her component of the design deliverables. The producer needs this information to compare expected progress (and costs) against actual progress. If there is any slippage, there is an opportunity to explore why and to take corrective measures. The meetings keep everyone informed and in the loop and have the added benefit of building team spirit and empowering the team with a sense of ownership of the product. By establishing the routine of a weekly meeting, status reports, and group evaluations, the producer prepares the team for continuing in this manner for the duration of the development.

Weekly Arithmetic

The producer begins a weekly routine of preparing a financial status report. The producer gathers progress reports from the team members (during the status meetings) and cost information from the payroll or accounting department—typically in the form of actual expenses broken down by labor category (producer, writer, art, sound, engineering, etc.) and further by individual, plus all out-of-pocket costs. The accounting department acquires this information from time sheets filled out by employees and invoices from vendors and independent contractors. The producer then analyzes the data to arrive at the answers to these questions:

- For each labor category, what was my original budget for this phase of development?
- As of this moment, how much have we spent in each category?
- As of this moment, how much of the total scope of work for this phase is complete in each labor category?
- Does my cost-to-date exceed my progress-to-date in each category?
- What is my estimate to complete this phase in each category?
- What is the variance in each category? (This means, what is the difference between the original budget and what is likely to be the total cost?)
- Am I over, under, or right on budget?

Obviously, the answer to the final question leads to all kinds of scenarios. Corrective measures may or may not be necessary. The producer should be prepared to take whatever steps are needed to right the ship.

This is an internal status report which the producer shares with the team and routes to upper management. It is a communication tool that keeps everyone informed about progress. As a management tool, it enables the producer to make tactical decisions every week during development.

Documents for Subsequent Phases

As the various chapters of the functional specification are completed, the producer analyzes them and derives a number of important documents needed for subsequent

This means "estimate to complete." It is the producer's estimate of how much more time is required of this team member or labor category.

Table 9.3 Project Status Report: Design Phase

4/21/00 Producer: Subricki

	Actual	Budget	Variance	ETC	% Burned
Hours					
Producer	280	320	40	40	87%
Director	160	160	0	0	100%
Writer	168	200	32	32	84%
Art	160	175	15	15	91%
Sound	60	70	10	10	100%
Engineer	55	40	(15)	0	137%
Research	160	160	0	0	100%
QA super	8	8	0	0	100%
Support	0	0	0	0	0%
Outside	0	0	0	0	0%
Totals	891	973	82	97	91%
Costs					
Producer	$14,000	$16,000	$2,000	$2,000	87%
Director	$9,600	$9,600	0	0	100%
Writer	$5,880	$7,000	$1,120	$1,120	84%
Art	$4,000	$4,375	$375	$375	91%
Sound	$1,200	$1,400	$200	$200	100%
Engineer	$3,300	$2,400	(900)	0	137%
Research	$1,280	$1,280	0		100%
QA super	$160	$160	0		100%
Support	0	0	0		0%
Outside	0	0	0		0%
Totals	$39,420	$42,215	$2,795	$3,695	93%

The $900 difference between the variance and the estimate to complete means this phase is going over budget.

phases. In practice, he or she begins as soon as the spec is begun and continues until it is complete. The three most important documents are the asset database, the final development plan, and the final budget. The producer cobbled together preliminary versions of all three during the discovery phase. At that time, he or she based them on an evaluation of the top-level design. Now, the functional specification is defining the product in detail. The producer can make a comprehensive list of all of the assets and arrive at an accurate scope of work. From this, he or she can develop an accurate and realistic development plan. From the development plan, the producer can build a precise budget. Until the last two items are complete, the developer and client cannot enter into a final and definitive contractual agreement and cannot begin the next phase.

Asset Database.   The asset database the producer generates during the design phase is the comprehensive list of all art, video, animation, and sound assets needed for the product. It serves several purposes. First, it provides the producer with a sobering view of the amount of art and sound production the team must do. This quantification of the workload makes it possible for the producer to arrive at a fairly accurate estimate of labor hours needed to create the assets. This, of course, feeds right into the budget. Second, the asset database becomes the work orders for the artists, animators, sound designers, and videographers. Each is given a portion of the list of assets and is responsible for creating those assets during the prototype and production phases. Third, the database becomes the tracking mechanism for progress. During development, the status of an asset is tracked step by step, from the moment it is assigned to an artist or sound designer to the day it is approved by the director and passed on to the programmer.

File-Naming Conventions.   Most studios have what is known as a file-naming convention, which is a system for labeling assets. A good asset-naming system is one in which the assigned name includes the name of the product, the node, the file type, and the version number of the asset. Having a file-naming convention is the essential first step in developing an asset database. Figure 9.10 is an example of a file name for the background graphic of the Main Menu for the product *Flight Fanatic,* described in Chapter 2.

Database Maintenance.   The producer, a production assistant, or a production manager is responsible for keeping the asset database up to date daily. Some studios employ database managers whose sole function is to maintain the asset databases of all the in-house projects. On a weekly basis during development, the producer compares the progress of asset creation, as revealed by the asset database, to the cost of development, as reported by the accounting department. That makes it possible for the producer to generate the weekly status reports.

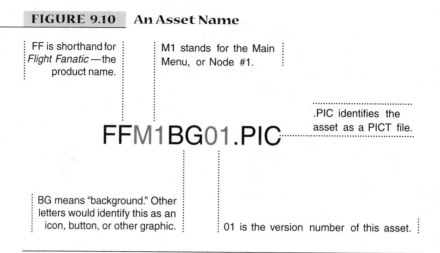

FIGURE 9.10   An Asset Name

FF is shorthand for *Flight Fanatic*—the product name.

M1 stands for the Main Menu, or Node #1.

.PIC identifies the asset as a PICT file.

FFM1BG01.PIC

BG means "background." Other letters would identify this as an icon, button, or other graphic.

01 is the version number of this asset.

The asset database pictured in Table 9.4 was made with Microsoft Excel. It's a simple, flat spreadsheet. Far more sophisticated database programs, such as *File-Maker Pro,* can be used to store and process all kinds of additional information about each and every asset. The producer should use whatever software meets his or her requirements.

Assets can be broken down by node, type, or both. During development, the producer may want information about all of the art assets for the entire product or about all of the art assets for a particular node. The database should be designed so it is possible to retrieve both kinds of information.

In Table 9.4, all of the assets are listed along the left column by file name. This is followed by a short description of the asset and the initials of the person responsible for creating it. The other columns track each asset's current status—designed, completed, approved, in sound (some animation needs to be joined with sound and made into a Quicktime movie), or in engineering. As long as this database is kept up to date, the producer can see at a glance how many assets need to be created, and what state they're in. This report shows that nearly all of the assets are completed and in engineering, with the rest in sound.

Other Activities

The producer completes other tasks that contribute directly to the final plan and budget. When the producer has determined what the scope of work is by studying the asset database, he or she predicts what graphics and sound resources may be needed to create those assets. By conferring with the technical lead on the project about the programming, the producer determines what equipment and labor are needed. The producer then decides about work assignments within the company, additional hiring, or acquiring resources from outside the company. During the

Table 9.4	Sample Asset Database								
	Art and Animation Assets	Start		892	892	892	456	892	892
		In Progress		0	0	0	82	810	82
	Node: Sign-on Screen		Owner	Design	Done	Apprvd	Snd	Final	Eng
1	7T P1 AP001 USA.MOV	TJ sign-on establish	SS	X	X	X		1	1
2	7T P1 GB001 USA.PiC	Background of sign-on screen	AW	X	X	X		1	1
3	7T P1 GG001 ALL.PIC	Coach icon	AW	X	X	X		1	1
4	7T P1 GG002 ALL.PIC	Sparks icon	AW	X	X	X		1	1
5	7T P1 GG003 ALL.PIC	Nick Park icon	AW	X	X	X		1	1
6	7T P1 GG004 ALL.PIC	Rudy Forest icon	AW	X	X	X		1	1
7	7T P1 GG005 ALL.PIC	Nate Cod icon	AW	X	X	X		1	1
8	7T P1 GG06A ALL.PIC	911 icon	AW	X	X	X		1	1
9	7T P1 GG06B ALL.PIC	911 selected	AW	X	X	X		1	1
10	7T P1 GG06C ALL.PIC	911 highlight	AW	X	X	X		1	1
11	7T P1 GG07A ALL.PIC	Go back icon	AW	X	X	X		1	1
12	7T P1 GG07B ALL.PIC	Go back selected	AW	X	X	X		1	1
13	7T P1 GG07C ALL.PIC	Go back highlight	AW	X	X	X		1	1
14	7T P1 GG008 ALL.PIC	Little red button highlight	AW	X	X	X		1	1
15	7T P1 GG009 ALL.PIC	Highlight around button, name plate	AW	X	X	X		1	1
	Node: Sign-in Screen								
16	7T N1 AP001 USA.MOV	TJ Nav Center establish animation	SS	X	X	X		1	1
17	7T N1 GB001 ALL.PIC	Long shot of BG	LE	X	X	X		1	1
18	7T N1 GB002 USA.PIC	Close-up of Dispatch center	LE	X	X	X		1	1
19	7T N1 AP002 USA.MOV	TJ Nav center help sequence	SS	X	X	X		1	1
20	7T N1 AU001 USA.MOV	Flood intro movie	LE	X	X	X		1	1
21	7T N1 AU002 USA.MOV	Zoo intro movie	LE	X	X	X		1	1
22	7T N1 AU003 USA.MOV	Warehouse intro movie	LE	X	X	X		1	1
23	7T N1 AU004 USA.MOV	Garage intro movie	LE	X	X	X		1	1
24	7T N1 AU005 USA.MOV	Academy intro movie	LE	X	X	X		1	1
25	7T N1 AU006 USA.MOV	Front Loader animation	DB	X	X	X		1	1

design phase, the producer must establish what any new or external resources are and what they will cost. In order to guarantee that the cost estimates and plan are accurate, the producer obtains firm, fixed bids for work, services, or supplies and agreements with independent contractors and freelance talent.

In all cases, the agreements must be contingent on the project moving forward. Absent a final contract with the client, the project could end at any time, and the producer should not be stuck with commitments to hire workers or to purchase equipment or supplies that are not needed.

Subcontractor Agreements. The producer may determine that he or she will have to hire freelance talent or independent contractors to do part of the work. The most common need is for graphic artists and programmers. He or she may also need to hire a music arranger/composer, a video crew, a photographer, or other specialized workers. He or she must meet those people and show them the work they'll be doing. They must provide an estimate for the work. There are two agreements the producer can reach with workers, either an employee contract or an independent contractor agreement.

If the worker is going to perform services on the developer's premises, using its equipment, and under the producer's supervision, even for a short time, the worker is an employee. The developer must treat the worker as an employee, which includes withholding and paying payroll taxes, social security, workmen's compensation, and other benefits. At this point, the producer must reach an agreement with the new hire concerning wages, work hours, the nature of the work he or she will perform (also known as normal duties), whom he or she will report to, the probable duration of employment, and, very important, who will own the rights to his or her creations.

If the worker will perform services on his or her own premises, using his or her own equipment and largely under his or her own supervision, then the worker may be an independent contractor. The producer must sign an agreement with the worker that specifies what he or she will deliver, when, at what cost, and, very important, that the developer owns all rights to the work. If this is not explicitly stated in the agreement with the worker, he or she may own at least part, if not all, of the rights in the work.

Vendor Estimates and Out-of-Pocket Costs. There is a boatload of miscellaneous costs associated with all development. These include travel, lodging, meals, shipping, phone, faxes, copying, supplies of all kinds (art, video, photography, office, manuals), new software, new hardware, legal fees, and insurance. The producer may have to book time at a sound studio, sound stage, video edit bay, or a location for a shoot. He or she may have to rent costumes or period automobiles. In order to include these items in the budget, the producer must contact all of these vendors and obtain estimates from them for their services or products. Do not use the lowest estimate for the budget. Be conservative. Get estimates in writing, and keep them in a file. Include these estimates in the final budget. The producer may have to take a shot in the dark about some expenses. How many times will he or she ship, by Federal Express, an overnight package to the client? How many round-trip airfares will be needed to visit the client? How many times will he or she buy pizza and sodas for a half dozen people still working at midnight? Include everything conceivable in the budget.

Final Plan

The producer modifies the preliminary development plan based on the new realities drawn out by the design phase and formulates a final plan. The design phase brings into sharper focus all of the tasks, their length, start and end dates, interdependency with other tasks, and the resources each requires. For example, it may become clearer during the design phase how much more art or animation must be generated or how much more software must be developed. The need for and availability of certain talent or a key independent contractor is discovered. The producer adjusts the preliminary plan accordingly.

One of the key things to focus on during this planning stage is the prototype. As you will read in Chapter 11, the prototype has three purposes: to test the design, the technology, and the development processes. The producer must determine now, during the design phase, what part of the final product he or she should produce during the prototype phase that serves those three purposes. Once the producer determines this, he or she prioritizes the order of tasks in the final plan to produce the desired prototype.

As described in Chapter 8, *Microsoft Project* is ideal project planning software to create the final plan. Table 9.5 is an example of a final development plan made with *Microsoft Project*.

Final Budget

Once the producer has created a final plan, which includes all of the tasks and the resources needed for those tasks, and has obtained reliable estimates of other costs, he or she can craft the final budget. The final budget is an accurate accounting of all the money the producer will spend to create the product. The budget itself is an internal document, not ordinarily shared with the client unless something about the agreement with the client gives it access to pay rates, overhead costs, and other proprietary information. The bottom line of the budget is the total cost. If the agreement with the client entitles the developer to a reasonable profit from the work, then the producer adds a profit to the bottom line of the budget, and that is the price he or she must agree on with the client. Under no circumstances should the developer ever agree to produce a product for a figure less than the bottom line cost of the final budget.

Table 9.5   Final Development Plan

| | | | February | March | April |
ID	Task	Time			
1	Brainstorming Session	1 day			
2	Notes of session - Agree	2 days			
3	Write Functional Spec	20 days			
4	Write Narrative Script	5 days			
5	Ruff BG Layouts	10 days			
6	Ruff Character Design	2 days			
7	Ruff Storyboards	10 days			
8	Design Graphics	15 days			
9	Production plan/Asset db	15 days			
10	Design Review	0 days	♦3/7		
11	Modify Spec	5 days			
12	Modify Layouts	5 days			
13	Modify Storyboards	5 days			
14	Design Review #2	0 days	♦3/19		
15	Design phase complete	0 days	♦3/20		
16	Voice Record (edit proto)	3 days			
17	Proto Art	20 days			
18	Proto Animation	20 days			
19	Build/Animate 3-D vehicles	15 days			
20	Sound Effects/Music - Proto	15 days			
21	Engineer Prototype	20 days			
22	Quality Assurance - Proto	4 days			
23	Prototype delivered	0 days	4/28 ♦		
24	Prototype phase complete	0 days	4/29 ♦		
25	Voice edit - full title	10 days			
26	All art	85 days			
27	All character Animation	105 days			
28	3-D animation	35 days			
29	SFX and Music	105 days			
30	E3 Demo	0 days			
31	Alpha 1.0	0 days			
32	Alpha 2.0	0 days			
33	Beta 1.0	0 days			
34	Beta 2.0	0 days			
35	The Engineering	105 days			
36	Quality Assurance	105 days			
37	Gold Master	0 days			

Date column headers: 1/9, 1/26, 2/2, 2/9, 2/16, 2/23, 3/2, 3/9, 3/16, 3/23, 3/30, 4/6, 4/13, 4/20, 4/27, 5/4

There are many different budgeting tools, but *Microsoft Excel* is one of the most useful, flexible, and pervasive. It is widely used, and the spreadsheet data can be exported to other databases. *Movie Magic* budget software from Script Systems in Burbank, California, is another excellent tool. Create a budget in the manner of a spreadsheet, with cost accounts and categories running down the first column of rows, and time, on a week-by-week basis, stretching off to the right. By inputting the number of hours each staff person is expected to contribute in the proper week, *Excel* calculates the total number of hours for each labor category. By factoring in actual hourly or weekly rates for each category, the spreadsheet calculates costs on a week-by-week basis. The budget, then, becomes a cash-flow chart for the project. See Table 9.6 for an example of such a budget.

When the producer has successfully managed the design phase, the functional specification; various graphic, sound and technical deliverables; an asset database; numerous legal agreements; a final development plan; and a final budget are completed. The producer is poised to begin the next phase upon approval of the deliverables by the client.

The Director during the Design Phase

While the producer provides each team member with a list of tasks, or deliverables, and a time frame for completion, the director provides each team member with creative and aesthetic *direction* for those tasks. In some cases, the director develops specific development methods for the completion of those tasks and instructs the team members on how to create certain deliverables. Remember that it is the director who develops and maintains the overall, high-level vision of the product, and he or she must communicate this vision to the entire team every day. In this discussion, the director is presented as the interactive designer of the product, as is often the case.

Direct Interactive Design

To begin with, the director works with the writer to develop the interactive structure of the product, and together they create the node map. This early exercise enables the director and writer to agree on such things as the global conventions, menus, buttons, icons, and other screen elements. They will also agree on such things as characters, backgrounds, and video. The writer, after all, has to describe these things in the document. Armed with a clear understanding of the logical, interactive design, the director begins focusing on the graphic and sound design, described earlier in this chapter.

Part of developing both the interactive structure and the graphic deliverables involves consultation with the technical director. The technical director can flag any problems with software or hardware that may result from the design and can

Table 9.6	Sample Budget							

				Budget Summary:			
Project Name: Budget Prepared By: Date:				Total Budget $0	Total Actual $0	Total Variance $0	Total Estimate $0

Account Number	Line Item	Rate per Unit	Type Unit	Amount Budgeted	Actual to Date	Variance to Date	Estimate Complete
100	Producer Unit	$0.00		$0	$0	$0	$0
100-01	Producer	$65.00	Hour	$0	$0	$0	$0
100-02	Technical Consultant	$65.00	Hour	$0	$0	$0	$0
100-03	Prod Coordinator	$30.00	Hour	$0	$0	$0	$0
100-04	Production Assist	$20.00	Hour	$0	$0	$0	$0
100-05	Rights Clearances	$0.00	Fee	$0	$0	$0	$0
100-06	Agents	$0.00	Fee	$0	$0	$0	$0
100-07	Other Producer Unit	$1,000.00	allow	$0	$0	$0	$0
110	Creative Director Unit	$0.00		$0	$0	$0	$0
110-01	Creative Director	$45.00	Hour	$0	$0	$0	$0
110-02	Assistant Director	$45.00	Hour	$0	$0	$0	$0
110-03	Game Designer	$20.00	Hour	$0	$0	$0	$0
110-04	Writer	$0.00	Hour	$0	$0	$0	$0
110-05	Character Designer	$0.00	Hour	$0	$0	$0	$0
110-06	Layout Artist	$0.00	Hour	$0	$0	$0	$0
110-07	Storyboards	$0.00	Hour	$0	$0	$0	$0
110-08	Composer/Arranger	$0.00	Hour	$0	$0	$0	$0
110-09	Other Creative Director	$0.00	allow	$0	$0	$0	$0
120	Talent	$0.00		$0	$0	$0	$0
120-01	Narrators	$0.00	allow	$0	$0	$0	$0
120-02	Singers/other	$0.00	allow	$0	$0	$0	$0
200	Art Department	$0.00		$0	$0	$0	$0
200-01	Art Dept Manager	$70.00	Hour	$0	$0	$0	$0
200-02	Art Director	$45.00	Hour	$0	$0	$0	$0
200-03	Digital Paint Manager	$30.00	Hour	$0	$0	$0	$0
200-04	Digital Artist	$25.00	Hour	$0	$0	$0	$0
200-05	Flood filler	$0.00	Hour	$0	$0	$0	$0
200-06	Subcontracted work	$0.00	allow	$0	$0	$0	$0
200-07	Other Art Department	$1,000.00	allow	$0	$0	$0	$0
300	Animation Department	$0.00		$0	$0	$0	$0
300-01	Animation Dept Manager	$30.00	Hour	$0	$0	$0	$0
300-02	Animation Administrator	$30.00	Hour	$0	$0	$0	$0

Table 9.6   (continued)

Account Number	Line Item	Rate per Unit	Type Unit	Amount Budgeted	Actual to Date	Variance to Date	Estimate Complete
300-03	Lead Animator	$35.00	Hour	$0	$0	$0	$0
300-04	Animator	$45.00	Hour	$0	$0	$0	$0
300-05	Asst Animator	$30.00	Hour	$0	$0	$0	$0
300-06	Subcontracted Work	$0.00	allow	$0	$0	$0	$0
300-07	Other Animation Dept	$0.00	Hour	$0	$0	$0	$0
400	Audio Department	$0.00		$0	$0	$0	$0
400-01	Casting	$65.00	Hour	$0	$0	$0	$0
400-02	Narration recording	$65.00	Hour	$0	$0	$0	$0
400-03	Narration edit	$65.00	Hour	$0	$0	$0	$0
400-04	Music Library	$250.00	Allow	$0	$0	$0	$0
400-05	Sound Effects Library	$250.00	Allow	$0	$0	$0	$0
400-06	Music Selection	$65.00	Hour	$0	$0	$0	$0
400-07	Music Edit	$65.00	Hour	$0	$0	$0	$0
400-08	Sound Effects Selection	$65.00	Hour	$0	$0	$0	$0
400-09	Edit	$65.00	Hour	$0	$0	$0	$0
400-10	Mix	$65.00	Hour	$0	$0	$0	$0
400-11	Layback	$65.00	Hour	$0	$0	$0	$0
400-12	Digital tape stock	$0.00	Reel	$0	$0	$0	$0
400-13	Other audio costs	$1,000.00	Allow	$0	$0	$0	$0
500	Engineering	$0.00		$0	$0	$0	$0
500-01	Engineering Manager	$70.00	Hour	$0	$0	$0	$0
500-02	Senior Engineer	$55.00	Hour	$0	$0	$0	$0
500-03	Engineer	$45.00	Hour	$0	$0	$0	$0
510	Title Engineering	$0.00		$0	$0	$0	$0
500-04	TE Manager	$30.00	Hour	$0	$0	$0	$0
500-05	Title Engineer	$30.00	Hour	$0	$0	$0	$0
600	Quality Assurance	$0.00		$0	$0	$0	$0
600-01	QA Manager	$45.00	Hour	$0	$0	$0	$0
600-02	QA Supervisor	$20.00	Hour	$0	$0	$0	$0
600-03	Technical Writer	$0.00	Hour	$0	$0	$0	$0
600-04	QA Tester–FT	$0.00	Hour	$0	$0	$0	$0
600-05	QA Tester–Temp	$0.00	Hour	$0	$0	$0	$0
700	Video Production	$0.00		$0	$0	$0	$0
700-01	Crew	$1,350.00	Day	$0	$0	$0	$0
700-02	Director	$350.00	Day	$0	$0	$0	$0
700-03	Lighting Director	$350.00	Day	$0	$0	$0	$0
700-04	Betacam stock, 30 min.	$30.00	Each	$0	$0	$0	$0
700-05	Lighting rentals, gels, etc.	$150.00	Day	$0	$0	$0	$0

(continued)

Table 9.6 (continued)

Account Number	Line Item	Rate per Unit	Type Unit	Amount Budgeted	Actual to Date	Variance to Date	Estimate Complete
800	Outside Services	$0.00		$0	$0	$0	$0
800-01	Image Capture–Scanning	$0.00	Hour	$0	$0	$0	$0
800-02	Video image capture	$20.00	Hour	$0	$0	$0	$0
800-03	MPEG Encoding	$0.00	Hour	$0	$0	$0	$0
800-04	Special purpose Software	$0.00	Allow	$0	$0	$0	$0
800-05	DISC Pressing	$20.00	Hour	$0	$0	$0	$0
800-06	Disc Pressing Media Costs	$15.00	Each	$0	$0	$0	$0
800-07	Other Digital Services	$1,000.00	Allow	$0	$0	$0	$0
900	Purchase, Rent	$0.00		$0	$0	$0	$0
900-01	New Computer Systems	$0.00	Allow	$0	$0	$0	$0
900-02	Disc Drives	$0.00	Allow	$0	$0	$0	$0
900-03	Cables, Connectors	$0.00	Allow	$0	$0	$0	$0
900-04	Off-The-Shelf Software	$0.00	Allow	$0	$0	$0	$0
900-05	Video Systems	$0.00	Allow	$0	$0	$0	$0
900-06	Furniture	$0.00	Allow	$0	$0	$0	$0
900-07	Other Purchases	$0.00	Allow	$0	$0	$0	$0
910	Other Expendibles	$0.00		$0	$0	$0	$0
910-01	Tapes (video)	$100.00	Allow	$0	$0	$0	$0
910-02	Tapes (audio)	$100.00	Allow	$0	$0	$0	$0
910-03	CD-ROM discs	$0.00	Allow	$0	$0	$0	$0
910-04	Syquest Discs	$250.00	Allow	$0	$0	$0	$0
910-05	Floppys–Mac	$0.00	Allow	$0	$0	$0	$0
910-06	Floppys–IBM	$0.00	Allow	$0	$0	$0	$0
910-07	Other Media	$250.00	Allow	$0	$0	$0	$0
920	Travel Expenses	$0.00		$0	$0	$0	$0
920-01	Airfare	$1,500.00	Allow	$0	$0	$0	$0
920-02	Rental Car	$0.00	Allow	$0	$0	$0	$0
920-03	Hotel	$185.00	Allow	$0	$0	$0	$0
920-04	PerDiem	$50.00	Allow	$0	$0	$0	$0
920-05	Client Entertainment	$0.00	Allow	$0	$0	$0	$0
920-06	Other Travel	$500.00	Allow	$0	$0	$0	$0
920-07	Travel allowance –	$7,000.00	Allow	$0	$0	$0	$0
930	Miscellaneous Costs	$0.00		$0	$0	$0	$0
930-01	Phones, Fax	$0.00	Allow	$0	$0	$0	$0
930-02	FedEx, other shipping	$26.00	Allow	$0	$0	$0	$0
930-03	Copies, binding	$0.00	Allow	$0	$0	$0	$0
930-04	Color Copies	$250.00	Allow	$0	$0	$0	$0
930-05	Printing	$0.00	Allow	$0	$0	$0	$0
930-06	Legal Expenses	$0.00	Allow	$0	$0	$0	$0
930-07	Miscellaneous Other	$1,000.00	Allow	$0	$0	$0	$0

recommend alternatives. He or she can also identify any graphic or sound parameters that may result from the current design.

Direct the Art and Sound Design

The director works closely with the art director to develop the look and feel of the product. The director provides the art director with screen layouts, which he or she derives from the node map and subsequent discussions with the writer. They may work on and modify these layouts together. Then, the director communicates the graphic vision of the product by describing the graphic design and style, color palette, fonts, icons, and characters during creative meetings. The director may provide drawings, paintings, photographs, videos, art books, or other samples to show the art director what he or she is looking for. They may review portfolios together or even visit a gallery or museum to get inspiration. This collaboration results in the graphic deliverables described earlier in this chapter.

The director directs the sound designer to identify and audition talent and select music and sound effects for the product. Again, this is based on his or her vision of the product. The director has the "big picture" and must share it with the team so each member can contribute his or her specific deliverable. In the end, the functional specification, the graphic design and the sound design, must coalesce to form a complete and unambiguous product design.

Production Methods

During the design phase, while developing the deliverables with the writer, art director, sound designer, and technical lead, the director devises production methods to employ to produce the art and sound in later phases. The director may, for example, decide that the best method for producing realistic animated characters is to use the process known as motion capture, during which live actors are connected to a device that captures the XYZ polar coordinates of their body joints while they move. This captured data is then applied to computer-generated animated characters, which move in exactly the same manner as the live actors. He or she may want to shoot live actors against a blue screen and then digitize every frame, separate the actors from the background, and composite them with an animated background.

Whenever the director concocts a method to obtain a certain effect, two things are important: that the process works and is suitable for this project and that the producer is aware of the details. The director should inform the producer of the staff, equipment, vendors, and other resources needed for each method so the producer can account for them in the final plan and budget. The director must instruct the team in the prototype and production phases to use these methods properly.

FIGURE 9.11

(a)

(b)

(a) Two live-action characters are shot against a blue screen. (b) Using digital compositing techniques, the blue area is replaced by an image of computer-generated characters to create the final scene.

Daily Walk-Around

The director should meet with team members in groups or individually and provide each with clear direction, ideally at the beginning of each day. The direction should include

- What the team member should work on (make this image, capture this video, record this sound)
- What it should look like or sound like (how big, how long, what palette)
- What method to use to create it (*PhotoShop, Illustrator, SoundEdit 16*)
- What file name to give it
- To announce when it's done so the director can approve it
- Who should get a copy of it or where to store it on the server

Usually, it does not take an artist or sound designer very long to create individual assets, so the director should get into the habit of making daily walk-arounds, visiting all team members to check on their understanding of the directions and their progress.

Pulling It All Together

By the end of the design phase, the director must gather together all of the design deliverables and orchestrate a formal design "pitch" to the client. The design pitch is a carefully planned presentation of the overall design, beginning with the functional specification and including the presentation of audition tapes and video, music samples, character designs, screen designs, and other graphic elements. The technical director may make a presentation of programming issues or even a brief demo, if possible.

The functional specification is usually far too long and detailed to go over page by page, so, if possible, it should be sent to the client several days before the pitch. During the presentation, the director interprets the design node by node on a high level, using the art and sound samples to illustrate the concepts.

This meeting is usually a give-and-take, question-and-answer session. Invariably, the client has suggestions that the producer and director must respond to, making great demands on the art of diplomacy.

The Writer during the Design Phase

At the very epicenter of all design phase activity is the writer. Look again at Figure 9.1 and Figure 9.2. Notice that the writer takes input from multiple sources and crafts a document that is part technical specification, part screenplay, part game design, and part database. It includes diagrams, tables, lists, node maps, algorithms, game logic, dialogue, narration, shot descriptions, pictures, storyboards, and asset names. The writer's readership—the development and management team—has very diverse needs. The writer must think and write logically, analytically, creatively, and, as if that is not enough, relentlessly. The clock is ticking during the design phase, and the writer must gather information from multiple sources, process the information, add creative flair, and write what is essentially a production manual on deadline. Refer back to part one of this book, and in particular Chapter 6, to recall the process and formalities of the functional specification.

Weekly Reports and Versions

As the writer interacts with team members to flesh out the details of each node, the functional specification takes shape. Very shortly after starting this process, the writer becomes the authority on the design, having a clearer picture than anybody else of the totality of the product. The writer must, by reason of this omniscient view of the product, keep the team informed generally about the growth and evolution of the product design. The producer has a special interest in the quantitative growth of the product, the director in the qualitative development. The writer should make formal presentations of the spec at the weekly meeting chaired by the producer. Publishing the spec weekly—especially electronically—is a great idea. Team members will critique the spec from two important perspectives: (1) whether the spec, as written, serves their special needs and (2) whether the design can be improved by tweaking something here or there. The writer should honor team feedback whenever and however possible. The team is the final audience.

Chapter Summary

In this chapter, you learned that the design phase is a team effort, managed by the producer, inspired by the director, and documented by the writer. Artists, sound designers, programmers, content experts, and others contribute their special talents and skills to the design. The prize at the end of this phase is the functional specification, which is the blueprint for the development of the product. The spec, as it is called, describes the product in minute detail.

There are many deliverables, which make their way into the spec. Some, such as screen designs, icon and button designs, and font specifications, are graphic in nature. Others, such as voice casting and music design, are sound deliverables. The node map is the graphical representation of the interactive design. The software evaluation and implementation schedule is a technical deliverable. Together with the dialogue, narration, and action and scene descriptions crafted by the writer, all of these deliverables contribute to the completion of the functional specification.

The spec leads to the creation, in turn, of many other documents, which guide business and project management. The producer analyzes the spec and determines the individual graphic and sound elements to create, putting these details into an asset database. The producer analyzes the asset database and the programming effort and determines the scope of work. He or she then constructs a development plan for the assets and programming. Finally, the producer fashions a final budget based on the development plan.

As usual, the producer has a firm hand on the process, the schedule, and the budget. The director keeps all team members functioning as a unit clearly focused on the creative vision of the final product. The writer absorbs input and contributions from all directions, processes the information, and writes a document that satisfies all readers.

Recommended Reading

Druin, Allison. *Designing Multimedia Environments for Children*. Wiley & Sons: New York, 1996.

Horton, William. *The Icon Book*. Wiley & Sons: New York, 1994.

Laybourne, Kit. *The Animation Book*. Crown: New York, 1979.

Lopuck, Lisa. *Designing Multimedia: A Visual Guide to Multimedia and Online Graphic Design*. Peachpit Press: Berkeley, CA, 1996.

Maestri, George. *Digital Character Animation*. New Riders: Indianapolis, IN, 1996.

Marcus, Aaron. *Graphic Design for Electronic Documents and User Interface*. Addison-Wesley: New York, 1992.

McCloud, Scott. *Understanding Comics: The Invisible Art*. HarperPerennial: New York, 1994.

The Development

Agreement

By J. Dianne Brinson and Mark Radcliffe

Edited by Larry Elin

In this chapter, you will learn about

- Tips for preparing proposals and bids, which lead to development agreements
- Legal issues to consider when entering into a development agreement
- Main sections and clauses in a development agreement and what those clauses mean

This chapter covers the special legal issues that a developer should consider when asked by a client to create a multimedia work. Most of these issues are equally applicable to development agreements between a developer and a publisher. Joint development projects are also covered. This chapter includes annotated versions of the letter of intent and the development agreement. As discussed in Chapter 9, the client and the developer often enter into the interim agreement, which makes it possible to design a product fully during the design phase. At the end of the design phase, the parties enter into the definitive agreement, or contract.

J. Dianne Brinson and Mark Radcliffe, authors of *Multimedia Law and Business Handbook,* graciously contributed the major portion of this chapter, which has been edited to link it more fully to the rest of this book. You will see many items that may need further study, and I recommend their book for that purpose.

The multimedia producer is responsible for the entire project, from beginning to end, and all parts of it, including the relationship with the client. The producer must be conversant with the legal documents that commit the developer to the client for the creation of a product. It is the producer who is responsible for fulfilling all of the terms of the contract.

Proposals and Bids

As discussed in Chapter 8, The Discovery Phase, don't spend a lot of time and effort on a proposal for a potential client without first qualifying the client. Make sure that the client is seriously considering the project and has the ability to pay for the work. Make certain that the person with whom you are dealing has the authority to approve the project. If that person does not have the authority, find out as soon as possible whether the person with authority is really interested in doing the project. Don't start work on the project until the client has signed a written contract. Your proposal to a client—in the form of the top-level design, the preliminary budget, and the preliminary development plan—is an *offer*. Until your client accepts the offer, there is no contract.

Some companies send requests for proposals (RFPs) to several multimedia developers. Responding to an RFP takes considerable time and effort. If you respond with a bid but do not get the contract, you will have no legal basis for getting reimbursement for your costs from the company that sent out the RFP.

Any proposal that you send to a potential client is protected by copyright. However, copyright protection does not cover the ideas used in the bid. If the recipient of a proposal photocopies all or part of your proposal, that's copyright infringement. If the recipient hires another multimedia developer to create a multimedia work based on the ideas used in your proposal, that's not copyright infringement. You may be able to get some protection for a proposal containing novel ideas by getting your potential client to sign a nondisclosure agreement.

Make your proposals in writing. Oral proposals are rarely complete (it is difficult in a phone conversation or face-to-face meeting to remember everything that you need to tell the client). If you make an oral proposal and it is accepted, you still should have the client sign a written contract. If the written contract contains terms that you did not mention in your oral proposal, the client may think that you are trying to change the deal.

Some multimedia developers have a standard proposal format that they use with all clients. The letter of intent, printed later in this chapter, is an example. Using a standard proposal saves time and eliminates the possibility that a key provision will be left out of a particular proposal. The agreements printed in this chapter could serve that purpose for your business, but have them reviewed by your own attorney before doing so.

If the bid you've included in your proposal is accepted, you will be bound by the price and terms of your bid. If you discover that you made a mistake in calculating the bid price—you forgot to add in the cost of hiring a music composer, for example—you will probably still have to do the work at the bid price and absorb the added cost yourself (and that will lower your profit). It is difficult to cancel contracts made through the bid process. This is precisely why the thorough, detailed analysis of the final design, as described in Chapter 8, is so terribly important.

The Contract

An agreement between a developer and a client should always take the form of a written contract signed by both parties. If your written proposal to a client is complete, you and your client can form a contract by having the client sign the proposal to indicate acceptance. You may want to finish your proposals with acceptance instructions, such as, "If you wish to accept this proposal and form a contract on the terms stated in this proposal, please sign below and return this proposal to me." It's permissible for you and your client to make handwritten changes to the proposal or mark provisions out, but both parties should initial any changes or deletions to avoid disputes later.

The balance of this section discusses the issues you should cover in your contract to create a multimedia work for a client.

Deliverables

In both the formal proposal and the contract, be as specific as possible about what you are to create for the client. Vagueness in the proposal and in the contract can camouflage misunderstanding that will come to light when you deliver the finished work to the client.

The inclusion of a detailed statement of deliverables will help you and your client make certain that you agree on the nature, content, quality, and uses of the work you are promising to create. Some deliverables that are frequently found in development agreements are

- Statements of technical issues (choice of programming language, graphic resolution, and so forth)
- Storyboards
- Prototype
- Beta version
- Gold master (final CD-ROM version)

Content

You should discuss the range of content options with the client before you enter into a contract. If the client is expecting you to use expensive content—an excerpt of Michael Jackson singing "Bad," for example—the contract should state that requirement (and you should raise your price or get the client to reimburse you for the costly license fees). Be careful not to commit yourself to obtaining rights in specific works, because those works may not be available for licensing. If the client requests specific works, make sure that you have the right to substitute different works if the requested works are not available.

Licensing costs for obtaining permission to use content owned by third parties can be substantial. It may be possible to obtain suitable material relatively inexpensively from stock houses and libraries.

Deadlines and Delivery Schedule

The contract should state when you must deliver the finished project to the client. In setting deadlines, remember that it will probably take more time than you expect to clear the rights to any third-party content that is used and to make certain that the components fit together.

Make certain that the deadlines are realistic. Serious delay on your part can be grounds for termination by the client—especially if the contract states that time is of the essence for performance of contract obligations. If the client is entitled to terminate the contract because of your failure to deliver the project on time, you may have to absorb the costs that went into the project before the termination. Normally, the client will have no obligation to reimburse you for those costs.

Payment

The contract should state the amount and form of your payment—whether it is on a time-and-materials basis, a fixed-price basis, or a royalty or other basis—and when payment is due. Some contracts provide for installment payments (for example, one third upon execution, one third at the delivery of the gold disk, and one third when the final product is accepted by the client). Other contracts call for payments at fixed development milestones, such as upon approval of the art and animation or upon approval of the alpha disc.

Acceptance Clause

For your protection, the proposal and contract should provide a procedure for objections to any deliverables. It's a good idea to require that objections be made in writing. There should also be a deadline for objections to the finished project. You need to know that after a certain period of time passes, it will be too late for the client to say, "I won't accept this. Do it again."

Ownership of Copyright

One of the most important issues to address in the contract is who will own the copyright. By addressing this issue in the written agreement, you will eliminate future legal disputes over ownership. In the next two subsections, Client Ownership and Developer Ownership, we'll discuss the ownership options.

Client Ownership

Your client does not obtain ownership of the copyright by paying for its development. For copyright purposes, when you create a multimedia work for a client, you work as an independent contractor, not as the client's employee. A work created by an independent contractor for a client is owned by the independent contractor unless the client obtains an assignment of the copyright.

A work can be automatically owned by the client only in very limited circumstances: if the agreement describes the work as a "work made for hire" and if the work is one of eight special types of works listed in the Copyright Act's definition of specially commissioned works made for hire. These rules apply only in the United States.

Assigning the Copyright

If the client is to own the rights in the multimedia work, the contract should provide for an assignment of these rights to the client. You should be prepared to sign a separate short-form copyright assignment for filing with the Copyright Office. Your client may want you to grant it a power of attorney authorizing the client to execute and file assignment documents. If you are married, live in a community property state, and work as an individual, your client may ask that you get your spouse to sign a statement acknowledging that he or she does not claim any ownership interest in the work's copyright. This sort of statement is known as a quitclaim.

Legal Effect of Assignments

If you agree to assign the copyright in the multimedia work to the client, you will not be able to sell copies of that work to other clients. Unless you retain the modification right or have the client grant you a license to modify the work to create new works, you will not be able to modify the work for sale to other clients. Once you assign the copyright, the client will have the exclusive rights to reproduce the work, distribute it, publicly perform it, publicly display it, and modify it for use in derivative works. However, you will still be able to reuse ideas that you used in the work.

Retaining Ownership of Components

If you are creating a multimedia work to fill a client's special needs, you may not object to giving the client ownership of the copyright. You may, however, want to retain ownership of components—for example, software engines—that you created for the work, or at least reserve the right to use the components in future projects. Unless you retain ownership of the components or get a license from your client to reuse them, your use of the components in future projects will infringe the client's copyright.

Example   Developer created an interactive training program that used a software engine for manipulating game images. Developer assigned the copyright in the work to Big Co. If Developer uses the software engine in a new multimedia project without getting a license from Big Co., Developer will be infringing Big Co.'s copyright.

Third-Party Components

Assigning the copyright to the client does not give the client ownership of components owned by third parties. You cannot assign rights that you do not own.

Example   The interactive training program that Developer created for Big Co. contained an excerpt of a song written by Joe Composer. Since Developer did not own the copyright in Joe's song, Developer's assignment of its copyright in the program to Big Co. did not give Big Co. ownership of the copyright in Joe's song.

Demo Rights and Credits

If the copyright is to be owned by the client, you may want to include a clause in the contract authorizing you to retain a copy of the work to show to future clients. Such demonstrations are public performances of the work. You may also want to specify how your credit should appear in the client's copies of the multimedia work.

Developer Ownership

If you are to retain the copyright in the multimedia work, the contract should state that you retain copyright ownership. If the contract says nothing about ownership of the copyright, you, as an independent contractor, will automatically own the copyright in the work. However, including a statement to that effect in your contract will help you avoid misunderstandings with clients who think that ordering and paying for a work gets them ownership of the copyright.

If the client contributes copyrightable material to the work, the client may be a joint author and thus a joint owner of the copyright. Stating in the contract that you will own the copyright in the entire work may help you avoid joint ownership claims by clients.

Reimbursement of License Fees and Costs

The contract should state whether any license fees, union reuse fees, and other costs you incur in creating the multimedia work will be reimbursed by the client.

Warranties and Indemnities

The client will probably insist that the contract include representations and warranties from you. Typical warranties in development agreements are as follows:

- You have the right to enter into the agreement.
- You have title to the multimedia work and all intellectual property rights in the work.
- You have the right to grant the client the assignment of copyright or to license the work.
- The work does not infringe third parties' intellectual property rights.

Warranty clauses typically include an indemnity provision in which the developer promises to indemnify and hold the client harmless for the breach of any of the warranties (in other words, pay for all costs arising out of the breach of the warranties).

Reason for Warranties

Clients have good reason for asking for warranties and indemnities. If you infringe any third-party intellectual property rights in making a multimedia work, your client will become an infringer by using the work (even though innocent of intent to infringe).

Example   Developer created a kiosk-type multimedia work called Cheese Expert for client, owner of a gourmet grocery. Cheese Expert contains pictures of Minnie Mouse and Mickey Mouse. Developer did not obtain permission from Disney to use Minnie and Mickey. Client's "public performance" of Cheese Expert in the grocery store infringes Disney's copyright and trademark rights.

Levels of Warranties

There are three levels of intellectual property warranties:

1. *Absolute warranty.* "The work does not infringe any third-party intellectual property rights."
2. *Know-or-should know warranty.* "To the best of my knowledge, the work does not infringe any third-party intellectual property rights."
3. *Actual-knowledge warranty.* "To my actual knowledge, the work does not infringe any third-party intellectual property rights."

As a developer, you should try to negotiate for the know-or-should know warranty or actual-knowledge warranty rather than the unlimited absolute warranty. Although you should do everything possible to ensure that your multimedia work does not infringe third parties' intellectual property rights, you can never be certain that a work composed of many components does not infringe others' copyrights. For example:

- The employee who created the software code for your work may have reused software code that is owned by a former employer.

- An independent contractor that you hired to create a component may have copied someone else's work.

- A composer who granted you a license to use his music throughout the world may turn out not to be the owner of the copyright of the music in all countries.

You should try to get absolute warranties from all your independent contractors and licensors.

Duration of Warranties

The contract should state whether the warranties continue during the term of the contract or are limited to the date on which the final product is delivered to the client.

Patent Warranties

Consider whether you want to warrant that your work does not infringe any patents. Patent applications in the United States are secret, so there is no way you can find out what patents might be granted during the term of your agreement. If you give a warranty that your work does not infringe any patents, you may be liable for infringing a later-issued patent that you did not know about. You may want to limit your exposure. One way to do that is to warrant only that, to the best of your knowledge, the multimedia work does not infringe any patents in effect on the date the finished product is delivered to the client.

Other Important Provisions

The contract should also contain several other provisions, as explained in the next subsections.

Modifications.   The contract should state who is responsible for correcting performance errors in the multimedia work. It should state whether the client has any right to require you to make changes to the multimedia work after it is delivered and whether the client must pay for modifications.

If you are retaining ownership of the copyright, the contract should state whether the client has the right to modify the work to correct errors. If the client does not have that right, modification by the client may infringe your modification right. If the contract provides that the client will own the copyright, the client as owner of the modification right will automatically have the right to make changes.

Many development contracts provide that the developer will make changes to correct performance errors for free during a warranty period and will provide maintenance for an annual fee after the warranty period ends.

Merger Clause.   The contract should include a merger clause to help eliminate claims that the real deal is something other than what is stated in the contract (for example, an earlier proposal that was modified during negotiations).

Termination Clause.   The parties may wish to provide that the contract can be terminated for cause (which should be defined) or even at will.

The termination provision should state how notice of breach that justifies termination should be given. The provision should include a "cure period" during which the breaching party has a right to cure the breach and avoid termination of the contract.

Nondisclosure Agreement.   If the client will be giving you access to proprietary or confidential information or trade secrets, you may be asked to include a nondisclosure agreement in the contract. If you will be disclosing trade secrets and other proprietary information to your client as well, you and your client should both sign a mutual nondisclosure agreement.

The nondisclosure agreement should state what information is to be considered confidential information and how confidential information must be treated (for example, whether the receiving party can disclose the information to all employees or only to certain employees or to consultants). It should also state the duration of the obligation to keep the information confidential.

Generally, confidential information is defined in one of two ways: (1) information marked confidential by its owner, or (2) information that the receiving party knows or should know is confidential. If you use the first definition, you need to include a method for identifying confidential information disclosed orally or by exhibition.

The following types of information are generally specifically excluded from the definition of confidential information:

- Information that is in the public domain at the time it is disclosed to the receiving party
- Information that later enters the public domain (but not through the fault of the receiving party)

- Information that is required to be disclosed by a court or government
- Information that is received from a third party without restrictions on disclosure

Another exception, which is more controversial, is "independent development." This is information that is independently developed by the receiving party. Some agreements require the party claiming that information is not confidential under this exception to bear the burden of proving that it independently developed the information.

Disclaimer of Implied Warranties. When goods are sold, according to the law of every state except Louisiana, certain warranties are implied as part of the transaction unless they are disclaimed. Because a contract for the development of a multimedia work could be considered a contract for the sale of goods, implied warranties may apply to a development agreement unless they are disclaimed.

Remedies. You may want to limit the remedies available to the client should you breach the contract.

Battle of the Forms. In the business world, contracts are often created based on an exchange of forms. The offeror sends a proposal to the offeree, and the offeree accepts by sending back a purchase order form. While the purchase order normally contains a number of terms that match the proposal's terms (price and delivery date, for example), it will generally include additional or contradictory terms as well.

The legal rules for determining what terms are included in a contract created this way are complex (attorneys call the process the battle of the forms). To avoid the battle of the forms, don't create a contract with a client by exchanging documents containing inconsistent terms. Make every effort to get the client to sign your proposal or negotiate a separate contract. If the client must use a purchase order, read it carefully, including its fine print, as soon as you receive it. If the purchase order form contains terms that are unacceptable to you, notify the client of your objection as soon as possible.

Joint Development Agreements

Individuals or companies that plan to work together on multimedia projects should enter into written joint development agreements documenting the terms of the relationship. A joint development agreement should state who will do what, when each party's performance is due, and how much time each party will devote to the project (particularly if the parties have other jobs or other projects).

In the United States, the Copyright Act provides that joint authors of a work have equal undivided interests in the work's copyright. However, the parties to a joint development agreement can provide that royalties and profits from a work will be divided in a manner other than 50–50—and one party can assign its interest in the copyright to the other.

According to U.S. copyright law, each single joint owner can, without getting the consent of the other owners, grant nonexclusive licenses to third parties to use the work in nondestructive ways. Nondestructive use is a use that does not diminish the value of the work. A joint owner who grants a license must share any royalties received with the other owners. Joint owners can provide by contract that the consent of all owners is required for granting licenses.

The rules for joint ownership of copyright vary from country to country. In many countries in Europe (Germany and France, for example), the consent of all joint owners of a copyright is necessary to obtain an enforceable license. This rule applies even if the work was created in the United States by U.S. citizens. This issue is very complex. You should try to avoid joint ownership if the work will be distributed overseas.

One risk that joint development agreements pose is that it is sometimes difficult to draw the line between a joint development agreement and a general partnership. Partners in a general partnership are all liable for the debts of a partnership. To avoid this problem, many joint development agreements state that the parties are not forming a general partnership. The purpose is to protect each developer from liability for general debts of the codevelopers (debts arising out of ventures or projects other than the joint development project).

The Letter of Intent

The letter of intent, or deal memo, is a temporary instrument. It gives both parties certain assurances moving forward. Since it includes references to nearly every important issue the two parties will have to agree on eventually, the parties can easily change the wording of any term to suit their current purposes. The phrase "to be negotiated later in good faith" is sometimes substituted for terms neither party is prepared to deal with immediately. If most of the terms in the letter are left intact, legal affairs from both parties have the basis of a definitive agreement—a contract.

Anatomy of the Letter of Intent

Following is a sample letter of intent. Although used successfully on many projects as an agreement between two parties, no one should use this agreement without first having his or her own attorney look it over. Comments are provided throughout to explain or call attention to important details in the agreement.

The letter of intent lists a number of issues the two parties agree on. The letter simply states that the two parties intend to reach a definitive agreement after certain details are ironed out.

Letter of Intent

This Letter of Intent summarizes the principal terms and conditions of the proposed Agreement between _____, (hereafter "Company"), and _____, a _____ corporation located at _____ (hereafter "Developer"), referred to jointly in this document as the "Parties." Subject to the conditions set forth below and to the successful negotiation and execution of a definitive agreement (the "Agreement"), which will fully reflect the understanding and agreement of the Parties, the Company and Developer intend to consummate the following Letter of Intent:

The "Work-for-Hire" provision in an agreement carries important copyright ownership issues. Everything done by the Developer under this basis becomes the property of the Company, unless it is specifically held out of the agreement.

1. Nature of Proposed Agreement

The Company intends to engage Developer to provide development services to produce a multimedia computer software product (the "Product"). The Top-Level Design for the Product and its target platform are attached to this letter in attachment "A". The Parties agree to make every effort to complete the Product according to the Preliminary Schedule attached to this letter as attachment "B". The development services will be provided by Developer on a "Work-for-Hire" basis for a fixed Development Fee, which is currently targeted by the Parties at approximately $_____. The preliminary budget is attached to this document as attachment "C".

The Parties acknowledge that the precise amount of the Development Fee and a Final Delivery Schedule cannot be determined until a Detailed Design for the Product (Functional Specification) and a Development Plan based upon that design are completed. The Parties, therefore, agree to develop the Product in Phases.

2. Development Phases

Developer will develop the Product in Phases. Each Phase has specific Deliverables from the Company and from Developer. The development will proceed through the following three phases: Design Phase, Prototype Phase, and Production Phase. Each Phase contains progress milestones, which trigger a payment for development services from the Company to Developer.

3. Design Phase

In the Design Phase, Developer produces and delivers The Detailed Design Specifications ("Specifications") which includes the Functional Specification document, screen layouts and designs, character designs, and color treatments. The Specifications determine the development plan, budget, delivery milestones, approval process, change order process, and other items in the Agreement. During the Design Phase, Developer creates the Development Plan and the Final Delivery Schedule and submits the Final Development Fee as a firm, fixed price.

The Parties acknowledge that the Design Phase is an iterative, subjective, creative process. Using the Top-Level Design as a point of departure, and affording The Company meaningful consultation, Developer will create Version 1.0 of the Detailed Design Specification. Developer will present the Specification to the Company. The Company will respond to the Detailed Design Specification, and Developer will modify Version 1.0 and produce Version 1.1 of the Detailed Design Specification.

The Company will compensate Developer $_____ for delivery of the Detailed Design Specification through Version 1.1 of the Detailed Design Specification. Thereafter, the Company will compensate Developer on a time and materials basis for subsequent Versions to the Detailed Design Specification. Developer will quote reasonable rates and estimates for completion of requested subsequent Versions.

4. Prototype Phase

In the Prototype Phase, Developer produces and delivers a Proof of Concept—a working "mini-" version of the product delivered in CD-ROM format, which includes final art, sound, animation, video, and software. The Proof of Concept is a subset of the final product—representing no more than 10% of the total size of the final product. The Proof of Concept will be suitable for demonstration purposes, focus testing, and preliminary marketing of the product. The parties acknowledge that the Proof of Concept is used to determine if the design of the product is acceptable and the intended outcome of the product can be realized if development moves forward. The parties may determine to redesign the product upon review of the Proof of Concept. In such an event the parties will negotiate in good faith any modifications to the design, the development plan, or the development budget.

The Company will compensate Developer $_____ for delivery of the Proof of Concept through Version 1.1 of the Proof of Concept. Thereafter, The Company will compensate Developer on a time and materials basis for subsequent Versions to the Proof of Concept. Developer will quote reasonable rates and estimates for completion of requested subsequent Versions.

5. Production Phase

In the Production Phase, Developer completes all art, animation and sound development, title engineering and quality assurance. Developer performs all work during the Production Phase according to the final, approved Detailed Design Specification. Developer affords the Company ample and regular access to the work to assure conformance with the Detailed Design Specification.

In the following paragraph, the parties agree that the Company will pay a Development Fee to the developer for its work, but that the total fee may change after the final design is complete. In addition, the Company will pay the Developer a royalty (a percentage of net profits) after recouping its costs, including the Development Fee.

6. Payments and Terms

Payments are made according to a schedule agreed upon by the Parties. The Agreement will provide that as compensation in full for the services performed and rights granted by Developer thereunder, the Company will pay Developer a Development Fee of approximately $_____. The exact fee will be determined during the Design Phase, and will be based upon analysis and evaluation of the final, approved Detailed Design Specification.

    The Company will also pay Developer a royalty of ___% of the Company's net revenues on the Product. "Net Revenues" will be defined in the Agreement, but will generally be equal to all sums received or due to the Company with respect to the Product, less cost of goods (Computed according to GAAP), credits for returns or promotional goods (subject to reasonable limitations), taxes, insurance, and shipping. In addition, before disbursing any royalties to Developer, the Company will be entitled to recoup all advances paid to Developer and to recoup other mutually agreed upon development costs paid by the Company.

One of the big issues a developer must reach agreement on is how design changes are paid for after development starts. Some contracts allow the client complete freedom to change and modify the product at any time, with no increase in cost or time. The following paragraph spells out how changes will be handled. If the client agrees in principle to this paragraph, the developer can sleep more easily.

7. Changes and Modifications

During the Production Phase of development of the Product, the Company may request certain changes and modifications. Changes and Modifications will generally fall into two categories: (1) Changes that must be made by Developer to the Product so that the Product conforms to the approved Detailed Design Specification or (2) Changes to the Detailed Design Specification.

Developer will make all changes necessary to conform the Product to the Detailed Design Specification at no cost.

Changes to the Detailed Design Specification will be considered either "Soft" Changes or "Hard" Changes. "Soft" Changes are those changes which do not materially affect the cost or time for development, and will be made at no additional cost to the agreed upon Development Fee. "Hard" Changes are those changes that deviate significantly from the Specification, add features or functionality, or materially add to the cost and time of Development. Developer will quote a reasonable additional fee to make "Hard" Changes, and the Company will pay for any elected "Hard" changes at the next agreed-upon payment milestone.

8. Expenses

The Agreement will provide that each party will bear its own expenses of performance.

9. Ownership

As between Developer and the Company, Company will be the sole owner of the Product and Developer will not own any part thereof. Developer will license to the Company all rights with respect to the Product which are necessary for the Company to reproduce, manufacture, market, and distribute the Product via computer media worldwide on the PC and Macintosh platforms. All rights not expressly granted in the Agreement will remain with Developer, including the right to develop versions of the Product for other platforms (including, but not limited to, interactive transmission) and the right to develop other versions of Product for the platforms described above (including, but not limited to "sequels"), provided that the Company will have a right of first refusal to publish any of the foregoing versions and to publish any subsidiary product (including, but not limited to, merchandise). All performers, employees, and independent contractors of Developer will sign agreements conveying sufficient rights to Developer so that no third party will have any colorable claim of rights with respect to the Product, and in particular, no right to receive royalties or other payments. The Agreement will also include warranties, representations and indemnities concerning Developer's ownership, noninfringement, and other matters.

10. Subcontract

The Company understands and agrees that Developer may subcontract certain portions of the development work.

The only binding portion of this Letter of Intent is paragraph 11, below, which initiates the Design Phase for a fixed fee, and paragraph 13, which guarantees that the agreement will be kept confidential.

11. Work during Pending Negotiations Notwithstanding Nonbinding Nature of Letter of Intent

The parties agree that Developer will commence work on the Design Phase of the Product promptly upon execution of this Letter of Intent and payment to Developer by the Company for The Detailed Design Specification in the amount of $_____. Developer will proceed diligently and use its reasonable best efforts to prepare the Product until such time as this Letter of Intent expires.

It is the intention of the parties that this Paragraph 11 shall be binding upon the parties upon execution of this Letter of Intent by both parties, notwithstanding the nonbinding nature of this Letter of Intent, and neither construed as creating, an obligation to enter into the Agreement or to otherwise proceed with the transactions proposed by this Letter of Intent beyond the limited extent agreed to under this Paragraph 11.

12. End User Technical Support

The Agreement will provide that the Company is to be solely responsible for providing technical support to end users of the Product but that Developer will provide reasonable assistance to the Company with respect to any end user problems for a period of 90 days after shipment of the product to retail channels. The parties may negotiate additional technical support to end users on a time and materials basis.

13. Confidentiality

The parties agree that this Letter of Intent, and the Agreement, if any, will be maintained in confidence by both parties except to the extent of any mutually agreed upon disclosure of information. The Agreement will contain a like provision.

14. Final Agreement

It is the intention of the parties that they will negotiate in good faith and execute the final Agreement by _____. In the event that the parties are unable to conclude a final Agreement by that date, this Letter of Intent and the intentions set forth herein shall expire.

This Letter of Intent merely summarizes certain of the principal terms and conditions proposed by the parties with respect to the transactions contemplated by the parties. This Letter of Intent is not an offer to enter into a contract, and no party's signature hereon is intended to be, and shall not be deemed to be, an acceptance of any offer by the other party. Except as to Paragraph 11 and Paragraph 13, the parties hereby expressly agree and acknowledge that this Letter of Intent is merely an expression of intent among the parties and not intended to be legally binding and that the actions contemplated by the Letter of Intent shall in all respects be subject to the execution of a definitive agreement in form and substance satisfactory to the parties and their respective counsel. Accordingly, except as to Paragraph 11 and Paragraph 13, the understandings contained herein will become binding, if at all, only at such time as such agreement has been duly executed by the parties, subject to any conditions set forth in such agreement being satisfied or waived.

Developer   Publisher

_____   _____
Signature: Signature:

_____   _____
Title: Title:

_____   _____
Date: Date:

Schedule A
Top-Level Design

The top-level design of the product is inserted here. It forms the basis of the agreement for what the product will be like. The top-level design will be used as the jumping-off point for the functional specification, which will form the basis of the final definitive agreement, the contract.

Schedule B
Preliminary Schedule

Note that the preliminary schedule and budget are very rough. Until there is a detailed design, it is impossible to arrive at a detailed schedule and budget. The dates and dollars are ballpark estimates, based on the top-level design.

Task	Approximate Time
Design phase Development of Functional Specification	8 weeks from start
Prototype phase Development of Proof of Concept	10 weeks from approval of Functional Specification
Production phase Art Begins	Upon approval of prototype

Art & Sound Finished	20 weeks from beginning art and sound
Alpha 1	16 weeks from beginning production phase
Alpha 2	18 weeks from beginning production phase
Beta 1	20 weeks from beginning production phase
Beta 2	22 weeks from beginning production phase
Gold Master	26 weeks from beginning production phase

Schedule C
Production Phases and Milestones
$400,000 Target Budget

Task	*Approximate Cost*
Design phase	
Development of Functional Specification	$ 40,000
Prototype phase	
Development of Proof of Concept	$ 75,000
Production phase	
Art Begins	——
Art & Sound Finished	$100,000
Alpha 1	$ 75,000
Alpha 2	$ 25,000
Beta 1	$ 25,000
Beta 2	$ 25,000
Gold Master	$ 35,000
Total	$400,000

Development and Publishing Agreement

This agreement has been used by a multimedia publisher for external major development deals in which the publisher is paying virtually the entire cost of the development. This agreement is possible if the developer and client have a detailed product design and the developer has been able to determine the precise cost and schedule. Do not use this agreement unless an attorney has examined it first.

Development and Publishing Agreement

This Agreement is entered into on the ____ day of _____, 2000, by and between Publisher, _____, a _____, Corporation with offices _____, ("Publisher") and _____ a _____ corporation with a place of business at _____. ("Developer").

Recitals:

Developer has proposed development of the interactive multimedia product described in Appendix A with the working name _____ which Developer is desirous of producing and distributing in interactive CD-ROM or other interactive form ("Title");

Publisher is in the business of developing, publishing and distributing CD-ROM-based and other electronic products. Developer is desirous of having Publisher provide funding to develop the Title and to publish and distribute the Title on the terms and conditions set forth herein, and Publisher is willing to provide such funding on the terms and conditions set forth herein;

NOW, THEREFORE, in consideration of the premises, conditions, covenants and warranties herein contained, the parties agree as follows:

1. Definitions

1.1 **"Add-On Products"** shall mean electronic software/multimedia products related to and intended to work with the Title.

1.2 **"Advances"** shall mean all funds advanced by Publisher to Developer to create the Title (as defined below) or Add-On Products under this Agreement.

1.3 **"Bundled Copies"** shall mean copies of the Title or Add-On Products distributed bundled with hardware, software or other products of Publisher or a third party.

1.4 **"Confidential Information"** shall mean the information of either party which is disclosed to the other party pursuant to this Agreement, in written form marked "confidential," or if disclosed orally, confirmed in a writing summarizing such information within thirty (30) days of disclosure and marked "confidential." By way of example and without limiting the generality of the foregoing, Confidential Information shall include trade secrets, know-how, inventions, algorithms, structure and organization of software programs, source code, schematics, contracts, customer lists, financial information, sales and marketing plans, and business plans.

1.5 **"Cost of Goods"** shall mean Publisher's actual cost of manufacturing and packaging copies of the Title or Add-On Products up to the time of shipment into the distribution channel, including the duplication costs for copies of the Title or Add-On Products on optical or magnetic media, packaging materials, manuals and other collateral materials and program components.

1.6 *"Deliverable Item"* shall mean each of the program components, materials or designs set forth in the relevant Delivery Schedule that Developer shall deliver to Publisher in accordance with the terms of this Agreement.

1.7 *"Delivery Schedule"* shall mean the schedule of Deliverable Items set forth in Exhibit B.

1.8 *"Effective Date"* shall mean the date first set forth above.

1.9 *"Net Revenue"* shall mean all revenues recognized in accordance with generally accepted accounting principles relating to the distribution or sale of the Title or Add-On Products or other products related thereto by Publisher or any of its affiliated, associated or subsidiary companies, less (a) units returned as defective, as a result of errors in billing or shipment, or otherwise returned in the ordinary course of business, (b) Cost of Goods, and (c) taxes collected by Publisher in connection with the Title or Add-On Products or other Title-related products for payment to any governmental authority. The foregoing deductions shall be consistent with the amounts paid in the industry for such items.

1.10 *"QA Testing"* shall mean quality assurance testing of an alpha or beta candidate or gold master for identification of bugs or errors.

1.11 *"Retail Copies"* shall mean all copies of the Title or Add-On Products distributed to third parties, except Bundled Copies, promotional copies and returns.

1.12 *"Specifications"* shall mean the functional specifications and description of features and content of the Title as set forth in Exhibit A.

1.13 *"Territory"* shall mean the entire world.

1.14 *"Title"* shall mean the interactive multimedia product described in Exhibit A known by the working name "_____." The Title shall also include any product for which Publisher exercises its right of first refusal as further provided below.

2. Advances.

2.1 Publisher agrees to pay to Developer an advance against royalties of _____ United States dollars (US$_____), to be paid in installments upon approval of deliverables on the schedule set forth in Exhibit B. Developer agrees that this advance shall be sufficient to produce a complete game without live action video. The amount of this advance may be adjusted as follows:

2.2.1 Publisher and Developer agree to meet and confer regarding reducing the amount of this advance and modifying the Delivery Schedule in the event that, during the development of the Title, it appears that the Title can be developed in a shorter time frame or at a lower cost than presently anticipated.

2.2.2   Budgeted amounts included in the advance for salaries and overhead expenses such as office space shall be reduced pro rata and/or charged against other projects on which Developer is working concurrently with the Development of the Title under this Agreement.

2.2   Advances for Video. Publisher shall have the option, in its sole discretion, to add live action video to the present specifications and budget. It is presently anticipated that the additional cost of such video would be approximately US$_____–US$_____. It is also agreed by the parties that the exercise of this option by Publisher shall not result in an extension of the delivery dates for the overall Title. To the extent that, at the time of exercise of the option, Developer believes that the schedule will slip as a result, Developer shall inform Publisher of this fact and the parties shall meet and confer regarding any adjustment to the Delivery Schedule. Developer shall investigate actual costs relating to such video, and shall rework the script to include such video, and shall submit a final cost estimate and script including such video at the time that game play is implemented and demonstrated on the target machine. Publisher shall make a decision within a reasonable time thereafter as to whether to include such video. If Publisher decides to do so, the parties shall mutually agree on a schedule of milestone deliverables and Advances relating to such video.

3. Proprietary Rights and Grant of License

3.1   The Title and all revisions thereof, if any, and all original music composed for and utilized in the Title are written and commissioned at Publisher's request and direction, and shall be considered works-for-hire.

3.2   All rights to the Title, including but not limited to the copyright, shall be the property of Publisher or its assignee. Publisher shall have all rights in the Title, including the right to make or license derivative works, and the right to produce the Title and derivative works in all forms now known or hereafter developed. Developer shall not acquire any right, title or interest in or to the Title in any format through the exercise of any rights or performance of any obligations by Developer hereunder. Publisher shall have the right to revise the Title, and Developer shall not have any right to make revisions of the completed Title without Publisher's prior written consent.

3.3   Developer grants and assigns Publisher any and all rights Developer may now have or may be deemed to have in the future with respect to the Title, including but not limited to the copyright to the Title and any and all portions thereof. To the extent that any such rights do not automatically vest in Publisher as works for hire and are not presently assignable, Developer agrees to assign such rights to Publisher in the future, and Developer agrees to deliver to Publisher at Publisher's expense all documents reasonably necessary to effect the assignment of Developer's rights contemplated herein.

3.4   Publisher retains the exclusive right to distribute, market, sell, display, advertise, and promote the Title in perpetuity throughout the world. The timing and manner of exercise of these rights shall be solely within the discretion of Publisher.

3.5   Notwithstanding the foregoing, Publisher recognizes that the underlying computer software engine in the game will be developed based on certain existing and future-developed proprietary computer software developed by Developer. Publisher shall be the owner of all work performed on such engine specific to the Title, and shall be granted a nonexclusive, perpetual, royalty-free, fully paid up license to use the engine in every way and manner contemplated under this Agreement in order to exploit the Title and Publisher's rights in the Title.

3.6   Publisher grants Developer the exclusive worldwide license to exploit the noninteractive game uses of the Title subject to Publisher's prior written approval and payment of a royalty to Publisher as provided below.

3.7   Developer's First Option. Developer shall have a first option to develop any Add-On Products and/or derivative interactive works which Publisher desires to have developed by an outside developer. For purposes of this section, "first option" shall mean that Publisher will promptly notify Developer in writing of the nature of such proposed Add-On Product or derivative interactive work. Publisher shall give Developer the right to develop such Add-On Product and shall negotiate the terms and conditions of such development in good faith. If Publisher and Developer are unable to agree upon the terms and conditions within thirty (30) days of Publisher's written notice, then Publisher shall be free to approach any other developer or third party regarding development of such Add-On Product or derivative interactive work.

4. Royalties

4.1   Royalties on the Title. The Advances shall be recouped by Publisher from royalties on revenues relating to the Title and Add-On Products. No royalties shall be paid to Developer relating to the Title or Add-On Products until all of the Advances paid to Developer have been recouped by Publisher. Publisher shall pay or credit royalties to Developer at the following rates:

    4.1.1   _____ % of Net Revenue on the Title up to _____ dollars (US$ _____);

    4.1.2   _____ % of Net Revenue on the Title from _____ dollars up to _____ dollars (US$ _____);

    4.1.3   _____ % of Net Revenue on the Title above _____ dollars (US$_____);

4.1.4 _____ % of Net Revenue on Add-On Products if the Add-On Product is created by a developer other than Developer;

4.1.5 _____ % of Net Revenue on Add-On Products if the Add-On Product is created by Developer.

4.2 Royalties from Developer to Publisher. Developer will pay Publisher a royalty based on all revenues generated from Developer's uses of the Title under the license granted by Publisher above. The amount of such royalty will be negotiated by the parties in good faith at the time Developer determines the nature of the ancillary product.

4.3 All royalty payments shall be made in U.S. dollars by a check drawn on a U.S. bank.

4.4 The above royalty rates shall include all royalties to be paid to third parties ("content royalties"). It will be Developer's responsibility to insure that all content and other third party royalties are paid when due.

4.5 Publisher shall render to Developer on a quarterly basis, within forty-five (45) days after the end of each calendar quarter during which the Title or Add-On Product is sold, a written statement of the royalties due to Developer with respect to such Title or Add-On Product. Such statement shall be accompanied by a remittance of the amount due, if any. Developer shall have the right, upon reasonable request, to review those records of Publisher necessary to verify the royalties paid no more than once per calendar year. Any such audit will be conducted at Developer's expense, by certified public accountants, and at such times and in such a manner as to not unreasonably interfere with Publisher's normal operations, and Developer and its auditor shall be required to treat information revealed during the audit as Confidential Information; provided, however, that if any such audit reveals an error of at least 5% in the payment of royalties, then Publisher shall pay the costs of the audit. If a deficiency is shown by such audit, Publisher shall immediately pay that deficiency. Nonpayment of any deficiency within thirty (30) business days of the date on which Publisher receives notice of such deficiency shall constitute a material breach of this Agreement. Once royalties become due from Developer to Publisher pursuant to section 4.2, statements and remittance of royalties from Developer to Publisher shall also be made according to the terms of this paragraph.

5. Development and Approval Process

5.1 Developer agrees to develop the Title with Publisher in accordance with the terms of this Agreement and Exhibit A, and to deliver the Title and the Deliverable Items set forth in Exhibit B to Publisher for approval, in Publisher's sole discretion, in the manner and on the dates specified in the Delivery Schedule. Developer and Publisher agree that no major additional enhancements to the Specifications set forth in Exhibit A will be required or made by Developer without the parties' prior mutual consent.

5.2   Upon receipt of each Deliverable Item except the alpha, beta, or golden master of a Title, Publisher shall, within ten (10) business days, provide Developer with either:

5.2.1   Written approval of the Deliverable Item; or

5.2.2   A written list of changes that must be made before Publisher will approve such Deliverable Item.

Failure to approve or provide a written list of changes within ten (10) days shall constitute approval of the Deliverable Item.

5.3   No Deliverable Item shall be considered to be approved by Publisher and no payment will be made for completion of such Deliverable Item until Developer has received written confirmation of such approval from Publisher, or a failure to approve or provide a written list of changes has occurred, and all preceding Deliverable Items have been approved by Publisher. If any Deliverable Item requires changes before it will be approved by Publisher, the steps set forth above shall be repeated until such Deliverable Item is accepted, or until Publisher exercises its termination or completion rights under section 5.7 below.

5.4   The alpha, beta, and golden masters of a Title must be fully tested by Developer for conformity with the Specifications prior to delivery to Publisher, and must meet the following criteria:

5.4.1   The initial alpha candidates must be delivered on or before the date set forth in Exhibit B, and must be fully feature and content complete, according to the description set forth in the Specifications.

5.4.2   The initial beta candidates must be delivered on or before the date set forth in Exhibit B and shall be feature frozen and contain all agreed upon changes from alpha and implement all corrections of any bugs or errors identified during QA testing of alpha that cause system or program crashes, or otherwise significantly interfere with the user's ability to use and enjoy the Title (priority 1 bugs).

5.4.3   The golden masters shall be delivered promptly upon implementation of all remaining corrections of previously identified and agreed upon bugs or errors.

5.5   Upon receipt of the initial alpha, beta, and golden master candidates, Publisher shall, within ten (10) business days, provide Developer with either:

5.5.1   Written acceptance into QA testing of the alpha or beta candidates, which will trigger Publisher's payment obligations, if any, as set forth in Exhibit B; or

5.5.2   Written acceptance of the golden master; or

5.5.3   A written list of changes that must be made before Publisher will accept the alpha or beta candidates into testing, or the golden master.

Publisher's failure to approve or reject the candidate or golden master in writing within ten (10) business days of receipt shall constitute approval.

5.6   If changes are required by Publisher before Publisher will accept the alpha or beta candidate into testing, or accept the golden master, then the steps set forth above shall be repeated until the alpha or beta is accepted into QA testing, or the golden master is accepted, or until Publisher terminates the agreement or exercises its completion rights, as described in section 5.7 below.

5.7   If Developer has not provided an acceptable Deliverable Item or alpha, beta, or golden master candidate within four (4) weeks of the date the Deliverable Item or candidate was originally due to be delivered, or if Publisher reasonably believes that the development of the Title is or will be at any time more than five percent (5%) over budget, Publisher shall be entitled to terminate this Agreement or exercise its completion rights as follows: If Publisher chooses to complete the Title, then Developer shall deliver to Publisher within five (5) business days of receipt of notice from Publisher the most current version of the source code for the Title, together with all related development and production materials, including video and audio master tapes, scripts, documentation, notes, hint sheets, and bug reports, and Developer shall cooperate fully with Publisher's efforts to complete the Title. Any amount spent by Publisher to complete the Title shall be considered an additional Advance, to be recouped from the royalties that would otherwise be paid to Developer relating to the Title. Such additional Advance shall be recouped at the relevant rate for the Title from Net Revenues until fully recouped. In addition, if Publisher completes the Title under the terms of this section, the royalty to be paid to Developer relating to the Title shall be reduced by five percent (5%). Publisher shall have sole discretion as to whether it chooses to complete the Title, if Publisher terminates under this section.

5.8   Upon acceptance of an alpha candidate, Publisher shall commence QA Testing. During this period, Publisher shall provide Developer with notice of any bugs or errors identified by QA Testing, and Developer shall work expeditiously to correct any bugs or errors so notified. When Publisher determines, in its sole discretion, that all agreed upon changes from alpha and all corrections of any bugs and errors identified during QA Testing of alpha that cause system or program crashes or otherwise significantly interfere with program operation have been made, Publisher will notify Developer that Publisher is ready to receive the initial beta candidates as set forth above. Upon such notification, Developer shall promptly prepare and deliver beta candidates to Publisher as set forth above, and such candidates shall be delivered in any event prior to the date set forth in Exhibit B. A QA Testing period shall then commence on the date that Publisher accepts the beta candidates into QA Testing. During this period, Publisher shall provide Developer with notice of any bugs or errors identified by QA Testing, and Developer shall work expeditiously to correct any errors so notified. When Publisher determines, in its sole discretion, that all bugs or errors identified during QA Testing have been corrected, Publisher will notify Developer that Publisher is ready to receive golden masters as set forth above.

5.9   Publisher shall have the right, at Publisher's expense, to send Publisher personnel to Developer's place of business upon reasonable notice during normal business hours for consultation with respect to the Title's development.

5.10   Developer shall be responsible for all development costs associated with the Title, including, but not limited to, the costs of any fees payable for software or other licensing rights or acquiring services or materials in connection with the Title. If any Deliverable Item contains any nonoriginal material, including music, Developer shall identify the material and the owner or copyright holder thereof at the time of delivery of such Deliverable Item, and Developer shall obtain, at Developer's expense, all authorizations necessary to secure from the owner or copyright holder of such material the rights for Publisher granted in section 3 above in connection with such material without additional costs to Publisher and without restriction. In addition, Developer shall deliver to Publisher along with the Deliverable Item containing such material, all documentation establishing Developer's and Publisher's right to use such material.

5.11   Incentives/Over budget.

5.11.1   If the development of the Title is over budget, Developer shall have the obligation to pay for the overage. If Developer fails to do so, Publisher may in its sole discretion cover the overage, but if Publisher chooses to do so, the salaries of Developer's Executive Producer and Producer will be cut 50% beginning immediately upon Publisher first obtaining information which would lead a reasonable person to believe that a budget overage will occur, and the amount not paid as salary shall be used to reduce such overage until such overage (or the grounds for belief that such overage will occur) is eliminated. If Publisher covers the overage and the project remains over budget at the time the golden master is accepted by Publisher, the royalties to be paid to Developer will be reduced one percent (1%) for every $25,000 or portion thereof that the Title is over budget. Any amount paid by Publisher to reduce a budget overage (or in any event in addition to the Advances set forth above) shall be fully recoupable from royalties that would otherwise be paid to Developer.

5.11.2   In the event that the Title is delivered before the time it is due and on or under budget as of the delivery date of the relevant deliverable item and for the Title as a whole, incentive payment(s) may be awarded to Developer in Publisher's sole discretion. This incentive payment or payments shall be limited at a maximum to the following: (a) If the Title is finished in acceptable form, under budget and early,

Publisher may pay Developer the remaining amounts in the budget for Developer salaries, which amount shall count as an Advance to be recouped hereunder; (b) If the alpha, beta, golden master, and demo deliverables are delivered on or before the dates that they are due and on or under budget, Publisher may pay to Developer a bonus of up to $2,000 for each of these deliverables (to a maximum of $8,000), which amounts shall count as an additional Advance to be recouped hereunder; and (c) For each top rating that the Title receives from reviews in reputable industry-recognized publications, Publisher may pay Developer an incentive bonus of up to $2,000 which shall not count as an Advance, provided, however, that the maximum amount payable to Developer under this subsection shall be $10,000, and such bonuses shall be paid only if all of the relevant deliverables are completed on or before the date that they are due and on or under budget.

5.12   Reports. Developer shall provide Publisher with monthly status reports, including updates of budget versus actual expenditures, and progress against the Delivery Schedule, on the first of each month within the term of the development of the Title. In addition, Developer shall inform Publisher promptly as soon as Developer becomes aware that there is a risk as to: (a) exceeding the budget, (b) failing to meet the schedule, (c) inability of the Title to perform up to the technical requirements contemplated in the Specifications or any other design materials or documents, or (d) inability to provide the feature functionality contemplated in the Specifications or any other related design materials or documents.

5.13   Equipment. Equipment purchased by Developer using funds from the Advances shall be owned by Publisher until such time as all Advances are recouped. The equipment presently owned by Developer is listed in Exhibit D. It shall be presumed that any equipment purchased by Developer from the effective date of this Agreement until the date development of the Title is completed is owned by Publisher pursuant to the terms of this section.

6. Product Name, Marketing and Promotion, and Credits

6.1   The parties agree to work together to choose the name under which the Title is distributed. Publisher understands that the choice of a name is important to Developer, and will use reasonable efforts to accommodate Developer's concerns. Notwithstanding the foregoing, the final decision as to the name of the Title shall be Publisher's. Publisher shall own the name of the Title as Publisher's trademark, but shall allow Developer to use such name in connection with any approved ancillary product.

6.2   Developer will provide Publisher with all commercially reasonable cooperation and support of Publisher's efforts to market and promote each Title. In particular, but without limiting the generality of the foregoing, Developer agrees at its own expense:

6.2.1   to permit the use of the images, voices, names, likenesses, and biographies of the persons involved in the creation of each Title and the persons involved in creating or appearing in the content incorporated in the Titles in connection with the advertising, marketing, publicity, and promotion of the Titles; and

6.2.2   to provide Publisher with demonstration videos, interactive and noninteractive demonstration discs or diskettes, photos or screen shots and abstracts of story lines of each Title, as reasonably requested by Publisher.

6.3   Publisher will consult with Developer regarding the packaging and marketing of each Title. Publisher will use reasonable efforts to accommodate Developer's packaging and marketing suggestions. Notwithstanding the foregoing, Publisher shall have the final decision on all packaging and marketing matters, and shall pay all costs related thereto. Developer shall not engage in any independent marketing or promotional activities without consulting with the appropriate Publisher personnel and receiving Publisher's prior consent.

6.4   Developer shall include Publisher's title animation on the first screen to be viewed by end-users of the Title.

6.5   Developer shall be given credits in the Titles consistent with industry standards, subject to Publisher's approval in Publisher's sole discretion. In particular, Developer shall be given at least the credits listed in Exhibit C, provided that Developer and any individuals named thereon carry out their responsibilities throughout the development of the Title.

6.6   Publisher shall include Developer's logo (as provided by Developer in suitable electronic format) on the packaging for the product. The size and placement of Developer's logo shall be within Publisher's sole discretion.

6.7   Publisher shall be responsible for all costs of focus group testing of the Title and Add-On Products.

7. Developer Copies

7.1   Developer shall be given a total of twenty-five (25) copies of the Title for each platform free of charge at the time the Title is first shipped for a platform in commercial quantities in the retail channel.

7.2   Developer shall be entitled to purchase a reasonable number of additional copies of the Title for each platform at Publisher's cost in any calendar quarter beginning with the calendar quarter after the Title first ships in commercial quantities in the retail channel. Such copies shall be supplied from stock on hand and shall not be resold by Developer, but shall be used for promotional purposes only, after consultation with the appropriate Publisher personnel. In the event Publisher does not have sufficient copies of the Title to satisfy Developer's request, Publisher shall deliver enough copies of the Title to satisfy the request from the next pressing of the Title.

8. Maintenance

Developer agrees to perform maintenance on the Title and Add-Ons created by Developer for as long as the Title is being offered for sale. Such maintenance shall include, but not be limited to, fixing any bugs or errors in the Titles within thirty (30) days of being notified of such a bug or error, and providing updated versions of the Title and source code containing such corrections. Such maintenance shall be provided at Developer's expense in the first ninety (90) days after commercial release of the Title for the initial platforms, and thereafter at Developer's reasonable and customary work-for-hire rates.

9. Source Code

Developer shall send to Publisher the most recent version of the source code for the Title at the end of each calendar month on a medium and in a format to be mutually agreed upon by the parties, until the Titles which have been finished and finally accepted by Publisher, and a final version of the source code has been provided to Publisher.

10. Customer Service and Information

10.1   Publisher will be responsible for providing reasonable and customary customer service for the Title. Developer agrees to provide such technical assistance and information to Publisher as shall be reasonably necessary for Publisher to provide such customer service.

10.2   Publisher agrees to provide to Developer upon request, but not more than once per quarter, a list of all registered users of the Titles, containing names, addresses, phone numbers, and other relevant marketing data, if known to Publisher. Such information shall be treated as Confidential Information under this Agreement.

11. Documentation

In addition to any documentation called for in the Delivery Schedule for any Title, Developer shall provide user documentation for the Title at Developer's expense.

12. Warranties, Indemnification, and Remedies

12.1   Developer warrants that it will proceed expeditiously to complete the Title, and that upon completion of the Title, it shall conform in all material respects to the Specifications and other descriptions prepared by Developer and contained in any accompanying written materials, and shall contain no viruses.

12.2   Developer represents, warrants and covenants that it has full right, power and authority to enter into this Agreement and to grant the rights granted herein without violating any other agreement or commitment of any sort; that it has no outstanding agreements or understandings, written or oral, concerning the Title; that Developer has not previously sold, licensed, encumbered or pledged the Title or any portion thereof as security to any third party; that the Deliverable Items provided hereunder shall be original; and that the Title does not and will not infringe or constitute a misappropriation of any trademark, patent, copyright, trade secret or other proprietary, publicity, or privacy right of any third party and Publisher's use, reproduction, sale, licensing and/or distribution of each Title as provided in this Agreement shall not violate any rights of any kind or nature of any third party.

12.3 Developer shall defend, indemnify and hold harmless Publisher, its successors, assigns, parents, subsidiaries, affiliates, licensees and sub-licensees, and their respective officers, directors, agents and employees, from and against any action, suit, claim, damages, liability, costs and expenses (including reasonable attorneys' fees), arising out of or in any way connected with any breach of any representation or warranty made by Developer herein or any claim that the Title infringes any intellectual property rights or other rights of any third party. Publisher shall give Developer prompt notice of any such claim or of any threatened claim, and reasonably cooperate with Developer in the defense thereof.

12.4 If Publisher receives notice of any claim, demand or suit, or of any facts which would lead a reasonable person to believe that there has been a breach of Developer's warranties as set forth herein, Publisher shall have the right to withhold from any payments due to Developer under this Agreement, and deposit in an interest-bearing escrow account with a commercial bank, reasonable amounts as acceptable to Publisher. Upon resolution of the claim, the amount in escrow including accrued interest thereon shall be distributed to Developer after deductions of any amounts required to be paid to Publisher or third parties under this indemnity.

12.5 Publisher hereby represents, warrants, and covenants that it has the full right, power, and authority to enter into this Agreement. Publisher shall defend, indemnify and hold harmless Developer, its successors, assigns, parents, subsidiaries, affiliates, licensees and sub-licensees, and their respective officers, directors, agents and employees from and against any action, suit, claim, damages, liability, costs and expenses (including reasonable attorneys' fees), arising out of or in any way connected with any breach of any representation or warranty made by Publisher herein. Developer shall give Publisher prompt notice of any such claim or of any threatened claim and shall reasonably cooperate in the defense thereof.

12.6 Neither Developer nor Publisher shall agree to the settlement of any such claim, demand or suit prior to final judgment thereon without the consent of the other party, whose consent shall not unreasonably be withheld.

12.7 The parties' indemnification obligations set forth in the foregoing paragraphs shall survive termination of this Agreement.

13. Termination

13.1   This Agreement will terminate on the thirtieth (30th) day after one party gives the other notice of a material breach by the other of any term of this Agreement, unless the breach is cured before that day; provided, however, that if the material breach relates only to a particular Add-On Product, then only the rights with respect to that Add-On Product shall be terminated. Publisher shall have the right to suspend payment for milestones or royalties from the time Publisher notifies Developer of a breach until the time such breach is cured by Developer.

13.2   This Agreement may be terminated by either party without prior notice if: (a) the other party files a petition for bankruptcy or is adjudicated a bankrupt, (b) a petition in bankruptcy is filed against the other party, (c) the other party becomes insolvent or makes an assignment for the benefit of its creditors or an arrangement for its creditors pursuant to any bankruptcy law, (d) the other party discontinues its business, or (e) a receiver is appointed for the other party or its business.

13.3   This Agreement also may be terminated by Publisher immediately upon notice pursuant to the terms of section 5.7 above.

13.4   In the event of any termination of this Agreement, Developer shall within five (5) days turn over to Publisher all copies of the source code, artwork, text files, graphics, design documents, bug reports and databases, and all other materials related in any way to development of the Title.

13.5   Notwithstanding any termination of this Agreement, Publisher shall retain the rights granted herein for the Title.

13.6   Termination of this Agreement shall not extinguish any of Publisher's or Developer's rights or obligations under this Agreement which by their terms continue after the date of termination. Termination of this Agreement shall be without prejudice to any other rights that either party may have at law or in equity, and shall not affect the rights of end-users to continue to use all distributed copies of the Titles.

14. Confidential Information

14.1   Neither party shall disclose any of the Confidential Information of the other party during or after the time this Agreement is in effect. Information shall not be deemed confidential if it:

14.1.1   is now or hereafter becomes, through no act or omission on the part of the receiving party, generally known or available within the industry, or is now or later enters the public domain through no act or omission on the part of the receiving party;

14.1.2   was acquired by the receiving party before receiving such information from the disclosing party and without restriction as to use or disclosure;

14.1.3   is hereafter rightfully furnished to the receiving party by a third party, without restriction as to use or disclosure;

14.1.4   is required to be disclosed pursuant to law, provided the receiving party uses reasonable efforts to give the disclosing party reasonable notice of such required disclosure, and cooperates in any attempts by the disclosing party to obtain a protective order or other similar protection against disclosure of the Confidential Information;

14.1.5   is disclosed with the prior written consent of the disclosing party.

14.2   Developer will not disclose or prerelease any Title or any Deliverable Item or component thereof to any person or entity without the prior written consent of Publisher.

15. Freedom to Compete

Subject to the terms of this Agreement, each party agrees that nothing in this Agreement will be construed as restricting or prohibiting either party from lawfully competing with the other party in any other aspect of its business, including, but not limited to, the development or distribution of other products or services, or the publishing of products competitive with those contemplated under this Agreement, and each party agrees to continue to compete vigorously in all other such aspects of its business.

16. Export Controls

Each party assures the other that it will comply with all export laws and restrictions and regulations of the Department of Commerce or other United States or foreign agency or authority, and not export, or allow the export or re-export of any Title in violation of any such restrictions, laws or regulations.

17. Assignment

This Agreement may not be assigned by Developer without the prior written consent of Publisher, except that Developer shall be entitled to assign this Agreement to the corporate entity to be created by Developer provided that such corporate entity assumes all rights and obligations of Developer hereunder, and provided that the same personnel are devoted to the Title by the corporate entity. An assignment by Developer in accordance with the foregoing requirements shall operate to relieve Developer of any personal obligations regarding this Agreement, except as such obligations may arise from Developer's affiliation as an officer, director, or employee of the assignee corporate entity. Publisher may assign this Agreement freely. Subject to the foregoing, this Agreement will bind and inure to the benefit of the parties and their respective successors and permitted assigns.

18. Integration

This Agreement sets forth the entire agreement between the parties with respect to the subject matter hereof, and may not be modified or amended except by written agreement executed by the parties hereto.

19. Severability

If any provision of this Agreement is declared by a court of competent jurisdiction to be invalid, void, or unenforceable, the remaining provisions of this Agreement shall continue in full force and effect, and the invalid provision shall be replaced by the legal provision which most closely achieves the intent of the invalid provision.

20. Governing Law

This Agreement shall be governed by the laws of the State of California applicable to agreements made and to be wholly performed therein (without reference to conflict of laws). In any action to enforce the terms of this Agreement, the prevailing party shall be entitled to recover its reasonable attorneys' fees and expenses.

21. Force Majeure

If the performance of this Agreement or any obligation under it (except payment of monies due) is prevented, restricted, or interfered with by reason of acts of God, acts of government, or any other cause not within the control of either party, the party so affected shall be excused from such performance, but only for so long as and to the extent that such a force prevents, restricts, or interferes with that party's performance. Notwithstanding the foregoing, the nonaffected party may terminate this Agreement immediately upon written notice if the force majeure circumstances continue for more than sixty (60) days.

22. Independent Contractor

Developer shall be deemed to have the status of an independent contractor, and nothing in this Agreement shall be deemed to place the parties in the relationship of employer–employee, principal–agent, partners, or joint venturers. Developer shall be responsible for any withholding taxes, payroll taxes, disability insurance payments, unemployment taxes, and other similar taxes or charges on the payments received by Developer hereunder.

23. Notices

The address of each party hereto as set forth above shall be the appropriate address for the mailing of notices, checks, and statements, if any, hereunder. Notices sent to Publisher shall be sent to the attention of _____. Notices sent to Developer shall be sent to the attention of _____. All notices which either party is required or may desire to serve upon the other party may be served personally or by certified or registered mail (postage prepaid), reputable commercial courier, or by facsimile transmission, and shall be effective upon receipt. Either party may change its address by written notice to the other.

24. No Brokers

All negotiations relative to this Agreement have been carried on by the parties directly, without the intervention of any person as a result of any act of either party (and, so far as known to either party, without the intervention of any such person) in such manner as to give rise to any valid claim against the parties hereto for brokerage commissions, finder's fees, or other like payment.

25. Waiver

No waiver by either party, whether express or implied, of any provision of this Agreement shall constitute a continuing waiver of such provision or a waiver of any other provision of this Agreement. No waiver by either party, whether express or implied, of any breach or default by the other party, shall constitute a waiver of any other breach or default of the same or any other provision of this Agreement.

26. Paragraph Headings

Paragraph headings contained herein are for the convenience of the parties only. They shall not be used in any way to govern, limit, modify, or construe this Agreement and shall not be given any legal effect.

27. Counterparts

This Agreement may be executed in two or more counterparts and all counterparts so executed shall for all purposes constitute one agreement, binding on all parties hereto.

IN WITNESS WHEREOF, the parties have caused this Development Agreement to be executed on the date set forth above by their duly authorized representatives.

Developer   Publisher

_____   _____
Signature: Signature:

_____   _____
Title: Title:

_____   _____
Date: Date:

Exhibit A: Specifications (including Budget)

Budgeted amounts for salaries and overhead expenses such as office space shall be reduced pro rata and/or charged against other projects on which Developer is working concurrently with the Development of the Title under this Agreement.

Exhibit B: Deliverable Items and Delivery Schedule

Exhibit C: Credits

Exhibit D: Developer Equipment

Chapter Summary

In this chapter, you learned about two legal instruments that clients and developers use when clients want to hire developers to create a multimedia product. The first is the letter of intent, or deal memo. The purpose of the letter of intent is to allow the developer to begin work on the design of the multimedia product and to be paid a fee for the design work. While working on the design, the developer controls the scope of the project so that it can develop the product for a target budget and within a desired timeframe. When the design is complete, it is submitted to the client for approval, along with a detailed budget and production plan. Typically, these detailed documents enable the client and developer to enter into the development agreement.

The development agreement is a comprehensive, definitive agreement. It contains numerous clauses and terms that protect both the client and the developer and defines remedies should the agreement or the project fail in any way.

The producer, who is most responsible for the success or failure of the development process, must be conversant with all of the legal agreements between the developer and the client as well as between the developer and its employees, subcontractors, unions and guilds, licensees, and licensors.

Recommended Reading

Brinson, J. Dianne, and Radcliffe, Mark F. *Multimedia Law and Business Handbook.* Ladera Press: Menlo Park, CA, 1996.

Brinson, J. Dianne, and Radcliffe, Mark F. *Internet Legal Forms for Business.* Ladera Press: Menlo Park, CA, 1997.

Both books are available from Ladera Press, www.Laderapress.com. Telephone (800) 523–3721.

11

The Prototype Phase

In this chapter you will learn about

- What the prototype is
- Difference between a prototype and a proof of concept
- Purposes of the prototype
- Planning and producing the prototype
- Testing the prototype
- Incorporating test results in the product design
- Roles of producer, director, and writer during the prototype phase

After the client has approved the functional specification and has signed a letter of intent or development agreement, the prototype phase begins. Because the producer has already prepared a plan and budget for the prototype during the design phase, the work can begin immediately. The prize of this phase is the prototype, a small, working version of the final product burned on CD-ROM. It contains final art, sound, video, animation, interactivity, and features, all of which gives the user an idea of what the final, complete product will be like. The prototype is the first tangible example of the product that up until now has been purely conceptual. The prototype is used to test various aspects of the product design, technology, and development processes before making the commitment in time and dollars to the full-blown product. If the prototype is successful, it is also used as a marketing and sales tool.

The completed prototype can be an exhilarating experience or a terrible disappointment, depending on the test results. Either way, the development team and client benefit.

The developer and its client test the prototype with focus groups of target users. If the prototype is successful—if it is everything everyone had hoped, and more—then there is excitement and energy moving on into the production phase. The client's marketing department can use the product to attract publishers, distributors, retailers, and end users. A version of the prototype can be put up on the company's web site and offered to customers as a free download. This is known to stimulate sales. Visit the web site, which includes links to publishers who provide downloadable demos of their products.

If it is a bust, the project can be abandoned before the parties invest unrecoverable time and money. If the results are mixed—and they almost always are—the parties use the focus test results to modify the design components of the product, the budget, schedule, and other things accordingly.

Typically, a prototype is about 10 percent to 15 percent the size of the final product, but the actual composition of a prototype is determined by criteria and needs, which may make size inconsequential.

The prototype phase is a miniversion of the production phase. It has a hard and fast deadline, deliverables, tasks, and milestones. The phase has three parts:

1. Create the prototype.
2. Test the prototype.
3. Modify the design based on test results.

The design modification may result in changes to the development plan, budget, and delivery date of the final product. During this phase, the producer, director, and writer continue their roles on the development team.

The Prize of the Prototype Phase

The prize of the prototype phase is a small, working CD-ROM version of the product, which is usually called a prototype but which may also be referred to as a demo or a proof of concept. Whether it's called one or the other depends on what the parties try to prove or test with the prototype when it is complete. If the CD-ROM is a working version of the product that includes the most intriguing and underlying technical features, it is a prototype. For example, let's imagine that the final design of a product calls for it to link automatically with a companion Web site that downloads time-critical data (stock quotes, for example) to the user's hard drive. The CD-ROM then uses this data, combined with personal user-profile information and financial management software, to make buy and sell recommendations to the user. If this feature works—if there is indeed a web site, if the prototype actually launches the Internet browser and connects to the site, and if the prototype in fact facilitates the download of data to the user's hard drive and crunches the data with user profile information—then the CD-ROM is a prototype. It works just as the final product will, only it's smaller.

If the CD-ROM simply appears as though it has the product's technical features but in fact does not, then it's a proof of concept or demo. Let's say the web site isn't up and the technical team hasn't solved some of the download issues. Maybe the business affairs folks haven't made a strategic relationship with a brokerage firm yet. So instead, when the user is using the product, a web connection and download is simulated. To the user, it looks as though something just happened, but actually, nothing did. This is not a prototype, but a proof of concept. A more cynical description of such a version is "smoke and mirrors" or "vaporware."

What is interesting is that to the user, it may look like something exciting happened in both cases. When asked during a focus test, users may respond anecdotally to questions about their experience with the product in identical ways even though in one case the feature worked and in the other the whole thing was faked. The creators of the product may be just as pleased with the focus test results from a proof of concept as from a prototype and may get those results with only half the effort. The developer and the client must know what their main purposes are before deciding to create a prototype or a proof of concept. In this chapter, we refer to the prize as the prototype.

Purposes of the Prototype

The prototype is both a development and a marketing tool. As a development tool, the prototype is useful for testing three important unknowns about the product: its overall appeal to the target user, the underlying technology that makes it tick, and the production methods employed by the director. If the product is an educational product, the prototype also proves whether the learning objectives are achieved with the current design. As a marketing tool, the prototype is useful for demonstrating what the product will be like to potential customers long before it is complete. This is particularly important if the product does not yet have a publisher or distributor or is so out of the ordinary it must be seen to be believed.

Development Purposes

The first development purpose is to test the interactive design with the target users, obtain feedback, and adjust the design to meet the expectations and desires of the end customers. This is known as a formative evaluation and can often be accomplished with a proof of concept or demo. As in the example above, there are many ways to create an experience that tricks users into believing they are seeing the real thing.

The second purpose is to test technology, particularly new, innovative, or trendsetting technology that may set the product far apart from or ahead of competition.

When such a result is needed, the technology must be developed and implemented in the prototype. It is necessary not only to determine how the technology enhances the user's experience, but also whether the technology behaves as expected, or at all. The development team can then make necessary adjustments to the design, the technology, or both.

For example, in the scenario described above, testing the prototype that downloads data from a web site to the user's hard drive may show that the overall experience is fine. The user likes this feature very much, especially since the downloaded information is time-critical. However, the test may also show that the data requires too much contiguous hard disk space, takes too long to download, uses incompatible file formats, or, for some inexplicable reason, causes the Web browser to crash. By catching these problems during the prototype phase, the programming team can address serious technology flaws at a very early stage rather than in the eleventh hour when it's way too late.

Finally, producing the prototype affords an opportunity to test production processes. The producer and director can determine if any product-specific production techniques they have employed achieve the desired effect. Again, they test to see whether the end results are pleasing to the target user during the focus tests, and they also watch to see whether the process was smooth, fast, inexpensive, and repeatable. In a previous chapter, we used the example of the motion capture method for creating life-like animation for 3-D, computer-generated characters. During the prototype phase, the director uses this method for a small, representative sample of animated scenes, which he or she includes in the prototype. The focus testers are asked to react to the characters. They respond that they like the animation—it's very realistic. The producer and director review the process, and determine that the method is a huge success. It takes less time and less money, and results in better animation, than animating with more traditional or conventional methods. They decide confidently to use the process in full development.

Instructional Purposes

Educational products usually have clear teaching and learning objectives, and developers use the prototype phase to determine whether the product's design will achieve those objectives. Many children's products are designed to teach something to preschool children, such as colors, shapes, the alphabet, counting, reading, early math, and so on. Other products teach more advanced subjects. Syracuse Language Systems, for example, is a leading developer of products that teach foreign languages using unique voice recognition software. Products published by The Princeton Review and Kaplan are designed to teach students how to pass tests such as the SAT and the GRE. The value of any educational product can and should be measured by its effectiveness as a teaching agent. The user should learn something by using the product—and preferably better and faster than by using another method. A user's SAT score should improve by correctly using Kaplan's product.

A product designed to achieve a specific learning objective is tested during the prototype phase to determine whether it really works. The developer tests the focus group members before they use the product to establish what their level of knowledge and understanding is. Control groups are assembled. One or more groups use the product, while others do not. The designated subjects then use the product and are tested again. In addition to the anecdotal remarks of the focus test subjects, the developer uses these test scores to ascertain whether the product's design is effective. Appropriate redesign may be called for.

Marketing Purposes

If a prototype proves successful, the marketing department exploits it in several ways. The multimedia business is extremely competitive, and all new products fight a steep uphill battle to reach the consumer. Product marketers seize every opportunity to demonstrate and publicize a new product to the long series of entities that stand between the completed product and the end consumer. A well-executed prototype is an ideal tool for the marketing department to make its case about the product to what is initially a cool, disbelieving audience. Among the audiences for the initial presentations are

■ *Publishers.* If the product is developed in-house, or if the developer's client is not a software publisher, then the prototype is used by the marketing department to attract a publisher. The publisher's role is to market products—to get products into the retail channels. Publishers rarely commit to a product until there is a working prototype so they can clearly see the product's potential value and marketability and can have confidence that the developer can finish it. Incidentally, if a publisher makes a commitment to a product at this point, it will almost certainly have a laundry list of changes, modifications, and enhancements it wants, which will ostensibly make the product more marketable.

■ *Retailers.* Retailers stock their shelves with multimedia products, but they have room for only about 10 percent of the total number of products developed each year. Only the very best make it into the retail channel, and even then, retailers have little patience if the product does not move off the shelves quickly. Marketers show the prototype to retailers and presell the product sometimes months before it is ready to ship.

■ *Product Reviewers.* There is a small but influential multimedia press. Some product reviewers are published in magazines, while others have web sites. Avid multimedia customers rely heavily on reviewers to tip them off that new products are coming and are good and worth buying or should be avoided. Marketers court reviewers, provide personal demonstrations of unreleased products, and hope for a positive write-up.

■ *Customers.* Savvy marketers have learned how to reach customers directly by putting downloadable versions of future releases on web sites. A well-executed prototype is the ideal demo. It tantalizes the customer. Many products have had such a stir surrounding their release generated by this tactic that the products sold out the moment they reached the stores.

The marketing folks may also use the prototype to begin writing their press releases, to make strategic cross-marketing or bundling deals, and even to shoot commercials.

Plan and Produce the Prototype

Most of the decision making for this phase occurs during the discovery and design phases, when the producer, working closely with the client and design team, determines the purpose, user, content, features, schedule, and budget for this particular prototype. The producer and the client may determine that the prototype must be used for customer focus testing, technology testing, and development method testing and must also be used by the marketing department at the Electronic Entertainment Expo. In such a case, both development and marketing purposes drive the decisions related to the size and makeup of the prototype. The end purposes determine what nodes from the total design should be in the prototype, which decision in turn determines the scope of work, level of effort, and cost. The deadline is the major multimedia convention called Electronic Entertainment Expo, or E3.

Put simply, the producer asks, "What chunk of this product can I produce at the lowest possible cost in the shortest possible time and still obtain the focus test results, development test results, and technology information I need? What's going to do the job for the marketing people? And can I get this done by E3?"

Select the Nodes

The producer, working with the director, writer, art director, and technical lead, selects the nodes from the product node map to include in the prototype. Most producers use the following criteria to determine the nodes:

■ What content, features, and technology show the most impressive aspects of the product? Which ones utilize the most innovative or potentially troublesome technology? These nodes should be included.

■ What content, features, and technology are redundant? Which ones will show only more of the same? These nodes should not be included.

- What can be done in a reasonable time for a reasonable cost? Nodes that cannot possibly be produced in time or that involve high cost should not be included in the prototype.

- What tasks are on the critical path of the larger development? Tasks that help move the overall development forward should be included in the prototype.

- What will get us to go/no go? This is essential. Any features or content that are considered key, unique elements of the product must be included in the prototype.

The prototype will almost certainly include company bumpers, the main title, and the first menu screen, if there is one.

Create a Plan for the Prototype

Once the producer has identified the nodes to be included in the prototype, he or she creates and evaluates the scope of work involved in producing those nodes. It is some subset of the total scope of work for the product and involves creating art, animation, video, and sound; programming; and integrating assets with software. There will be multiple CD-ROM burns, followed by quality assurance testing. The producer must identify those tasks in the larger plan that contribute directly to the prototype and put those tasks into gear first.

Create a Budget for the Prototype

Based on the scope of work, and using the same assumptions used for the final product budget, the producer creates the budget for the prototype. Very often, the producer allocates a portion of the final development budget to the prototype, generally based on the percentage of the whole product represented by the prototype. If the prototype consists of about 20 percent of the whole product, then the tendency is to allocate 20 percent of the whole budget to the prototype. This is not the most accurate method. Some work performed for the prototype will be used throughout the product, such as screens, buttons, icons, sounds, and certain software that will be used globally, that is to say, in many places throughout the product. The prototype will certainly include some of the more complex software because the prototype is supposed to be used to test this type of programming. Research and rights clearances that benefit the whole product must be done for the prototype. Overall efficiency is sluggish at the beginning of the development process, so everything takes a little longer and costs a little more for the prototype than for the final product. Even though the prototype may be quantitatively 20 percent of the final product, it may actually cost 25 percent to produce and result in 30 percent progress toward the final product. The producer must be very careful to determine the costs accurately.

Reach Agreement for the Prototype

The producer must be certain that the client agrees to pay for the prototype, either in a definitive agreement (contract), the letter of intent, or another agreement, if necessary. The functional specification, completed in the design phase, makes it possible for the parties to reach a final contractual agreement, but it does not guarantee it. Contract negotiations routinely drag on. The letter of intent signed before the design phase included a preliminary budget for the product, including the prototype. However, that was done before the final product design was completed and before any decisions had been made about the scope of the prototype. That budget was a target budget, or a range, but not an actual cost.

Absent any other agreement, the best alternative is for the producer to draft a letter that stipulates what the prototype will consist of in terms of nodes, content, features, and so forth; when the prototype will be complete; and what the total cost will be. He or she posits the letter as clarification of the letter of intent based on all of the product details that emerged during the design phase. The producer gets the client to sign the letter agreeing to pay for the prototype if it meets the criteria described in the letter. Most clients are interested in keeping the project going, not in gumming it up. If the client is pleased with the developer's performance so far, it is usually happy to sign such a letter.

Edit the Spec for the Prototype

The writer trims down a version of the functional specification to include only those nodes that are in the prototype. This is simply a matter of removing any chapters and sections that describe things not included in the prototype. Copies are distributed to the development team. This step simplifies the development and quality assurance of the prototype, as no one will be forced to thumb through a huge document looking for the scattered nodes of the prototype.

Create Asset Development Work Orders

Choosing nodes for the prototype moves development of assets needed for the prototype to the front burner. The producer creates asset lists for those nodes in the prototype and provides them to the director, art director, and sound designer. Department managers (the manager of the art department, the manager of the sound department) use these asset lists to generate work orders—also called marching orders—for their staffs. If any freelance talent, voice talent, actors, or independent contractors are needed for the prototype, the producer hires them at this time, and he or she includes the work orders in their employment contracts or deal memos. Link from the web site to Ladera Press, which makes available sample employment agreements.

The programmers, meanwhile, begin writing code for the product. They often use "placeholder" art and sound until the actual art and sound assets come in. The programming team should solve the big problems first. If there is programming that is new, unique, or complex, the programmers should deal with it right away, before they are deluged with assets from the art and sound departments.

The Prototype Quandary

During development of the prototype, the producer has an interesting quandary to deal with. What does the producer do, during the prototype phase, when an artist completes all of the art for the prototype and has the wherewithal to continue creating art for the final product? Should the producer pay the artist to keep developing art for the final product? Should the artist be assigned to another project, instead?

In this particular example, three things can happen and two of them are bad. If the prototype tests poorly, and the project is abandoned, any work beyond that paid for by the client to complete the prototype will be borne by the developer. If the prototype tests are mixed, and it is clear that with some modifications the product can be successful, then some work on the prototype and some of the additional work may be subject to replacement. The developer may have to absorb the additional costs. If the prototype tests well and few if any modifications are called for, then any additional work performed on the product during the prototype phase will be useful and time well spent. The producer must decide what to do based on his or her own level of confidence about the product and its chances in testing.

Cull Scripts for the Prototype

The writer provides the sound designer with audio scripts and the director with video scripts for the nodes to be included in the prototype. The writer derives these scripts from the functional specification. Sometimes it is cost efficient to record all of the narration or dialogue for a product, even for nodes not in the prototype. In this case, the writer provides complete scripts. SAG and AFTRA recording talent, for example, are paid a minimum rate—currently about $522 per day for a four-hour minimum day. In that space of time, the sound designer could record all of the audio, and the talent would not have to return later for a second session. The focus test results, and other changes and modifications requested later, could bring the talent back for more recording. It's the producer's call.

Create File or Project Space

The producer makes sure there is space on the studio's file server to accommodate all of the assets and software for the title. The producer must create properly named directories on the designated device so that the staff can place their finished and approved assets or software in the right place. Every studio has its own system for setting up these directories, but typically each node has a directory, and within that directory there are subdirectories for art, sound, animation, video, text, and software. If the producer has created the asset database similarly, then he or she can poll the directories and compare the contents of each with what they should contain when the node is complete. In this way, the producer can track progress.

Create Art, Sound, and Software

With work orders in hand, the artists, sound designer, music composer, videographers, and programmers get to work. The producer tracks day-to-day costs and progress, while the director instructs the staff on the proper development of their work. The writer keeps the functional specification up to date as changes and modifications occur during development. Unless there are major changes called for after the focus tests, the writer is in a maintenance mode from this point on.

A healthy practice for the producer and director is to make sure everyone is working on the same node at the same time. In other words, the producer and director should prioritize the nodes so that the art, sound, video, and software are created for the top-priority node first, and then the next, and so on. Seems like common sense, but until it is formalized, the producer and director cannot be sure what the department heads or their staff will do. I once worked on an animated feature film when this wasn't practiced. Because of a management snafu, background paintings were completed for one sequence while the animation and ink & paint were completed for another. Neither sequence could be shot until the two departments caught up with each other.

In addition to the prototype nodes, the programmers also work on such generic technical details as installation procedures for the product, quitting the product, and perhaps saving the product or loading saved versions.

Manage Development

The producer maintains the practice of weekly status meetings and reports established during the design phase. He or she gathers progress information from the asset database on a daily basis and from the responsible parties during the meetings and compares the progress with expenses. As long as there is no slippage, the producer doesn't have to take any action. Otherwise, the producer takes whatever action is necessary to correct the process. Corrective action can take many forms. If art is falling behind, the producer can hire additional artists or approve overtime. If the composer does not have the music ready, he or she can arrange to use needle drop (library) music for the prototype. One of the most difficult things to assess is progress on the software development. Even programmers often compare it to pregnancy: nothing seems to be happening for a long time and then, suddenly, there's a fully formed human. Unless the producer is a programmer, it is difficult for him or her to know exactly what the state of the software development is except from reports by the programmers themselves.

The director continues the practice of daily meetings with artists, animators, sound designers, programmers, and others. He or she gives them specific instructions about the day's activities and follows up later with a walk-around. During the walk-around, the director approves any work completed or gives directions for changes or fine-tuning. The director takes special interest in any new or untested development methods and supervises them personally.

The writer must keep the functional specification up to date with modifications made to the design. During development, it is typical for artists, sound designers, and programmers to discover new, better, or more accurate ways to produce an effect described in the spec. During art development, for example, an artist may discover that a piece of art created for one screen will work just as well for another, thereby reducing the asset list by one element. A sound designer may find a better sound effect than the one called for in the spec. A programmer may suggest a different on-screen device for users to input their ages than the "slider" described in the spec. The director agrees. The writer must modify the spec to reflect all of these small changes made during development.

When the art and sound departments begin to provide the programmers with assets, programmers often find that those assets must be modified in some way before integration with the software. Additional art is often needed. These discoveries must be documented in the functional specification by the writer and in the asset database by the producer.

Product Tweaking

A very exciting time is when some part of the product—even a very small part—suddenly comes alive on the monitor of one of the programmers. It is possible that months have gone by during which the product was discussed, designed, negotiated, written about, and sketched. Finally, there it is, looking, sounding, and behaving as designed. The team may decide that it isn't perfect—that "tweaking" it in some fashion will enhance the experience for the end user. Now is the time to do it. This is a very common practice, particularly for game products, which depend very much on feedback from users before the timing, attributes, and behaviors are adjusted just right.

The producer should keep a watchful eye on tweaking so it does not consume the staff and cause the development schedule or budget to suffer. Tweaking should never become too much of a trial-and-error exercise.

Quality Assurance

At some point, a sufficient amount of the prototype is complete for it to be burned on CD-ROM. Once the product is burned on CD, the quality assurance department (QA) takes over and tests the product. Each tester must be given a copy of the functional specification, which has been updated with any changes, modifications, and tweaking. QA testers are responsible for finding bugs. They do this by repeatedly playing with the product while reading the functional specification and comparing what the spec says should happen with how the product actually behaves. They try different combinations of keystrokes, mouse moves, and other unintended and unnecessary stimuli. The objective is to try to break the product. They perform these tests on a number of different computers, each with different combinations of monitors, hard drives, processors, joy sticks, printers, sound cards, video cards, and so forth. The objective here is to see whether product performance is platform dependent.

There are several classifications of bugs the QA testers may find. A priority 1 bug causes the system to crash. Clearly, these are serious bugs. A priority 2 bug is anything that does not conform to the spec and is obviously a problem. If the sound for a video does not play, for example, or if a button branches to the wrong node, these would be considered priority 2 bugs. Priority 2 bugs must be fixed. A priority 3 bug is one in which an event does not conform to the spec but isn't obviously a problem. Perhaps some music plays when the user branches to a node and it sounds fine, but it is not the music specified in the spec. Priority 3 bugs need to be fixed eventually. Priority 4 bugs are those that do not occur all the time, are difficult or impossible to repeat, or occur with such irregularity that they may be impossible to fix and are unlikely ever to happen to a customer. Priority 4 bugs are low priority.

The testers "log" the bugs they find for the first version of the prototype. This procedure may involve entering the bugs into a sophisticated database or simply writing the description of the bug down on a piece of notepaper. The QA supervisor is responsible for compiling the complete list of bugs for the first burn and for merging and purging the list. Several testers may find the same bug. It needs to be reported only once. The QA supervisor then goes over the bug reports with the producer and/or the director. They then assign the bug to a responsible party to fix. It is usually clear when an artist, a sound designer, or a programmer should fix a bug.

After the staff person fixes the bug—or, more appropriately, thinks he or she has fixed it—the QA supervisor amends the bug report to show that the bug needs to be retested after the next burn. The supervisor provides each tester with a list of bugs to retest. Typically, every burn results in the elimination of some bugs and the emergence of others. So the process is repeated for burn after burn, until all the bugs are fixed. When no priority 1, 2, or 3 bugs are found, the burn is considered the final prototype.

Focus Test the Prototype

In anticipation of the final burn, the producer arranges for a focus test. A focus test is a formal unveiling of the product to a small but representative sample of target users. Members of this focus group use the prototype in an environment where their frank impressions and appraisal of the product can be acquired and evaluated. Test staff stay with the subjects during the sessions and help them if they get stuck. They make note of any parts of the product that the subjects have difficulty with. While the subjects interact with the prototype, test staff query them about their experiences. Usually, they work from a prepared list of questions. Questions have to be developed so that the focus group subjects are not led to certain kinds of responses.

Obviously, the whole point of the focus test is to find out whether the product appeals to the target market. Do they like it or not? What do they like the most? The least? What would they like improved? What confused them? What delighted them? Would they recommend this to a friend? How much would they expect to pay for a product like this? There could be many other questions and the staff is free to dig deeper if a subject has more to say. Subjects often have incredibly insightful things to say about a product, especially if the product is targeted at them.

The following are necessary for a focus test:

- Working prototype
- Computer stations where focus testing can take place
- Focus group subjects
- Questions for the subjects
- Staff to ask the questions
- Video cameras to tape the sessions
- Date to conduct the tests
- Gifts or stipends for the subjects
- Methodology for evaluating the results
- Date to evaluate the results

There are testing services that will do all of this, or the producer can manage the process.

Tips for Focus Testing

If possible, conduct the focus tests outside the office environment. The office can be a distraction. If there are more than one test station, keep them in different rooms. Do not allow the test subjects to hear each other comment about the prototype during the tests.

Choose subjects who are in the target market. It's common practice at many companies to recruit employees' children to test kids' products. Their children, in turn, bring friends from school. Be certain the children have some experience with multimedia products and have a basis of comparison with other products, otherwise the results will be difficult to evaluate. For a strategy game developed at Media Station, Inc., the company recruited teens from the local game arcade to test the product. This proved very successful. Each brought a friend and all exhibited a keen understanding of the game market. Their feedback was extremely valuable.

Project Pass, the jointly developed math curriculum from GTE and the NFL, was focus tested with the target users, seventh graders, and their teachers, for an entire school year. Results were used to modify the entire product during the following summer, and the curriculum was rereleased in the fall.

Develop questions that tell you, first of all, about your subjects. Do they own and use computers? What kind? Do they use multimedia? What genres do they prefer? How often do they play? How much do they spend on multimedia annually? How do they decide what products to buy? Develop this part of your questionnaire to obtain a profile of your testers. If they love your product, you will have a profile for your target market.

Next, develop questions that are product specific. These you will have to determine for yourself. However, to the extent possible, you should develop questions that you can evaluate quantitatively. Questions that can be answered "yes," "no," or "undecided" can be tallied later. You will have to qualify the answers to other questions. For example, a question like "What would you do to make the product better?" will result in extremely useful anecdotal feedback. In either case, the staff person who asks the questions must be careful not to phrase them or to inflect his or her voice in any way that could influence the answer.

If possible, videotape the session. Use the videotapes later to watch body language, to listen for telltale inflections in subject's responses, and to review testing methods. It is always a good idea to reward the subjects with a small payment such as tee-shirts, movie tickets, and pizza and soda while testing.

Evaluating Focus Test Results

The focus test creates both quantitative and anecdotal data. Quantitative results are often simple to interpret and act upon. For example, the producer may discover that of the twenty-three focus testers, twenty-two dislike the music. He or she should consider finding another composer. If the focus test poses the right questions, results will show whether users like the subject, content, features, user interface, narrator, characters, animation, graphics, games, scoring, challenges, obstacles, levels, and game world. The producer will know whether users think the product is too boring, too easy, too hard, too confusing, or too childish. If the test subjects are sophisticated and knowledgeable users, the producer will know how the product stacks up, in the eyes of the target market, against competitors.

Anecdotal remarks are very important. Here, the data can be qualified. Let's say you're testing your new racecar driving game. A respondent may say something like, "I like it, but it doesn't seem to have the same feel as such and such a product. It's, I don't know, stiffer and not as natural feeling." Others may say the track doesn't have enough hairpin turns or there aren't enough competitors to pass. You have to take these comments for what they're worth. If that other product is a hit, play it yourself and compare your product. Stiffer? Fix it!

Incorporate Test Results

The two most unlikely results of the prototype focus tests are that the product is horrible and so development should stop now or that the product is perfect and so development should continue. Instead, the producer is probably pondering a number of results that indicate that the product is pretty good but requires some level of surgery to be a hit with users. It may require changes that range from adding or subtracting entire nodes, to redesigning some of the art or interactive structure, to hiring a new composer and reorchestrating all of the music. Perhaps the game needs minor tweaking to make it play faster. Based on the producer's interpretation of the focus test results, some changes will be absolutely necessary while others will be important, but not essential. Before development can move on to the production phase, the producer must decide what changes to make and the impact of those changes on the schedule and budget, and he or she must quickly reset the plans to move forward.

Prioritize the Changes

Compile a list of the modifications and divide them into three categories:

1. Changes that must be made as a number-one priority, no matter what
2. Changes that should be made, unless the cost is prohibitive
3. Changes it would be nice to make if there is time and if they don't cost anything

Prioritize all of the changes in all three categories. Further divide the changes into type (art, animation, video, sound, interactive design, programming, game play) and node. Be certain to indicate whether the change impacts the entire product or just some small part of it.

Evaluate the Changes

The design and development team must then evaluate the changes from the following perspectives:

■ In what way do these changes affect the aesthetic design of the product? Here, the director considers the art, video, animation, sound, and interactive design. The director should determine the impact of the changes on individual nodes and on the product as a whole. Sometimes, making what appears to be a simple change on one screen creates a ripple effect felt everywhere.

■ In what way do the changes affect the technical approach? The producer and the technical director must determine whether another technical approach is needed. Do we now have to hire another programmer? Do we have to license other software?

■ In what way do the changes affect the production processes and methods? The director determines whether any production methods change, and if any do, how are the effects to be created now?

■ In what way do these changes affect the schedule and budget? Are these expensive and time-consuming changes? Will we have to back-peddle and redo a lot of work, or do these changes merely force us to adjust our future development plans? The producer must adjust the asset database, the development plan, and the budget to reflect the changes.

■ In what way do these changes affect the current design documents? How much rewriting and restructuring is required? Are new audio and narration scripts needed? The writer must modify the functional specification to reflect the changes.

It is critical that the management team evaluates the necessary product modifications correctly, quickly, and efficiently because the next phase, the production phase, will be guided by the decisions it makes at this juncture.

Reach Agreement on Changes

The developer must reach an agreement with the client on what changes to incorporate into the product. Some changes, incidentally, will come directly from the client. Agreement can be reached with the execution of a change order, which is referenced in the letter of intent and, if there is a contract in place by now, in the contract, as well. In a change order, the producer itemizes all of the changes to the functional specification called for by the focus test results and categorizes the changes as "hard" or "soft" changes. Hard changes are those that deviate from the approved spec and add cost and/or time to the final budget and plan. Soft changes are those that can be made without affecting the budget or plan. An example of a soft change is when the change affects a node that has not been worked on yet and the new scope of work is the same as the original scope of work. It's a wash.

Modify the Specification

If the client and developer reach agreement on the changes, the writer must immediately modify the functional specification to reflect the agreed-upon changes. The producer must get approval of the modified spec immediately. Once done, the producer modifies the asset database, the development plan, and the budget prior to moving the team on to the next phase, the production phase.

Chapter Summary

In this chapter, you learned about the prototype and the important role it plays in creating a product that will be acceptable to target users. The prototype is a small, working version of the final product that the developer tests with potential users to determine several important things before investing time and money on the final product. The developer tests the overall design, technology, and development processes. If the product is an educational or instructional product, the creators test its effectiveness as a teaching and learning tool. They test the prototype with focus groups and obtain early feedback from target users about the potential marketability of the product. If the prototype is successful, the marketing people use it to fulfill their needs before the final product is complete. They use it to attract a publisher or retailers, to get publicity from reviewers and at trade shows, and to entice customers with downloadable versions of the product.

During the prototype phase, the producer, director, and writer carry on with their important roles. The producer manages the development process, tracks progress, and compares progress against costs. He also arranges for the focus tests of the prototype, the gathering and evaluation of focus test results, and modifying the product before moving on to full development. The director supervises the staff on a day-to-day basis, giving each staff member clear direction on what and how to create the assets he or she is responsible for. The writer maintains the functional specification, incorporating changes.

When test results are in, the developer prioritizes them and costs them out. If the client agrees to the changes and any additional cost or time required to implement them, the client signs a change order authorizing the developer to proceed with development.

Recommended Reading

Dempsey, John V., and Sales, Gregory C., Eds. *Interactive Instruction and Feedback*. Educational Technology Publications: Englewood Cliffs, NJ, 1993.

The Production Phase

In this chapter, you will learn about

- The gold master, the prize of the production phase
- Deliverables, including asset creation, programming, and prerelease burns
- Roles of the producer, director, and writer
- Managing the change process
- Prioritizing tasks
- Meaning and importance of Alpha and Beta versions
- The quality assurance cycle
- Writing for package design, inserts, and readme files

So far, we have covered three important phases that lead up to the production phase. During client discovery, we defined the product with a top-level design and we established the preliminary time line, costs, milestones, roles, and responsibilities and finally signed a contract or letter of intent with the client. During the design phase, we wrote a functional specification, created graphic designs and layouts, found talent, cleared rights, built an asset database, and finalized the budget. We determined the critical path and created a final development plan. During the prototype phase, we created a small working version of the product for creative, technical, and business purposes and then tested it with focus groups. After the prototype was tested, the results analyzed, and modifications determined, the functional specification, asset database, development plan, and budget were adjusted to reflect modifications needed for the final product.

The production phase begins. It consists of a methodical attack on a mountain of work. Artists create graphics and animation. Photographers shoot pictures and the director shoots video. Sound designers record audio, select or create sound effects and music, and then mix tracks. Programmers write software or use existing engines or authoring tools and combine the assets with the software in a process called integration. Quality assurance testers step in at appropriate times to uncover and log bugs. Through it all, the producer, director, and writer continue to manage the process, supervise the creative efforts, and document the modifications, respectively.

In this chapter, we cover the deliverables, tasks, and milestones of the production phase and discuss the specific roles of the producer, director, and writer. By the end of this chapter, you should have a very clear picture of the entire process and the importance of conducting development in phases.

The Production Phase Prize

If the developer and the client have used the formulaic approach to multimedia development described so far, the production phase is a time for orderly, well-directed work toward a common goal—the gold master. The gold master is the final, fully tested and client-approved disc, which is sent by the developer to the disc replication facility. There, the disc is used as the master copy, from which thousands or even hundreds of thousands of products are made. These CD-ROM products are burned, labeled, packaged, shrink-wrapped, and shipped to stores all over the country or the world.

During the production phase, the production staff contributes thousands of labor hours to get to gold master. The development team at Media Station expended over 6,000 labor hours, for example, on the *Tonka Search and Rescue* CD-ROM. The team is directed and managed by the director and producer, who use the functional specification as their production bible.

There are two requirements that govern and dominate the activities of the development team while it tackles the various tasks, creates the deliverables, and makes the milestones leading to the gold master. First, the gold master must conform to the product described in the functional spec exactly, unless the developer and the client agree to modifications along the way. When that happens, the writer must edit the spec to reflect those changes accurately. Second, the gold master must be bug-free. There must be no art, sound, or programming problems of any kind.

Production Phase Deliverables

In order to make a gold master, the team must create a number of deliverables, which fall into three categories: assets, programming, and prerelease burns. The development staff works from the asset database and under the direction of the director to create thousands of individual graphic, video, textual, and sound elements. The programmers work under the direction of the lead engineer to write software, integrate licensed software, or use authoring tools to make working versions of the final product, incorporating assets provided by the production staff when they are available. When a certain percentage of assets and programming is complete, the programmers create a "disc image"—a collection of all the files needed for the product—and they burn a disc. Table 12.1 shows various production phase deliverables and who is responsible for each.

Table 12.1 The Production Phase Deliverables		
Deliverable	Responsible Party	Comments
Background art	Artists	Artists work from paper designs completed during the design phase.
Icons	Artists	
Buttons	Artists	
Graphics	Artists	
Screen text	Writer, possibly artist	Artist may create bitmap.
Photographs	Photographers and artists	Artists digitize photos.
Video	Videographer and artists	Artists may capture video.
Voice-over	Sound designer	
Music	Sound designer	
Sound effects	Sound designer	
Quicktime, AVI, or MPEG movies	Sound designer and artist	Work together to sync the picture to the sound.
Special-purpose software	Programmers	
Database engines	Programmers	May include writer or researcher.
Authored nodes	Programmers	
Installation software	Programmers	
Alpha burns	Programmers	
Beta burns	Programmers	
Bug reports	Quality assurance testers	Work with producer to assign and track bugs.
Readme files	Writer	May be the responsibility of the publisher.
Package art	Artist	
Insert or manual text	Writer	

The phrase *burn a disc* refers to the physical creation of a CD-ROM, during which a laser burns tiny pits in the substrata of a recordable disc. The arrangement of these pits carries the digital information.

Testers from the quality assurance group then test the disc and log bugs, as described in Chapter 11. Subsequent burns are made when more assets and programming are completed and when bugs discovered in the previous burns are corrected. This process continues until the product includes all assets and programming, complies with the functional spec, and is bug free.

Progress Payments and Approvals

Client approval of a deliverable is called a milestone and may trigger a progress payment from the client. The developer and client agree on the milestones that trigger payments during their contract negotiations. At a minimum, the deliverable may require the approval of the client before it can be incorporated into the final product. Nearly every contract gives the client final approval of all creative elements. As deliverables are completed, the producer arranges to send the material to the client or to assemble the material for a client visit and evaluation. Some clients take a very proactive role in seeing or listening to deliverables and providing the development team with feedback. Other clients are less vigilant (some to the point of being irritatingly difficult to nail down). It is the producer's responsibility to obtain the client's approval of all deliverables as quickly as possible for the purpose of maintaining the schedule. When a milestone—*the approved deliverable*—activates a progress payment, the producer is responsible for notifying accounts receivable to invoice the client as soon as the client's approval has been obtained.

The producer should obtain client approval in writing. It is a good practice to send a form letter such as the one in Figure 12.1 along with the deliverable with a short statement and space for the client to sign. You may reword this form to fit your requirements. Have the client return it to you. Indicate that work cannot continue until this approval has been received. This paper trail will help you avoid unpleasantness later if the client suddenly wants to make a change to the deliverable. Never rely on verbal approvals.

If the client refuses to approve a deliverable, you must establish the reason for the refusal. According to the deal you should have signed with the client, the only reason not to approve a deliverable is nonconformity to the functional specification. You recall that during the design phase, important art and video elements were drawn as layouts, designs, and storyboards. Some were created for the prototype. Audio samples were provided during the design and prototype phases. And all elements are described in detail in the spec itself. Have the client spell out exactly what the reasons are for nonapproval. Again, use the written form in Figure 12.2.

If the refusal is based on a fair and sound comparison of the actual delivered element and the expectations set up by the design and description of the element in

FIGURE 12.1   **Example of a Client Approval Form**

ABC Developer, Inc.

DELIVERABLE APPROVAL FORM

I have reviewed the _____ materials for the CD-ROM

product _____. The materials comply with the

functional specification and are hereby approved for the final product.

FOR XYZ PUBLISHERS

Name _____

Title _____

Date _____

---

the functional specification, the client may have a strong case for you to create it again. If not, the refusal may call for a change order.

Managing Changes

 Throughout product development—but expecially during the production phase when so many elements are sent to the client for review—the client requests changes. The requests may be for aesthetic, marketing, educational, or other reasons. The changes may be small and inconsequential from the developer's standpoint, or they may represent major overhauls of the design. Using the functional specification as a touchstone, the producer must ascertain whether the change impacts the schedule, the budget, or both. Whenever the client requests a change, the producer should send the change order form to the client to obtain a written documentation of the request. The change order form (see Figure 12.3) adds to the paper trail, which documents the development history and all but eliminates some of the more contentious moments that can occur between the parties.

The development team and the client must be made aware that absolutely no changes occur without the direct, purposeful involvement of the producer and the use of change order forms. There is a strong temptation for an artist, sound de-

FIGURE 12.2 **Example of a Client Nonapproval Form**

ABC Developer, Inc

DELIVERABLE NONAPPROVAL FORM

I have reviewed the _____ materials for the CD-ROM

product _____. The materials are not approved

for the final product for these reasons:

FOR XYZ PUBLISHERS

Name _____

Title _____

Date _____

signer, or programmer, and even the director, to make a casual change requested by the client during an informal phone call or over lunch. This establishes a poor precedent with the client, who has no idea how a relatively minor change impacts development. All assets and software programs are elements of a grander scheme, and one small, unauthorized alteration can have a maleficent ripple effect. If someone surreptitiously alters an image, sound, or software event described in the functional spec, testers will log it as a bug, causing needless work for a number of people later on.

When the client fills out and returns a change order, the producer gathers the appropriate team members, who evaluate the change request and determine its impact on the budget and schedule. The response to the client may be made using a form like that in Figure 12.4.

The director must look at the change request and determine whether it has any negative or positive impact on the overall design of the product. A small change on one screen in one node may affect the overall look and feel or consistency of the interface design or may cause other repercussions throughout the product. The director, who has the clearest overall vision of the product, must evaluate the change from that point of view. The lead programmer must review the change to determine

FIGURE 12.3   **Example of a Change Order Form**

ABC Developer, Inc.

CHANGE ORDER FORM

Date

Project Name   Project #

Client   Contact

Address   State   Zip

Phone   Fax   E-mail

Client Change Request

In space below, please describe the current design. Include the node number and page number from the functional specification. Include a sketch if appropriate.

Describe the current design

In space below, describe the changes you would like to make. Include a sketch if possible.

Describe desired change

---

whether any major software rework is required. The art director determines whether and how much additional art is needed. The sound designer evaluates the sound needs. Almost any change causes the writer to modify the functional specification.

The producer estimates time and cost based on the team's evaluation. If the developer and its client have agreed to handle cost changes on a time and materials basis, the producer completes the hours and rates on the change order form and sends it back to the client for approval or negotiation. The change is then in the client's court. The client must decide whether the change is worth the extra cost and time.

Production Phase Tasks

The producer and director prioritize tasks. Some tasks must precede others in the production pipeline. Generally, the programmers and software engineers can only

FIGURE 12.4 **Example of a Change Order Response**

Developer Evaluation

	Description	Hours	Rate	Cost
Software				
Sound				
Art				
Animation				
Video				
Writing				
Testing				
Other				
Total Cost				

Estimated impact on schedule

Note. Approval of this change must be received by the developer by _____ in order to avoid delays in the development schedule.

Client Approval

I agree to the additional cost and to the changes to the delivery schedule (if any) provided above. I understand that I will be invoiced for the additional work upon completion and approval of this change.

FOR XYZ PUBLISHER

Name

Title

Date

do so much before they need graphic and sound assets to complete their work. Therefore, asset production is a top priority.

Interdependencies of Tasks

Many asset production tasks are interdependent. For example, before an animator can draw characters that talk on camera, he or she needs a voice track to work from. To create a voice track for the animator, the sound designer hires talent, records the voice, selects the "takes," edits to length, and saves the sound file in the proper digital format. The animator then reads the voice track and determines the precise frame that each phoneme occurs on, recording the information on an exposure sheet. The animator then draws the proper mouth on the character so that when the animation and sound files are locked together and played simultaneously, the character's mouth shape matches the sound synchronously. Of course, before any of this can happen, the writer must write the dialogue. (Computer software from a company called Lips Inc. (LipsInc.com) does much of this work automatically. The software "reads" the sound track and not only determines what the proper mouth position should be, but also actually drives a computer graphics program to create the proper mouth.)

Artists generally create background art before animators draw character animation that will play over it. Animators draw the character animation using background art as a guide. Animators can see where their characters interact with objects in the background and can match perspective. If a character must reach out and open a door or point at something in the scene, for example, the art containing the door is drawn first, giving the animator a layout to work on.

The animation must be completed before the sound designer can add music and sound effects. All of these tasks must be completed before the animation is digitally saved as a movie.

Before the director can shoot any video, the writer must write the scene descriptions and dialogue and the producer must arrange for settings, locations, props, set dressings, costumes, makeup, and, of course, talent. After the video is shot, it must be edited, digitally captured, and properly compressed, often by someone in the art department.

As you can plainly see from these examples, many tasks are both interdependent and interdepartmental. A very detailed development plan for the production phase will list these tasks, in the proper order, with the appropriate responsible party. See Table 12.2. This chronologically arranged list enables careful scheduling and coordination. There will be work handoffs between various staff people all day long, every day, and without a detailed task list, it is quite easy and typical for important tasks to be forgotten, dropped, or lost in the shuffle.

You will remember that many tasks have already been completed during the design and prototype phases. Animation and video have already been storyboarded. Screens and characters have already been designed and laid out. Talent has already been cast. These tasks are not included in Table 12.2. Furthermore, there may be many tasks that are project specific or are required because the director dreamed up a special development method. These are not included.

Production Phase Task List

A widely used method for animating 3-D characters is motion capture, a technique that involves using real actors to perform actions, which are tracked by various detection devices that are attached to the performer. Computer software gathers the motion data and then applies the movement data to 3-D computer-generated characters. This method is fast and accurate, but it does involve several additional tasks not included in Table 12.2.

Table 12.2 Production Phase Task List				
		Tasks	Responsible	Comments
animation tasks	1	Write scripts	Writer	
	2	Hire talent	Producer	
	3	Hire composer	Producer	
	4	Write and produce music	Composer/arranger	
	5	Record dialog	Sound designer	Director directs
	6	Select voice takes	Director	
	7	Edit and format voice takes	Sound designer	
	8	Read track	Director	May have assistant do
	9	Exposure sheets	Director	
	10	Create backgrounds	Artists	
	11	Animation	Animators	
	12	Ink & paint	Artists	
	13	Compress and format movies	Artists	Quicktime, AVI, MPEG, etc.
	14	Sync movie to sound	Sound designer	
	15	Add SFX and music	Sound designer	
	16	Output final movie	Sound designer	
3-D animation tasks	17	Build 3-D models	3-D animator	
	18	Animate characters	3-D animator	
	19	Create texture maps	Artist	
	20	Animate camera and lights	3-D animator	
	21	Render animation	3-D animator	
	22	Output final movie	3-D animator	
video tasks	23	Provide scripts	Writer	
	24	Hire talent	Producer	
				(continued)

Table 12.2   (continued)

		Tasks	Responsible	Comments
video tasks	25	Hire crew	Producer	If not staff crew
	26	Build sets	Producer	If needed
	27	Rent props, dressings	Producer	If needed
	28	Rent equipment	Producer	If not owned
	29	Hire caterer and transportation	Producer	
	30	Purchase expendables	Producer	
	31	Shoot video	Director	
	32	Select takes from dailies	Director	
	33	Edit video	Editor	Unless edit after capture
	34	Add audio, EFX, music	Editor	
	35	Capture and compress audio	Editor or artist	
still graphics tasks	36	Locate photographs, art	Researcher	
	37	Acquire photographs, art	Producer	
	38	Hire photographer	Producer	
	39	Hire talent	Producer	
	40	Arrange for setting, etc.	Photographer	
	41	Take photographs	Photographer	
	42	Scan photographs	Artist	
	43	Size, color correct, format	Artist	
	44	Create icons	Artist	
	45	Create buttons	Artist	
	46	Create other graphics	Artist	
	47	Create bitmap text	Artist	
	48	Create text files	Writer	
sound tasks	49	Hire talent	Producer	
	50	Record narration	Sound designer	
	51	Edit and mix with music	Sound designer	Music completed for animation
	52	Save in proper format	Sound designer	

		Tasks	Responsible	Comments
programming tasks	53	Author title using stand-in assets	Programmers	
	54	Substitute final assets	Programmers	
	55	Write special software	Programmers	
	56	Debug software	Programmers	
	57	Write installation programs	Programmers	
	58	Burn Alpha disc	Programmers	
	59	Burn Beta disc	Programmers	
	60	Debug title	Programmers	
	61	Burn gold master	Programmers	
quality assurance tasks	62	Develop testing plan	QA supervisor	
	63	Configure testing hardware	QA supervisor	
	64	Schedule testing/burns	QA supervisor	
	65	Test burns, log bugs	Testers	
	66	Prioritize/assign bugs	QA supervisor and producer	
	67	Retest	Testers	

Table 12.2   (continued)

Role of the Producer and Director during Development

The production phase involves more people doing more tasks over a longer period of time than the other phases combined. The management effort balloons significantly during the production phase, not only because of the total volume of work, but also because the work should be front loaded. The producer must make certain that a great deal of work is completed in the early weeks of the production phase and then trails off over time. The chart pictured in Figure 12.5 graphically shows the proper planning of labor hours and activity over time for the whole development process. Notice how the workload is very high as the production phase begins and then gradually decays as the end nears. A well-constructed development plan loads resources for the completion of tasks to result in this kind of bell curve. By the waning weeks of development, the team should consist of the quality assurance testers and a skeleton crew of a programmer, artist, and sound designer who tweak the product and fix bugs.

FIGURE 12.5

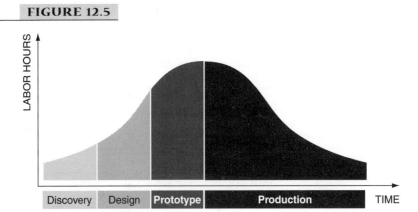

A well-constructed plan for labor distribution during the development process results in a bell curve.

When there is no plan, or a poorly executed one, the loading of resources may look like the chart in Figure 12.6. When this occurs, the development studio is probably in crisis mode, with most of the team spending sleepless weekends trying to cobble together the product at the last minute.

FIGURE 12.6

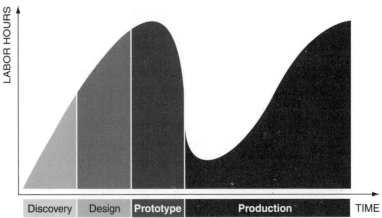

A poorly constructed plan for labor distribution during the development process results in a crisis of a heavy workload at the end of the production process.

The director must supervise the staff so that their work is of a consistently high quality and fits into the final product properly. The director's job is complicated by the volume of work and the number of staff persons who need his or her constant direction.

Task Assignments

In order to plan and execute the production phase as depicted in Figure 12.5, the producer puts many balls into the air simultaneously. Every task that can be completed in parallel with others must be. On the very first day of the production phase, the producer works with the director to provide task assignments and creative direction to the team. The producer must provide each team member—either individually or through his or her department supervisor—both the specific assignment and the desired completion date. This is often done using the marching orders described in Chapter 9. The producer should make certain that each team member knows how his or her work fits into the big picture, how it will be used by another team member in another department, and how and when to notify the director that the task is complete and ready to be approved. When a team member is properly informed, he or she will be both motivated and less likely to improvise.

Sample Work Assignment (Marching Order)

Look at Figure 12.7, the sample work assignment. Even with an attached asset list and storyboards, and with the functional spec referenced on the work assignment, the artwork itself is open to the interpretation of the individual artist. The director should speak to the artist or to the art director to make certain that the individual artists are clear about the assignment. By providing guidance before the work starts, the director ensures that the work will not have to be redone. Of course, this goes for the sound designers, photographers, and programmers as well.

Follow-Up

The producer should follow up with task assignments periodically during the day or week, depending on how long the tasks take. The producer can verify that the staff is still on track and on target and can update the asset database when assets have been completed and approved.

Progress Tracking

As described in Chapter 9, the producer tracks progress by obtaining reports from department heads indicating what assets have been produced and approved. The reports come in the form of database printouts and oral reports made during the weekly team meetings. From the accounting department, the producer gets a weekly cost report. By comparing the two, the producer knows whether the development target is met and the costs are in line.

FIGURE 12.7   Sample Work Assignment

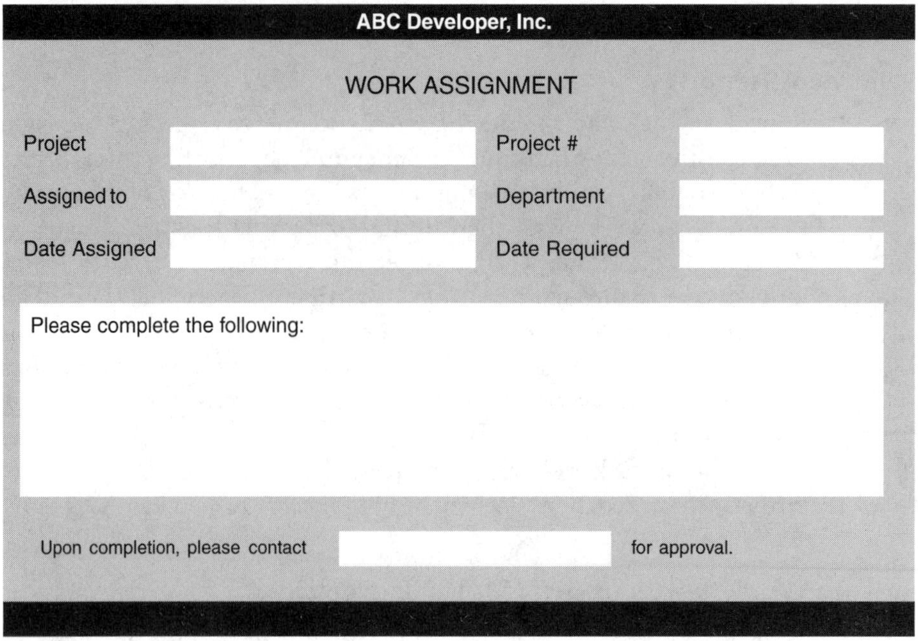

ABC Developer, Inc.

WORK ASSIGNMENT

Project		Project #
Assigned to		Department
Date Assigned		Date Required

Please complete the following:

Upon completion, please contact _____ for approval.

Alpha and Beta Discs

At some point during the production phase, about 80 percent of the assets and programming are complete. At this point, the lead programmer creates a disc image and burns a CD-ROM. This first version of the title is called the Alpha 1.0 burn. Not only is 20 percent of the title missing, but also the disc is full of mistakes, bugs, and first attempts that are certain to bring sighs of shame and disgust. However, the purpose of the initial Alpha burn is to underscore what needs fixing, tweaking, and finishing. Alpha 1.0 undergoes rigorous testing by the quality assurance department, which is seeing the revised functional specification and the disc for the first time since the prototype several months before.

This begins a cycle of Alpha disc burns and testing (Figure 12.8). With each disc burn, more assets and programming are added, while bugs are fixed on the previously tested portions. The bug-testing, logging, and bug-fixing process was covered in depth in Chapter 11. Successive Alpha burns have not only fewer bugs, but also more assets and features. As the disc gradually grows to 100 percent of the assets and features, it is called a Beta. Beta 1.0 contains 100 percent of the title's assets and features but has not been completely debugged. It still contains priority 2, 3, and 4 bugs. Subsequent versions of Beta discs have fewer bugs. When the producer is certain that a Beta disc is bug-free and meets all of the other requirements of a gold master, it is declared Beta 2.0, the gold master candidate.

FIGURE 12.8   **The Quality Assurance Cycle**

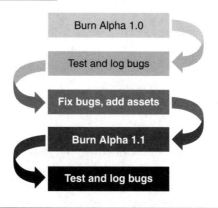

Unless required to do so by the contract, the producer sends Alpha and Beta discs to the client at his or her discretion. Depending on the client's multimedia experience, these prerelease burns can be either reassuring or shocking. The producer may be contractually obligated to send some versions of the Alpha and Beta to the client and usually does so with "release notes," a written description of the disc that acknowledges all known bugs and shortcomings.

Clients are notorious for finding changes they'd like to make, even at this late date. The producer's job often entails holding off the client's rush to judgment. Often, bugs exaggerate problems that go away when the bugs are fixed. Programmers, artists, and sound designers use this time to fine-tune and tweak the product to make it look, sound, and behave better with each successive burn. The longer the producer can delay a client from asking for changes, the more likely it is that the client won't want any.

The Gold Master

The producer sends the gold master candidate to the client for final approval. The client evaluates the disc from every possible perspective. This is the last opportunity to delay the release for any reason. By this time, everyone associated with the project is well aware of the product's quality and conformity to the original (and subsequently modified) design specification. The appropriate authority approves the disc and releases it for manufacturing. The producer then sends the official gold master to the client's disc manufacturing facility.

Readme Files

Readme files are simple text files that the developer puts on the gold master disc. A readme file may be last-minute information about the product or about how to install the product, or it could include corrections to printed material packaged with the product. The consumer can open these files and read the message. The producer should be certain to double-check all printed information—especially 1-800 telephone numbers, URLs, and e-mail addresses of technical support—and if any corrections are necessary to have the writer create a readme file with the proper information.

Package Design

During the production phase, and before the gold master date, the marketing manager begins the process of package design. CD-ROMs are sold in shrink-wrapped cardboard boxes that vary slightly in size and shape but are generally 9 inches wide by 10½ inches tall by 1½ inches deep. Boxes may be a little wider or narrower, taller or shorter, or deeper. Boxes are available with flaps, cut-outs, embossing, and any number of other options. Packaged with the CD-ROM, which is protected in a plastic jewel case, are a manual, instructions, or other printed material. CD-ROMs are often sold with other promotional material, coupons, toys, and so forth. Syracuse Language Systems, which publishes language-learning products that feature voice recognition software, at one time packaged its products with a microphone.

Printed on the front of the box is an eye-catching graphic, the title of the product, and other standard information, which normally includes

- The logo of the publisher
- The logo of the developer (sometimes on the back or side)
- The genre of the product
- The intended target age of the user
- The platform and operating system the product runs on
- Slogans and product blurbs

On the back of the package, the publisher prints screen shots: scenes from the product that give the consumer an idea of the look and feel. Listed or highlighted are the product's main features. Also included are

- A table detailing the minimum system requirements
- Contact information, such as the address, phone, and e-mail of the publisher
- Copyright notices
- Bar code with inventory control number

FIGURE 12.9

Sample package art for *The Legend of Kyrandia,* developed and published by Westwood Studios, an Electronic Arts company.

Very nearly every package contains these elements. Package design entails deciding specifically what images to use, how to lay them out on the box, what type faces to use, what colors to use, and what features to highlight. Remember that the retailer stocks shelves according to genre, so a product's competition will be right next to it on the store shelves. The package designer chooses a prevalent color for the front of the package that will contrast it with other packages in the same genre. You recall that a product's features are often determined by its competition in the marketplace. These are the features the marketing manager certainly wants on the back of the box.

The producer, director, and writer are involved in these decisions to some extent. In many cases, the producer is ultimately responsible for the commercial success of the product and has a vested interest in the design of the package because it plays a major role in attracting consumers in retail venues. The PC CD-ROM and console game markets are extremely competitive, and it is vitally important that the product attract attention on the crowded retail shelf. The director, who has a clear creative vision of the product and whose work is wrapped in the package, is emotionally vested in the package design. The writer is tasked with writing the copy that appears on the package.

Tips for Writing Package Copy

As large as the package may seem, there is relatively little space for large bodies of copy. The copy must be printed in large type so it can be read easily from arms' length. Furthermore, consumers don't have the time to read very much while standing in the store aisle. Package copy must be clear, concise, and exciting. It is meant to sell the product as much as inform about it. Package copy is more akin to advertising copy than to any other style or form.

The marketing department determines the unique selling points of the product and prioritizes them. These become the features bulleted on the back of the box. Not surprisingly, the features are often exactly those that the designers visualized while writing the concept document many, many months before. Typically, a short block of copy extols the product. Note the copy and bullets from the package back in Figure 12.10.

FIGURE 12.10

Sample package copy illustrates similarity to features of advertising copy: clarity, conciseness, and excitement.

 ## Archiving

The very last piece of business, usually the responsibility of the producer, is the proper archiving of all materials used in the development of the product. Do not underestimate the importance of doing this or the time (and space) needed to do it properly. Archiving is necessary for the following reasons:

■ Some products require modification after release. These modifications can be very simple or quite complex, depending on what they are and why they are required.

■ Many products have follow-on projects, such as sequels, which may require the same assets as the first.

■ Many products require localization: versions of the product in a foreign language for international distribution. Localized products require the same assets, some of which will have to be modified to show translated text or different icons or buttons. Voice-over and narration will have to be replaced.

■ There may be legal or business disagreements, and it may be necessary to look again at memos, letters, approval forms, or other documents.

■ People move around freely and oral tradition and human memory quickly fade. Corporate memory must be kept in a file cabinet.

For these reasons, all physical and electronic production elements must be properly labeled and stored. Any method that suits your purposes, culture, or capacities should be used. Do consider storing the elements off site, as long as you can access them easily. The following documents should be properly labeled, categorized, and archived:

■ All concept documents and other creative design elements, including drawings, sketches, node maps, and meeting notes

■ All meeting agendas and follow-up memos

■ All memos and letters exchanged with the client

■ The proposal and bid

■ Letter of intent and development agreement

■ Initial and final versions of the functional specification

■ Copies of invoices from vendors, receipts, expense reports, and all other proofs of expenditures on the product

■ Deal memos and subcontracting agreements with independent contractors

■ Releases signed by talent

■ Copyrights, licenses, and permissions

■ Copies of weekly status reports, both internal and external

■ All approval and nonapproval forms signed by the client

■ Shipping receipts

The following physical production elements must be archived:

■ Final layouts, character designs, storyboards, and exposure sheets

■ Video tapes, photographs, film, audio tapes

■ All versions of CD-ROM burns. Make certain each is properly labeled as Alpha 1.0, Beta 2.4, and so forth and dated

The following elements must be stored electronically:

- All graphics: backgrounds, buttons, icons, animation files. It is best to archive only the last and final version of these assets, in the highest resolution possible. Layered *PhotoShop* files are preferable to flattened, indexed files. This makes it possible to modify images.

- All sound files. Ideally, sound files should be stored in a multitrack, premixed format, which would allow a future sound designer to substitute a new voice track for the old.

- Captured but uncompressed video. Again, this makes it possible to reuse the video in a future application but also to modify it, if desired.

- Source code. Source code is any computer programming readable by a human. The source code must be archived so any future changes to it can be effected.

Even if you have plenty of on-site storage for these elements, it is prudent to put it all on CD or some other media and store it off-site, with the documents and physical production material. Once you have archived the production material, you are done.

Chapter Summary

This chapter covered the production phase of product development. After three phases of planning and testing, the production phase is methodical, orderly asset development, programming, and testing the product as it nears completion. The prize at the end of the production phase is the gold master, which is sent to the disc manufacturing facility, where replicates are burned, packaged, shrink-wrapped, and sent to retailers.

During the production phase, the team creates art, sound, and programming deliverables under the management and supervision of the producer and director. The producer sends the deliverables to the client for approval. When the client has approved a deliverable, the event is a milestone in the development of the product. Some milestones trigger a progress payment, depending on the agreement between the developer and its client. When the client requests a change to a deliverable, there is a change order process that ensures a clear understanding of the requested change, documentation of the impact of the change (on budget and schedule), and a go-ahead from the client.

The producer identifies all of the tasks and the correct order the tasks must be completed so the team can create the deliverables. Either directly or through department heads, the producer provides each team member with work assignments and other information so that each staff person works on the right elements at the right time and understands how the element fits into the larger product. The director provides creative direction for the creation of each element, which ensures that the element will meet his or her approval when complete and will not have to be done over.

When a meaningful amount of the assets and programming have been completed, the programmers burn a disc and hand it over to the quality assurance testers. The first of these discs is called the Alpha disc. The testers hammer away at the product and encounter bugs. They log the bugs, which are then reviewed by the producer and assigned to the appropriate staff for fixing. Another disc is burned and tested, and the process continues until the product is bug-free. Eventually, the disc meets all of the criteria for being the gold master.

During the production phase, the marketing department begins package design, which may involve the writer, art director, producer, and director.

The last piece of business is the proper archiving of all development materials. There are many compelling reasons for archiving. There may be a follow-on project, localization, or minor modifications. There may be a need to reestablish a paper trail to solve a business or legal disagreement. Once archiving is complete, the members of the development team are truly done with their project.

part *three*

Appendixes

The Student Project

Appendix A is a portion of a functional specification written by two students at the S. I. Newhouse School of Public Communications as part of their final project for a course called *Writing and Designing Multimedia*. About 15 percent of the functional specification is reprinted here. In addition to writing this design document, the students created a fully working prototype of their product in a multimedia lab. This specification is included here as a good example of a design document that can be written and executed by students during a single semester. My comments appear in gray boxes.

The complete functional specification for this student project was 57 pages long.
Fewer than 10 pages are reprinted here.

Cancer: A Survival Guide

TABLE OF CONTENTS

Executive Summary

Global Conventions

Node Map

Navigation and User Interface

Bumper

Welcome Screen

Main Menu Screen

Interactive Glossary

Interactive Tours

Journal

Frequently Asked Questions

Resources

Credit Page

EXECUTIVE SUMMARY

Cancer: A Survival Guide is an educational CD-ROM that gives patients and their families a personal introduction to the people, products, and procedures that they may encounter in their fight against cancer. This self-help product features a journal for patients to record their daily experiences with the disease. The interactive journal gives patients a greater sense of control at a time when they are likely to feel that they have lost control.

The product looks and feels like a scrapbook. This metaphor, consistent with the journal feature, gives the CD-ROM a very personal and photographic nature.

Cancer: A Survival Guide is designed for 15- through 30-year-old cancer patients. Authors of self-help guides and other literature for cancer patients have largely ignored this age group. *Cancer: A Survival Guide* provides several features that are not available on the Web or even in written materials. First, this CD-ROM helps to alleviate patient fear by providing a very personal introduction to the people, places, and things associated with the disease. Patients "meet" doctors and nurses who show them some of the procedures involved in cancer treatment. More important, they "meet" and hear the stories of other survivors.

Second, the journal feature of the product gives patients a greater sense of control over their lives and their disease. The journal encourages them to record medical information such as their temperature or blood count in daily entries. The CD-ROM creates charts from the information entered by the patient. The charts track these important details over time and in relation to their treatment schedule. Best of all, these charts can be printed out and can even be shared with the patient's doctors interested in tracking their progress. The daily entries also include a place to record any personal thoughts or feelings that the patient wishes.

This CD-ROM is distributed through doctors' offices and serves as a primary resource for these patients. It provides patients with a sense of control and a foundation for other research into the disease. *Cancer: A Survival Guide* is a home base for those who are fighting cancer.

Global conventions are all those things that will be used repeatedly in the title. Global conventions can include graphic and sound elements, buttons, icons, cursor states, and other behaviors. Once described here, these things do not have to be described everywhere they will appear.

GLOBAL CONVENTIONS

Background

A notebook background with a spiral binder on the left border is used for every screen after the bumper.

Tabs

Six notebook tabs appear on every page past the "cover" of the journal. The tabs are labeled for the section of the journal to which they will lead the user. The words on the tabs are black but turn white on rollover. On mousedown, they become outlined in black, and on mouseup, the tab leads the user to the selected section. On mouseup, the page moves from left to right and is accompanied by a page turning sound.

Table A.1 Interactivity Table for Tabs			
User	**System**	**Description**	**Comments**
Clicks on journal tab	Goes to "journal" section	Unselected journal, selected journal, and rollover journal, page turning sound	Upon rollover, moves to rollover state. Moves to selected state upon mousedown, plays a page turning sound, and wipes to the "journal" section upon mouseup.
Clicks on glossary tab	Goes to "glossary" section	Unselected glossary, selected glossary, and rollover glossary, page turning sound	Upon rollover, moves to rollover state. Moves to selected state upon mousedown, plays a page turning sound, and wipes to the "glossary" section upon mouseup.
Clicks on tour tab	Goes to "tour" section	Unselected tour, selected tour, and rollover tour, page turning sound	Upon rollover, moves to rollover state. Moves to selected state upon mousedown, plays a page turning sound, and wipes to the "tour" section upon mouseup.
Clicks on questions tab	Goes to "questions" section	Unselected questions, selected questions, and rollover questions, page turning sound	Upon rollover, moves to rollover state. Moves to selected state upon mousedown, plays a page turning sound, and wipes to the "questions" section upon mouseup.
Clicks on resources tab	Goes to "resources" section	Unselected resources, selected resources, and rollover resources, page turning sound	Upon rollover, moves to rollover state. Moves to selected state upon mousedown, plays a page turning sound, and wipes to the "resources" section upon mouseup.
Clicks on contents tab	Goes to "contents" section	Unselected contents, selected contents, and rollover contents, page turning sound	Upon rollover, moves to rollover state. Moves to selected state upon mousedown, plays a page turning sound, and wipes to the "contents" section upon mouseup.

Exit

The program can be exited only through the "Contents" page. The Exit button is represented by a door. The door opens and makes a door opening sound on rollover. On mousedown, the program goes to a credits page and is exited after a seven-second delay.

NAVIGATION AND USER INTERFACE

This section describes the overarching structure, branching logic, and user interface details of the title.

Bumper

When the CD-ROM begins, a cornfield and blue sky fades up with the words "A Closely Trained Ant Production." The sound of giggling ants is heard, and the song "Ants Marching" begins playing as a half-dozen animated ants with a guitar march across the screen. At the same time, the letters rearrange to spell out "A Liston Treacy-Lenda Production." After the ants have marched off screen, the bumper dissolves into the welcome screen.

Welcome Screen

A survivor welcomes the user to the product. In a short *QuickTime* movie, the survivor tells her own story, introduces the CD-ROM, and gives encouragement to the new user (patient). Following is a script for the survivor.

> Hi. My name is Rebecca and I was diagnosed with cancer in 1998. I know how scary it is to hear the word cancer from your doctor. That's why I wanted to make *Cancer: A Survival Guide*. In it, you will meet some of the people who are soldiers and allies in the fight against cancer. You will also find a tool to locate resources and a journal to record your own experience. Good Luck.

Main Menu Screen

The first page of the "scrapbook" contains five options for the user. Each option is represented by an icon of the section that it leads to. The icons, which appear to be taped to the scrapbook, are labeled and are active buttons that take the user to different sections of the scrapbook. The table of contents also contains a button that closes the book and exits the CD-ROM.

Table A.2   Interactivity Table for Table of Contents

User	System	Description	Comments
Clicks on journal icon	Goes to "journal" section	Journal plain, journal roll, pencil scribble, page turning sound	Upon rollover, moves to rollover state and plays a pencil scribbling sound. Upon mousedown, plays a page turning sound and wipes to the "journal" section upon mouseup.
Clicks on glossary icon	Goes to "glossary" section	Glossary plain, glossary roll, pencil scribble, page turning sound	Upon rollover, moves to rollover state and plays a rimshot sound. Upon mousedown, plays a page turning sound and wipes to the "glossary" section upon mouseup.
Clicks on tour icon	Goes to "tour" section	Tour plain, tour roll, camera clicking, page turning sound	Upon rollover, moves to rollover state and plays a camera clicking sound. Upon mousedown, plays a page turning sound and wipes to the "tour" section upon mouseup.
Clicks on questions icon	Goes to "questions" section	Questions plain, questions roll, chime, page turning sound	Upon rollover, moves to rollover state and plays chime. Upon mousedown, plays a page turning sound and wipes to the "questions" section upon mouseup.
Clicks on resources icon	Goes to "resource" section	Resource plain, re-source roll, pages flipping, page turning sound	Upon rollover, moves to rollover state and plays the sound of pages flipping. Upon mousedown, plays a page turning sound and wipes to the "resources" section upon mouseup.
Clicks on exit icon	Goes to "exit" section	Exit plain, exit roll, door opening, page turning sound	Upon rollover, moves to rollover state and plays the sound of a door opening. Upon mousedown, plays a page turning sound and wipes to the credits page upon mouseup.

Tour Main Menu

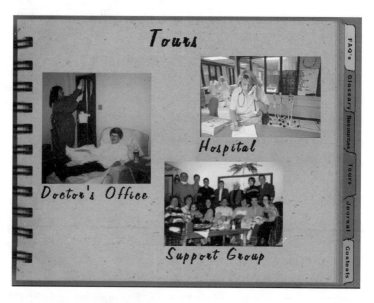

When users click on the Interactive Tour button from the main page, they reach another menu page of the scrapbook. From this page, the user can take virtual tours of a hospital, a doctor's office, and a support group. Users meet people who give explanations and assistance at each of these places.

Table A.3	Interactivity Table for Tour Main Menu		
User	**System**	**Description**	**Comments**
Click on doctor's office icon	Goes to "doctor's office" section	Doctor's plain, doctor's roll	Upon rollover, moves to rollover state. Upon mousedown, goes to the "doctor's office" section.
Click on hospital icon	Goes to "hospital" section	Hospital plain, hospital roll	Upon rollover, moves to rollover state. Upon mousedown, goes to the "hospital" section.
Click on support group icon	Goes to "support group" section	Support plain, support roll	Upon rollover, moves to rollover state. Upon mousedown, goes to the "support group" section.

As you can see from the pages reprinted here, the students demonstrated a clear understanding of the components of a multimedia product. They began by identifying a subject (cancer), target users (cancer patients), a need (support), and a genre (educational). They then determined the contents, features, and structure (the application) and the look and feel and functional controls (user interface) of their product. They did a nice job of using the journal as a visual and structural metaphor.

The Multimedia

Industry

Market Segments and Businesses

The multimedia industry consists of those market segments, and the business interests within them, that create, distribute, and sell products and services (offerings) to consumers and to businesses, that are interactive multimedia applications, or that enable interactive multimedia experiences.

Multimedia offerings are those that share the following characteristics:

- People experience the offerings (applications, web sites, CD-ROMs, games, videodisks) by using digital computer technology.

- The offerings are made up of text, sounds, pictures, animation, and video.

- The offerings are interactive.

Multimedia offerings are distributed online (over the Internet), offline (on a local device such as a CD-ROM), or in a hybrid environment, which combines the two (CD-ROMs, for example, that connect to companion web sites).

At the highest level, the multimedia market has two segments: consumer and corporate. The consumer multimedia market is further segmented into consumer entertainment, education, information, and commerce. The corporate multimedia market is segmented into corporate communications, training, public relations, and commerce.

The market segments are distinct from each other because of differences in:

- The purposes and objectives of the offerings

- The distribution system for delivering the offerings to the users

- The venue (location) where users typically experience the offerings
- The technology (hardware and software) needed to experience the offerings
- The extent to which the segment offerings use video and sound
- The extent to which the offerings are interactive
- The dominant business model that generates revenue for those businesses in the segment

Within the market segments, various businesses provide products or services either directly to consumers or to businesses within the market. The businesses (and/or entities) in these market segments include, but are not limited to the following:

Enabling Technologies

- Hardware manufacturers
- Hardware peripheral manufacturers
- Other enabling technology creators (both hardware and software)
- Software developers
- Software publishers
- CD-ROM disc manufacturers
- Audit bureaus

Content Providers

- Product and Web developers and their vendors
- Audio/visual production and postproduction studios
- E-commerce web sites
- Corporate web sites
- Advertisers
- Advertising agencies
- Rights holders to intellectual property

Distribution Providers

- Software distributors
- Software retailers
- Internet service providers (ISPs)
- Portal web sites
- Telephone companies
- Cable companies

Some of these businesses are more prevalent, or even unique, in some market segments, while others cross over. PC manufacturers, for example, sell computers into every segment. Audit bureaus measure traffic on the World Wide Web.

Internet (Online)

The Internet is the network of networks, originally established by the Defense Department's Advanced Research Projects Agency in the 1960s. The fastest-growing component of the Internet is the World Wide Web ("Web"), which currently (2000) has over 100 million users in the United States.

Purposes.   The Internet is used for communications, commerce, information storage and retrieval, promotion and advertising, and entertainment. The web site for this book, for example, intends to provide additional, updated information relevant to the material in the book. Research organizations continue to study Web usage to determine trends.

The Technology and Distribution System.   The Web links users to each other and to web sites resident in web servers everywhere in the world by means of carefully developed communications and messaging protocols. The only requirement is that users have computers capable of running the protocols and connected to the Internet by telephony through an Internet Service Provider—a local company equipped with servers (computers), which in turn are connected to each other via telephony. The protocols are packaged in software and provided to users in the form of "browsers," which provide value added in the form of "search engines," software tools that enable users to find specific topics wherever those topics are located in the network of servers. The exponential growth of Web users caused the emergence of "portal sites," which provide users with a jumping-off point, or "main menu," for entering the Web. The book web site has regularly updated information about the number of users, web sites, and principle activities on the World Wide Web.

The Level of Multimedia and Interactivity.   The Web is home to many multimedia applications. Web sites, for example, feature text, sounds, images, video, and the means to interactively access data, input data, and link to other sites. Because the data is transmitted from site to site or from server to client largely via landlines, the speed of transmission is limited to what the lines can handle. In some cases, the bandwidth, or carrying capacity, of the lines is great and at other times quite limited. Because of this, certain media, particularly video, are limited in size and frame rate. Latency, the speed of response of the multimedia application, is also affected by bandwidth limitations.

The Venue.   Researchers continue to study where Web users access the Web most often. Studies show that many people access the Web from their place of work and use it for communications and information retrieval. From home, users access the Web for communication, commerce, and entertainment.

The Dominant Business Model.   Internet companies are searching for business models that generate revenue for themselves. Currently, Internet businesses earn money in a variety of ways. Consumers pay a flat monthly rate to an ISP for access to the Web, and ISPs pay access charges to telephone companies to speed customer Web traffic on to other servers. Portal companies, which provide the enabling software and search engine services to consumers at no cost, sell advertising space on their sites. The rates for placing the advertisements are determined by the number of consumers who visit the portal sites, though what constitutes a visit is hotly debated. The various entities whose self-interest is determined by the definition are trying to reach agreement on such terms as a "hit" and a "click through." Meanwhile, some of the most successful web sites provide goods and services through e-commerce, which is the Web version of catalog shopping. Consumers access the sites, review products, place orders, and receive the goods by post in a few days. There is an enormous venture capital investment in all kinds of companies within this mix. Very few companies have shown a profit. However, many individuals have fared well by trading stock in Internet companies whose values rise due to speculation rather than performance.

Consumer CD-ROM (Offline)

The consumer CD-ROM market consists of those offline products developed and distributed principally for personal home and office use.

Purposes.   Consumer CD-ROM products are predominantly developed for entertainment, games, education, reference, and office utility.

The Technology and Distribution System.   CD-ROM is an acronym for Compact Disc Read Only Memory, an optical storage medium developed primarily by the Dutch company Philips, N.V., to store digital information. The principle behind optical storage technology is that digital information can be physically (rather than magnetically) stored on a plastic disc by burning pits, in a tightly controlled manner, into the subsurface of the disc. Because digital information is binary, using only two numbers—0 and 1 (called bits)—to represent all other values, bits can be represented by two states: either "on" or "off." The presence of a pit in the disc is interpreted as "on," or 1, while the absence of a pit is interpreted as "off," or 0, when the disc is scanned by a laser in a CD-ROM player, or drive.

A CD-ROM can hold 650 megabytes (5,200,000,000 bits). Audio, pictures, text, and, of course, computer software can all be represented digitally. Under software control, the laser in a CD-ROM drive can scan the contents of the disc in a non-linear manner. The compact disc is a small, inexpensive, durable, transportable, easily replicated storage medium; it is therefore ideal for interactive multimedia applications.

The Venue. Typically, CD-ROM drives are part of a home computer system. Consumer CD-ROM products are used in the home and office.

The Level of Multimedia and Interactivity. Consumer CD-ROM products tend to have a high level of multimedia and interactivity, largely because of the demands of the competitive market (see below). Products in all genres tend to feature full-color graphics, animation, and video; high-quality stereo sound; and interactive features that would not be possible over the Internet.

The Dominant Business Model. The consumer CD-ROM market currently follows a retail model, similar to book and home video publishing. CD-ROM products are packaged and sold at retail outlets directly to consumers. Approximately 75 percent of CD-ROMs are sold this way. Internet wholesalers and retailers are also selling the products in the manner of catalog sales. The principal players in the CD-ROM consumer market are shown in Table B.1.

Education

The education segment consists of products and applications for formal educational purposes, both in classroom and home venues. It consists of both offline (CD-ROM) and online (Internet) multimedia.

Purposes. As discussed in Chapter 3, educational multimedia is intended to impart knowledge and skill to users. In educational multimedia (as separate from corporate training), the users are in academic or home environments and the learning objective is related to cognitive, affective, and psychomotor development. Educational multimedia is often, but not always, a component of an educational program of study. An educational CD-ROM used in a classroom, for example, will be collateral to lectures, texts, manipulatives, and other teaching tools. An educational web site accessed by a master's degree candidate in a distance learning scenario, may be part of a program of study that includes independent research and intensive two-week encounters with the professor during the summer.

The Technology and Distribution System. Educational multimedia utilizes both online (Internet) distribution and offline (CD-ROM) distribution. Educa-

Table B.1	Principal Players in CD-ROM Market	
Player	Role	Compensation
Rights holders	Rights holders own the copyrights to intellectual property, such as characters, games, stories, and images. Rights holders license the use of their property to others for use in multimedia products. Lucasfilms, for example, owns the rights to the *Star Wars* stories, characters, and film footage. Lucasfilms licenses the rights to use the property to multimedia publishers, such as Hasbro Interactive.	A fee, plus a royalty based on sales
Developers	Developers create multimedia products by designing them; producing all of the audio, video, text, and other assets; and writing and testing the software. Developers may perform this work under contract with a client (which may be a publisher). Or, the developer performs this work and then attempts to find a publisher that will release the product into the retail channels.	A fee, usually regarded as an advance against royalties
Publishers	Publishers package and market CD-ROM products to distributors and retailers. Publishers often take the greatest financial risk, footing the bill for product development, packaging, shipping, advertising, and marketing costs. Publishers also take responsibility for on-going customer support. They also reap the greatest rewards: the largest percentage of the gross revenue and ownership of the copyright to the final product.	Net profits from sales of sell-through of products to consumers
Distributors	Distributors accept products from publishers and take orders for products from retailers. They warehouse the product inventory, deliver it to retailers, and often stock the shelves as "rack jobbers." When products are returned or unsold, the distributors return the products to the publishers. Some publishers bypass distributors and perform these functions themselves.	Percentage of gross sales of sell-through to consumers
Retailers	Retailers accept products from publishers and distributors and stock their shelves. Typical retail outlets include computer stores (CompUSA), software stores (Media Play), consumer electronics stores (Best Buy), and mass merchandisers (Wal-Mart). Retailers sell the products directly to consumers.	Percentage of gross sales to consumers

tional multimedia is developed for use on home computers equipped with CD-ROM drives and Internet connections. Typically, courses in which contact (both virtual and real) with the instructor is integral and which require frequent updates and changes are offered on the Internet, and courses which require a deeper audio/visual experience but do not require contact with the instructor are available on CD-ROM. CD-ROM courses tend to be self-contained and self-directed. Currently, many children's educational programs are available on CD-ROM (see the many examples in the book), as well as language instruction and other self-improvement subjects. Most distance learning programs that utilize the Internet are directed at adult learners. Many MBA programs, for example, are available in distance learning environments.

The Venue. Educational multimedia is experienced in the home and in class-rooms and labs. Many grade schools, for example, have computer labs in which the students use multimedia applications in a self-paced manner. In these scenarios, the instructor acts as a coach and facilitator, while the student explores the multimedia product at his or her own speed. Other educational products are designed to be used by students at home with little or no contact with an instructor. Distance learners access their lessons from the home but have constant contact with the courseware and their instructors through the Internet.

The Level of Multimedia and Interactivity. Because educational multimedia is designed by instructional designers for maximum efficiency, educational applications tend to have no less than and no more than the level of multimedia and interactivity necessary to achieve the learning objective. The products tend to be no-frills. Low development budgets also contribute to this. Some educational products, particularly those that have gained favor in the consumer market as "edutainment," have stronger production values and are not victim to the tight purse. Products from Humongous (owned by GT Interactive), The Learning Company (owned by Mattel), and Knowledge Adventure (owned by Havas) are in this category. Each has published educational software that has succeeded in the consumer market on a level with many popular entertainment products.

The Dominant Business Model. There are three dominant business models in educational multimedia. Products, particularly CD-ROM, are sold directly to consumers at retail. Several major software publishers dominate this market, including The Learning Company, Broderbund Software (both owned by Mattel), and Knowledge Adventure (owned by Havas). Courses, which include multimedia components (usually over the Internet), are offered to students by institutions for the price of tuition and fees. More than 195 accredited schools offer distance learning (DL) programs in this way. In fact, over half of the estimated one million DL students are enrolled in graduate business programs. Finally, packaged multimedia courses, which usually include other components, are sold to schools by courseware developers. The schools then use the courseware in classrooms. Courseware may be distributed via Internet, CD-ROM, or both. Computer Curriculum Corporation and Edmark (owned by IBM) are two major developers of multimedia courseware for classroom use.

Console Games

Purposes. Console games are produced and sold strictly for entertainment purposes.

The Technology and Distribution System. Console games are so called because the hardware platform is a single-purpose appliance designed and sold specifically to play games that are designed and developed for that platform. The appliance contains special purpose computer chips, processors, boards, and other proprietary devices that enhance the speed and display capabilities of the game. Although game consoles feature very powerful computer processing, the hardware is dedicated to the single purpose and incapable of performing other computer functions. Typically, the game console is connected to a home television monitor and is controlled with a special-purpose game controller, rather than a keyboard and mouse. Newer game consoles, such as Sega's Dreamcast, are available with a 56K modem. The software products developed for the game consoles are burned on optical discs technically identical to CD-ROMs, but the software is encrypted in such a way that it can be read only by the appropriate player.

There are three competing console game technologies, each championed by its Japanese corporate inventor: Sega, which manufactures the Dreamcast platform; Sony, which manufactures the PlayStation; and Nintendo, which manufactures the Nintendo 64. These companies license developers and publishers, which create and market games for the products. The licensors are paid a royalty for every game sold by the developers and publishers.

The Venue. Console games are generally played at home. Because the console is connected to a television, the game appliances are generally not colocated with the family's primary television, but rather in a game room or bedroom.

The Level of Multimedia and Interactivity. Console games exhibit the highest level of multimedia and interactivity of all the multimedia segments. Competition between the large Japanese companies that dominate the market forces them to improve and enhance the graphics and game play of their products continuously. Console games now feature stunning real-time 3-D graphics and extremely fast processors that make interactivity lightening quick. Dreamcast and PlayStation game consoles employ 128-bit technology, Nintendo uses 64-bit. Compare this with the typical computer display, which uses 24-bit. The game consoles are so powerful, in fact, that game developers must use special workstations in order to write code for the games. Sony, for one, sells a proprietary game developer workstation for PlayStation games.

The Dominant Business Model.   Like the consumer CD-ROM market segment, console games are a retail market. Added to the mix are the consoles themselves, which are sold in consumer electronics stores, specialty stores, and mass merchandisers. The market is tightly controlled by the big three Japanese console game manufacturers. They sell the console players directly to consumers and license the right to produce games for those platforms to publishers and developers they choose carefully. They also develop and sell programming tools and libraries, as well as development workstations, to the developers.

Corporate Training

Corporate training is a huge industry, but only a portion of it includes multimedia development. As in instructional programs of all kinds, multimedia plays a role in corporate training only when the medium meets the objectives of the instructional program better than other possible approaches. Corporate training programs are created for internal consumption, so multimedia applications in this segment differ wildly in size, cost, production values, and other bases of comparison.

Purposes.   Corporate training utilizes multimedia solutions to teach new skills, knowledge, or concepts to a workforce. The multimedia component may be only a small part of a general training program that includes conferences, classes, textbooks, manuals, tutorials, and other approaches.

The Technology and Distribution System   Corporate training may utilize offline (CD-ROM) or online (Internet or intranet) multimedia technology and distribution or both. Offline solutions are used when a high degree of multimedia (video, sound) and interactivity is required but it is not necessary to update the material very often. Online solutions are chosen when the material does not require robust multimedia and interactivity and the material requires frequent updating. The venue and distance also contribute to this decision.

The Venue.   Corporate training takes place on the job, at home, in special training venues, and during business travel. The training may involve group collaboration and interaction or may be personal. Because of this, the technology chosen and the design of the training program are profoundly affected by the venue.

The Level of Multimedia and Interactivity.   The level of multimedia and interactivity is determined by the subject matter, learning objective of the program, the size and sophistication of the audience, and other criteria. Some corporate training programs are very humble; others are very rich, sometimes approaching and exceeding the production values of commercial products.

The Dominant Business Model.   Corporate training programs are developed for internal consumption and evaluation. Training programs are not created to generate revenue, but to generate a return on investment in the form of a better-educated, more efficient, more skilled, higher motivated workforce. The results are often nonquantifiable. The clients for corporate training programs are corporations in need of solving a performance gap within their workforces. Responsibility to solve the problem may fall to a department within it, such as human resources or a special training department. When the solution calls for a multimedia solution, the corporation may hire an outside developer to create the multimedia components. In such situations, the developer works for its client on a work-for-hire basis, usually for a fixed fee.

The Multimedia

Studio

The multimedia development studio is a full-service company capable of designing and developing a multimedia application (a CD-ROM product or a web site) for a client (internal or external). The multimedia studio is only one of the many businesses that are components of the various segments of the multimedia industry. It is, however, the most likely place for a producer, director, or writer to work; although software publishers and other clients usually employ producers to manage and/or work closely with development studios.

Structure

Functional Areas

Multimedia development studios are generally structured to accomplish effectively and efficiently the following parallel and codependent functions:

- Corporate management
- General administration and operations
- Finance
- Business development
- Creative development
- Studio production
- Technical development
- Research and development

There is more than one organizational model. Some multimedia companies, particularly small developers, have very flat organizations in which a small number of individuals share responsibilities for the critical tasks associated with each of the functions above. As companies grow larger, the tendency is toward a hierarchical structure. A small company that is likely to expand is well advised to establish a hierarchical structure it can grow into. Culturally, the two models are diametrically opposed, and it is usually impossible to morph a flat organization into a hierarchical one.

Corporate Management. The top individual at a multimedia company may be the Chief Executive Officer (CEO), the president, or the owner, depending on its size and corporate structure. The corporate officers in charge of the functional areas above usually compose the management team. Other corporate officers who make up the typical management team of a large company are the Chief Operating Officer (COO), the Chief Financial Officer (CFO), the Chief Creative Officer (CCO), and the Chief Technical Officer (CTO). Other members of top management may include legal counsel, manager of human resources, director or manager of business development, and others who hold key positions. On hierarchical organizational charts of medium- to large-sized companies, these managers often appear on the same level, each responsible for a department. The officers report directly to the CEO or president. In small companies, these functions are managed by a smaller number of individuals, most of whom are responsible for several areas.

General Administration and Operations. General administration and operations is usually headed by the Chief Operating Officer, the General Manager, or the Executive Producer. General administration and operations is a catchall of functions and activities related to the infrastructure of the company. The infrastructure of the company consists of policies, practices, and procedures that are put in place, rarely change, and enable the company to function properly from one day to the next. These functions are not project-specific. General administration and operations include

■ *Office management:* This position is responsible for locating, planning, purchasing, and renting facilities, equipment, and manuals and for supervising secretarial and clerical services and custodial and grounds services. This function also establishes and maintains relations with outside vendors, such as office suppliers, travel agencies, caterers, and limousine services.

■ *Human resources:* This position is responsible for corporate/employee relations, such as hiring, training, reviewing, insuring, promoting, and disciplining, or terminating employees. Human resources ensures that the company complies at all times with state and federal labor laws, with individual employment contracts, and with union agreements.

■ *Business affairs:* This position reviews and administers all contracts and works closely with legal (usually outside attorneys) to ensure that all agreements entered into by the company are drafted properly.

■ *System administration:* This position is responsible for keeping company computers running properly, keeping the internal network (intranet) up and running, archiving and backing up files, installing and upgrading software, and other company-wide computer services.

■ *Public relations:* This position is responsible for communication between the company and the public. Press releases, statements to the press, the production of company brochures and company literature, and material on the company web site usually fall under the purview of public relations.

Business Development.   Business development is responsible for generating revenue through sales of development services to clients, the establishment of strategic relationships with other entities that lead to revenue-generating opportunities, and the development of new product ideas with profit potential. Business development includes

■ *Marketing:* This entails researching and interpreting market trends and creating product ideas that meet market needs. It includes the development of programs that expose the public (customers) to the company's products or services. It also includes establishing pricing policy and distribution channels.

■ *Sales:* For the multimedia development studio, this involves winning contracts to develop products for external clients. Sales are garnered by approaching potential clients, approaching existing clients to develop additional products, and advertising, which can attract hidden clients.

■ *Concept development or acquisition:* This involves developing product concepts internally or acquiring concept ideas externally and then seeking development partners (publishers) who can fund development or handle publishing the product when complete.

■ *Licensing:* This involves identifying copyrighted material from which derivative multimedia products can be developed.

Creative Development.   The Chief Creative Officer, Creative Director, or Executive Producer usually heads creative development. Those involved in creative development are responsible for developing product ideas, game ideas, characters, stories, and interactive and graphic designs, which either meet the needs of clients or can be further developed into wholly owned intellectual property. Creative development may include

■ *Writers:* Writers write concept documents, proposals, top-level designs, functional specifications, and any other documents needed to realize a creative concept.

■ *Directors:* Directors are usually assigned to specific projects, products, or product lines or develop new ones.

■ *Game designers:* Game designers may also be programmers and may be responsible for technical development.

■ *Graphic designers:* Specialized designers, such as character designers and concept artists, may be part of creative development.

Finance.   The Chief Financial Officer is usually in charge of all financial activities. Small companies may have a single bookkeeper or even use an outside accounting service. Banks, lending institutions, investors, state and federal tax bodies, and other parties require that the company books be kept and its financial statements reported accurately from time to time. The accounting function includes payroll, accounts payable, accounts receivable, and individual project cost accounting.

Studio Production.   Multimedia companies usually separate asset production from software development. Typically, production comes under the management of the Executive Producer or General Manager. The production department of a medium-to large-size developer includes

■ *Producers:* Individual producers who are in charge of specific projects, products, or even product lines. In large studios, there may be senior producers, associate producers, and assistant producers, each having different levels of responsibility.

■ *Asset management:* Production assistants or production managers keep track of asset production and maintain asset databases for the benefit of production tracking by the producers.

■ *Art department:* Headed by the art director, this department is responsible for generating all graphics and animation and may be responsible for photography and videography.

■ *Sound department:* Headed by the senior sound designer or other manager, this department is responsible for creating all sound elements.

■ *Quality assurance:* Headed by QA Supervisor or Manager, this department is responsible for testing all products before release.

Technical Development.   The Chief Engineer or Senior Programmer typically heads technical development. The department, made up of programmers, is responsible for writing all project-specific software and integrating software with assets to create multimedia products. This department works closely with the production studio. Like producers, programmers also may be classified as senior programmers, junior programmers, lead engineers, etc.

Research and Development.   The Chief Technology Officer heads research and development. This activity is the development of software solutions that may or may not be project-specific. The software engineers involved in research and development break new ground; solve difficult, long-term problems; or look for better, faster, more elegant software for future products.

Administrative and Functional Organization

Large multimedia companies with hierarchical organizations usually have two concurrent structures. One serves the administrative purpose of placing specific job functions in departments under the management responsibility of one person. Each employee of the company, then, has only one individual to whom he or she reports for job assignments, to request time off, for a performance review, and so forth. However, during the development of a multimedia product, employees are joined together across department lines to form development teams. Functionally, each employee reports to someone else, usually the producer, director, or project manager. Figures C.1 and C.2 show the administrative and functional organization charts.

FIGURE C.1

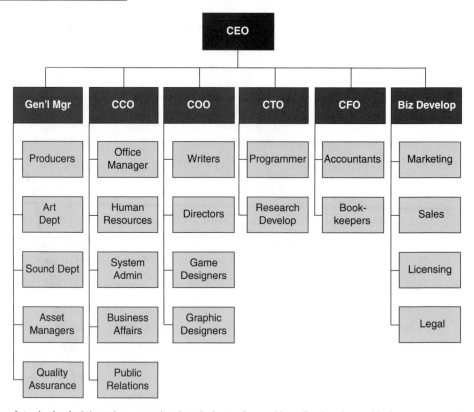

A typical administrative organizational chart of a multimedia developer. Various corporate officers assume responsibility for departments.

FIGURE C.2

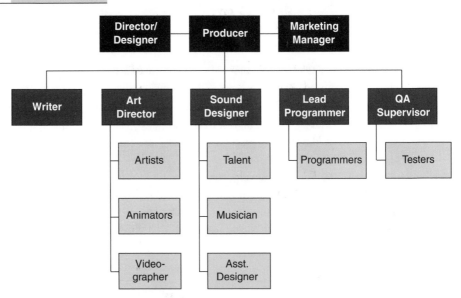

A functional organizational chart, showing how staff from different departments are assembled into a team to develop a multimedia product.

Job Descriptions

Table C.1 provides job descriptions for key members of the development team, specifying responsibility, authority, and accountability. It is critically important that every person know and understand not only his or her own job description, but also the job description of the other members of the team. If an individual is responsible for a particular task or job function, that person must have the authority to make decisions related to performance of that function. For example, a producer cannot be given responsibility for managing the development budget but not the authority to select the most cost-efficient subcontractors, vendors, and equipment. Likewise, if an individual has and exercises authority, that person must accept accountability for his or her success or failure.

Table C.1	Job Descriptions of Key Development Team Members		
Job Title	**Responsibility**	**Authority**	**Accountability**
Producer	Client contact and relationship Contract review and approval Production plan Production budget Milestone tracking Asset management Resource management Bug tracking Manage change order process Report to upper management	Represent company Approve/not approve conditions Set deadlines Determine expenditures Manage process Create and maintain asset database Start/stop/hire/terminate Assign bugs Ascertain costs and time for changes Know and understand hourly rates and metrics	Good relationship with client No onerous conditions in contract Make deadlines Make profitable Measure and report against costs Complete and detailed database Proper headcount loading Bugs assigned and fixed Changes implemented Accurate reports and forecasts
Director/Designer	Creative vision Design within budget Direct art, animation, sound Approve art animation and sound Know and understand the processes	Design interactivity Establish look and feel Supervise artists and sound designers Ask for changes, fixes Determine how things are to be done	Quality product Quality product within budget Give good directions Smooth production process
Writer	Write functional specification Maintain functional specification	Determine dialog, interactive design, descriptions Determine what changes and modifications have been made	Spec that can be used by all Spec that is up to date and current
Art Director	Work with director, writer, technical lead to determine needs Determine costs and time for art production Communicate art needs to writer, director, producer Maintain constant flow of art production Technical quality of art—correct palette, etc. Communicate art changes to writer, director, producer Create art	Determine art needs for project—scope and details Sign off on art production Manage activities of other artists Look at and approve all art Determine when changes are necessary Manage own time and effort to create art	Complete understanding of scope of work Accurate art cost and time testimate Complete asset database of art Art production on schedule Bug-free art Keep database and functional spec current Quality art—on time and budget

Table C.1 (continued)			
Job Title	**Responsibility**	**Authority**	**Accountability**
Technical Director	Consult with design team to determine technical requirements Write technical specifications	Suggest technical approach Determine the technical approach for a project	Technical requirements well understood Technical approach well documented
Lead Programmer	Work with design team and contribute on technical requirements Determine costs and time for technical work Engineer title	Determine technical requirements for project Sign-off technical costs and time Manage own time and effort to engineer title	Technical requirements well understood Accurate cost and time estimate for technical work Quality engineering—on time and budget
Sound Designer	Work with director, writer, technical lead to determine needs Determine costs and time for sound production Communicate sound needs to writer, director, producer Maintain constant flow of sound production Technical quality of sound—correct format, etc. Communicate sound changes to writer, director, producer Create sound	Determine sound needs for project—scope and details Sign off on sound production Determine sound needs for project—scope and details Manage activities of other sound—talent, musician, etc. Listen to and approve all sound Determine when changes are necessary Manage own time and effort to create sound	Complete understanding of scope of work Accurate sound cost and time estimate Complete asset database of sound Sound production on schedule Bug-free sound Keep database and functional spec current Quality sound—on time and budget
Quality Assurance Supervisor	Set-up spec Schedule disc burns Manage testing process Log bugs in bugtracker Manage database	Determine set-up Set and change dates and versions Schedule testers Determine nature of bugs Assign, cancel bugs	Get approval from producer and/or client Keep burns on schedule Keep testers busy Keep bugs in process Quality, bug-free product

Glossary of Multimedia Terms

Advance against royalty: A payment made by a publisher to a developer to fund development of a product. The publisher recoups the advance before paying the developer a royalty (a percentage of profits) on sales.

Adventure game: One of the genres of computer games in which the player controls a character who is on a quest.

Algorithm: A procedure for solving a problem or accomplishing a task using a mathematical or logical procedure. Programmers often devise algorithmic solutions to programming problems, especially when the procedure calls for a repetitive process.

Alpha: The term generally applied to the first CD-ROM burn, or version, of a product. It contains most of the final assets and features. Every studio has its own quantitative and qualitative criteria for what can be called an Alpha.

Analog: The representation, storage, and transmission of data, video, or audio by means of waveforms.

Application: A software product or program. Often used as a term for a multimedia product.

Artificial intelligence(AI): A computer application that simulates "thinking," in that the program assimilates and processes new knowledge.

Asset: An individual graphic, text, sound, or video file used in a multimedia product. Multimedia products contain thousands of individual assets.

Assignment of copyright: The transfer of ownership of a copyright from one party to another.

Authoring: The process of knitting together the various nodes, or chunks of information, in a multimedia product by means of software programming or of using an off-the-shelf authoring tool, such as *Macromedia Director*.

Bandwidth: The measure of the amount of digital data that passes through a transmission system. Typically, bandwidth is expressed in terms of thousands or millions of bits per second.

Beta: A term used to describe a CD-ROM burn, or version, that contains all of the intended assets and features and that is in the process of being tested and corrected for bugs.

Bid: That part of the developer's proposal to a client that stipulates the price, or cost, of developing the multimedia product.

Bit: A 0 or a 1. It is the smallest expression of digital data.

Bitmap: A graphic representation made up of an array of pixels, or square dots, arranged in a grid pattern. Think of the placard cheering section at a college football game.

Boilerplate: Clauses in a contract that are so common and generally accepted that they are rarely rewritten.

Branching: The act of moving from one node, or chunk of information, to another in a multimedia product.

Browse mode: The mode of navigation through a multimedia product wherein the user may branch anywhere at anytime with complete exploratory freedom.

Browser: Software that reads and displays HTML documents on the World Wide Web.

Bug: A problem with the multimedia product discovered during the testing process; a nonconformity to the functional specification.

Bumper: A company logo or animation that identifies the publisher, developer, or other party to the development of the multimedia product. It is often the first thing a user sees and hears.

Burn: Refers to the making of a CD-ROM by recording information on a blank disc using a special laser device. "Let's burn a disc tonight, and test it in the morning." "Do you have last night's burn?"

Button: A graphic representation in a multimedia product that is displayed on the screen and can be selected by the user by clicking on it. This action usually initiates some response by the product.

Button states: Alternative versions of a button's graphic representation, which appear based on user interaction. For example, a button may appear a certain way when it first occurs on the screen and change appearance when the user moves the cursor over it. It may change appearance a third time when the user selects the button by clicking on it. In order, these states are called the steady state, cursor present, button selected.

Byte: A digital expression made up of 8 bits.

CBT: Computer-Based Training. Some or all of a training or instructional program is accessed interactively by the user on a computer.

CD-ROM: Compact Disc-Read Only Memory. The CD-ROM can hold approximately 650 megabytes of digital data. Once data has been burned onto a CD-ROM, the data cannot be altered.

Clearances: The term for obtaining the rights to use copyrighted material.

Client: On the World Wide Web, one of the millions of users.

Client: In multimedia deals, the entity that pays for the development of a multimedia product. Usually a publisher.

Compile: The act of converting the programmer's software code (source code) into machine-readable binary code (object code).

Compression: The process, scheme, or technique of reducing the amount of data, or digital information, needed to represent an image, video, or sound. Various compression techniques are used, and many of them use algorithms (see above).

Concept document: A very short (one to two pages) document that describes the idea for a multimedia product, focusing on the subject, genre, and audience.

Content: The subject matter, body of knowledge, information, concepts, ideas, story, or game that compose the multimedia product. Not to be confused with the assets that represent the content on the screen or through the speakers.

Contingency: A percentage of the anticipated costs of developing a product, usually 10 percent, which is added to the budget to pay for unexpected additional costs.

Copyright: The exclusive right of the author of a work to own and control its reproduction, modification, distribution, public performance, and public display.

Cursor: The graphic symbol on the screen that the user controls with the mouse, keyboard, joystick, or voice commands.

Customization mode: A mode of navigation through a multimedia product wherein the user may set parameters or specify preferences. This has the effect of self-delineating the experience so that only content of interest to the user is available.

Critical path: The sequence of tasks that are dependently linked, one with the next, from the beginning of a project to the end.

Cross platform: An application that is designed and developed to function on more than one hardware/software configuration.

Database: A collection, list, library, or matrix of information, which can be accessed, queried, sorted, and otherwise manipulated to provide the user with customized results.

Deal memo: *See* Letter of intent.

Debug: The process of testing an application and finding and fixing bugs.

Deliverable: During multimedia development, a deliverable is a production item, element, or material that is created for the purpose of moving the project forward.

Demo: A working sample of a multimedia product.

Derivative work: A work (product, for example) that is based on another, copyrighted work.

Developer: A company that provides end-to-end product development services, including design, asset production, software development, integration, and testing.

Development: The entire process of creating a multimedia product from inception through gold master.

Digital: The system of representing information solely with numerical values, typically in binary (0 and 1) mode.

Digitize: The act of converting an analog signal (such as audio or video) or a physical element (a photograph, for example) into digital format.

Distance learning: An educational or instructional application accessed by users from remote locations.

Distributor: A company that accepts products from publishers and ships them to retailers. Also called a wholesaler.

Download: The transfer of data from a server to a client, such as a personal computer.

DVD: Digital Versatile Disc (also called Digital Video Disc). Regarded as the successor to CD-ROM, it is capable of holding 18 gigabytes of data.

Edutainment: A word coined to apply to multimedia applications that are both entertaining and educational.

E3:   The Electronic Entertainment Expo, a major conference for the multimedia and computer game industries, held annually in late spring.

Fair use: In copyright law, the limited use of copyrighted material without the permission of the copyright owner, under special circumstances.

Feature: An interactive capability or a unique interactive experience offered to the user of a multimedia application or product.

File server: A computer that is connected to a network and acts as the central repository for data that can be accessed by many users from remote locations.

Flow diagram: A graphic representation of the structure of a multimedia application or product showing the nodes and the links that connect them. Also called a node map.

FMV: Full Motion Video. Video displayed at 30 frames per second.

Formative evaluation: Product testing undertaken during the development period that leads to modifications to the design and/or further development.

FTP: File Transfer Protocol. A utility program on the Internet that allows users to send and receive files from other remote servers.

Functionality: The control provided to the user over a multimedia product. Usually provided by a combination of real and virtual devices.

Functional specification: The detailed design document that describes a multimedia product in its entirety.

Game design: The detailed design document that describes a multimedia game product. It includes the game logic and algorithms.

Genre: One of a number of commonly accepted categories of multimedia products. Among the genres are games, educational, office utility, and reference.

Global(s):   User interface elements or interactive features that are used consistently throughout a product. For instance, if a user can exit an application at any time by clicking on a certain button that is always present, this is a global.

Gold master: The final CD-ROM disc containing all assets and programming that is in full compliance with the functional specification.

Guided tour mode: Navigation through the multimedia product that is controlled by the computer program.

Hotspot: A region or area on the display screen that has been programmed to respond to the action of the user, usually when the user clicks the mouse while the cursor is positioned in the region.

HTML: Hypertext Markup Language. The standardized coding that enables documents to be sent and received over the World Wide Web.

HTTP: Hypertext Transfer Protocol. This is the standard protocol used for transferring files between servers and clients on the World Wide Web.

Hybrid: A CD-ROM that is cross-platform or that has the capability of linking directly with a companion Web site.

Hyperlink: The connection between two hypertext documents.

Hypermedia: Hypertext documents that are linked and that contain audio and visual media as well as text.

Hypertext: The documents of a database that are connected with programmed links, enabling users to access one document from another.

Icon: A graphic that represents an idea, concept, person, place, or thing.

Instructional design: The academic discipline that designs instructional programs and systems suitable for the learners, the subject matter, and the learning environment.

Integration: The act of combining assets with programming to create the final multimedia product, usually done by the programmer.

Intellectual property: Work that is protected by copyright, trademark, patent, or trade secret.

Interface: In multimedia, that part of the application or product that is visible to the user and that makes contact with and control of the multimedia product possible.

Internet: The global network of computer networks, originally built by the Advanced Research Projects Agency of the U.S. Defense Department.

IP: Internet Protocol. The set of standards that enables the transmission of packets of information from one Internet site to another.

Java: A cross-platform programming language developed primarily by Sun Microsystems for use in developing multimedia Internet applications.

JPEG: Joint Photographic Experts Group. A standard image file format developed for the purpose of digitizing photographs and maintaining the highest possible quality with the least amount of data.

License: A right to use copyrighted material, granted by the copyright owner, for use in a product or application.

Linear: In media, a sequence of noninterruptible scenes or events. Motion pictures, television shows, and radio programs are linear.

Link: The connection between two hypertext documents.

Localization: The reproduction of a multimedia product in a new language, often by substituting all dialogue, narration, text, and graphic assets with new ones in the foreign language.

LOI: Letter of Intent. An interim agreement between two parties that often precedes a contract or other, more definitive agreement.

Look and feel: The aesthetic characteristics of the multimedia product, generally describing the graphic and sound style, but also referring to the overall gestalt of the product.

Menu: A node in a product that allows the user to access other nodes, in the manner of a central jumping-off point. The homepage of a web site is an example of a menu.

MIDI: Musical Instrument Digital Interface. A sound creating, recording, and transmission standard.

Milestone: An event during the development of a multimedia product when one or more deliverables have been approved by the client. Often used as a trigger for a progress payment.

Moral rights: Rights related to copyright that protect the author from unauthorized modifications to the work. Although a European concept, often found in agreements related to art and music. Important in foreign agreements.

MPEG: Motion Picture Experts Group. A video compression standard.

Multitask: The ability to perform more than one task at a time.

Navigation: The act of traversing a multimedia product. Moving from node to node.

Needs analysis: The process of determining the purpose and objective of an educational or instructional application.

Node: In hypertext, a document that is linked to another document. In multimedia, any chunk of data, or software event, or combination of the two that the user can access.

Node map: A graphical representation of the structure of a multimedia application, showing the nodes and the links that connect them. Also called a flow diagram.

Nonexclusive rights: A license to use copyrighted material that allows the copyright owner to license the same rights to another party for the same purpose.

Nonlinear: In media, a user-paced and interactively accessible collection of scenes or events.

Offline: In media, the ability to access only the data that is stored locally, on one's own computer.

Online: In media, the ability to access data on remote file servers.

PC Data: A company that tracks the PC market, including the sales of CD-ROM products broken down by genre.

Phase: A step in the development process that has specific deliverables, milestones, and tasks. The successful completion of a phase makes it possible to go on to the next phase.

Placeholder: Temporary assets used by programmers to represent finished assets until they are available.

Platform: The combination of equipment and software that makes up a multimedia station. Macintosh computers, PCs, and Nintendo 64s are all platforms.

Prize: The main goal or objective of a development phase.

Proof of concept: A small, playable version of a product that may not have the actual, final computer code working but appears to behave as though it does. Used for testing the concept of the product, not the technology.

Proposal: A document that contains the developer's top-level design, preliminary budget or cost estimate (bid), and development schedule.

Prototype: Like a proof of concept, but the prototype does use the actual, intended computer code for its operation.

Publisher: The company that accepts the financial risk of developing, packaging, and marketing a multimedia product.

QA: Quality Assurance. The process of testing a multimedia product to assure compliance with the functional specification.

Recoup: The act of obtaining repayment of money previously advanced to a developer by a publisher. Typically, the publisher recoups an advance by withholding royalty payments due the developer until the advance is fully paid back.

Rights: Refers to the copyright to a property. Also called the intellectual property rights.

ROI: Return on Investment. The measure of profitability of a capital investment, expressed as a percentage.

Rollover: A perceptible change in the appearance of a button when the user moves the cursor over it.

Royalty: A percentage of sales, based on various formulas, paid to a developer by a publisher. Other parties may also receive royalties, including musicians, artists, talent, and the copyright owner.

RPG: Role-Playing Game. In a role-playing game, the user controls a character on the screen and may be joined by companions in a quest or puzzle-solving adventure.

Server: *See* **File server.**

Simulation: A multimedia application that uses natural laws or a predicated system of rules to generate results.

Slippage: When anticipated or promised deadlines or completion dates are likely to be missed.

Software: Computer code, written by programmers, that causes the multimedia product to operate. Includes the computer operating system, the source code, the object code, databases, and any other computer language instructions.

Source code: The programming written by the programmer before it is compiled. Source code can be read by a programmer and, therefore, debugged.

Storyboard: A series of drawings that depict action or a sequence of events, like a comic strip.

Streaming: A method of transmitting audio and/or video over the Internet is such a way that it plays immediately on the client computer.

Summative evaluation: The evaluation of the effectiveness of an instructional product that takes place after it is released.

Technical specification: A document, usually prepared by the lead programmer or technical director, that describes the programming methods to be used to solve a particular programming problem.

Time and materials: A term often used in development agreements that refers to the labor, equipment, and supplies costs for completing a project.

Title: In multimedia, another term for an application or product.

Top-level design: A document that describes a multimedia product in terms of the product's target market, subject, genre, general content, features, and look and feel. Used to generate interest and agreement between parties.

Tracking: The process of keeping track of progress on the development of assets and software for a multimedia product.

URL: Uniform Resource Locator. The address of a document or file located on the World Wide Web. When hyperlinks connect one hypertext document to another, the URL is imbedded in the link command.

Warranty: A promise that facts are true.

Web browser: A computer software program that allows the user to access the Internet.

Work for hire: The copyright law that grants the copyright in a work to the hiring party, or employer, when the work is created as part of the employee's normal job duties.

WWW: The World Wide Web—a network of computers, servers, and html documents.

WYSIWYG: What You See Is What You Get. Refers to development systems that show the creator what the final work will look like to the user.

References

Binmore, Ken. *Game Theory and the Social Contract.* MIT Press: Cambridge, 1994.

Boyle, Tom. *Design for Multimedia Learning.* Prentice Hall: London, 1997.

Brinson, J. Dianne, and Radcliffe, Mark F. *Multimedia Law and Business Handbook.* Ladera Press: Menlo Park, CA, 1996.

Brinson, J. Dianne, and Radcliffe, Mark F. *Internet Legal Forms for Business.* Ladera Press: Menlo Park, CA, 1997.

Brown, Barbara. (1998). "Digital Classrooms: Some Myths about Developing New Educational Programs Using the Internet." *THE Journal, 26* (5). Retrieved August 12, 1999 from the World Wide Web: http://www.thejournal.com/magazine/vault/a2007.cfm

Castle, Louis. E-mail interview with author. June 19, 1999.

Dempsey, John V., and Sales, Gregory C., Ed. *Interactive Feedback and Instruction.* Educational Technology Publications: Englewood Cliffs, NJ, 1993.

Dombrower, Eddie. *Dombrower's Art of Interactive Entertainment Design.* McGraw Hill: New York, 1998.

Druin, Allison. *Designing Multimedia Environments for Children.* Wiley & Sons: New York, 1996.

England, E., and Finney, A. *Managing Multimedia.* Addison-Wesley: Harlow, England, 1999.

Feldman, Tony. *An Introduction to Digital Media.* Routledge: London, 1997.

Fisher, Roger. *Getting to Yes: Negotiating Agreement Without Giving In.* Penguin Books: New York, 1991.

Goldberg, Ron. *Multimedia Producer's Bible.* IDG Books: Foster City, CA, 1996.

Gotbaum, Victor. *Negotiating in the Real World: Getting the Deal You Want.* Simon & Schuster: New York, 1999.

Head, Alison. *Design Wise, A Guide for Evaluating the Interface Design of Information Resources.* Cyberage Books: Medford, NJ, 1999.

Horton, William. *The Icon Book.* Wiley & Sons: New York, 1994.

Johnson, Kerry A., and Foa, Lin J., Ed. *Instructional Design: New Alternatives for Effective Education and Training.* Macmillan: New York, 1989.

Johnson, D. W., and Johnson, R. T. "Cooperative Learning and Feedback in Technology-Based Instruction." In Dempsey, John V., and Sales, Gregory C., Ed. *Interactive Instruction and Feedback.* Educational Technology Publications: Englewood Cliffs, NJ, 1993.

Korolenko, Michael. *Writing for Multimedia: A Guide and SourceBook for the Digital Writer.* Wadsworth: Belmont, CA, 1997.

Laurel, Brenda. *Computers as Theater.* Addison-Wesley: Reading, MA, 1991.

Laurel, Brenda, et al. *The Art of Human–Computer Interface Design.* Addison-Wesley: Reading, MA, 1990.

Laybourne, Kit. *The Animation Book.* Crown: New York, 1979.

Lopuck, Lisa. *Designing Multimedia: A Visual Guide to Multimedia and Online Graphic Design.* Peachpit Press: Berkeley, 1996.

Maestri, George. *Digital Character Animation.* New Riders: Indianapolis, Indiana, 1996.

Marcus, Aaron. *Graphic Design for Electronic Documents and User Interface.* Addison-Wesley: New York, 1992.

McCloud, Scott. *Understanding Comics: The Invisible Art.* HarperPerennial: New York, 1994.

McLuhan, Marshall. *Understanding Media, The Extensions of Man.* The New American Library of Canada: Toronto, 1966.

Nelson, Ted. *Computer Lib/Dream Machines* (Rev. ed.). Microsft Press: Redmond, WA, 1987.

Nielsen, Jakob. *Hypertext and Hypermedia.* Academic Press: Boston, 1990.

Norman, Donald A. *Things That Make Us Smart.* Addison-Wesley: Reading, MA, 1993.

Norman, Donald A. *The Psychology of Everyday Things.* Basic Books: New York, 1988.

Osborne, Martin, and Rubenstein, Ariel. *A Course in Game Theory.* MIT Press: Cambridge, 1994.

Reynolds, A., and Iwinski, T. *Multimedia Training: Developing Technology-Based Systems.* McGraw Hill: New York, 1996.

Sammons, Martha C. *The Internet Writer's Handbook.* Allyn & Bacon: Boston, 1999.

Schwier, Richard A., and Misanchuk, Earl R. *Interactive Multimedia Instruction.* Educational Technology Publications: Englewood Cliffs, NJ, 1993.

Snider, M. (1999, June 7). Lowenstein: Adults power video-game sales. *USA Today,* p. 2D.

Stansberry, Domenic. *Labyrinths: The Art of Interactive Writing and Design, Content Development for New Media.* Wadsworth: Belmont, CA, 1998.

Tapscott, Don. *Growing Up Digital: The Rise of the Net Generation.* McGraw Hill: New York, 1998.

Tapscott, Don., Ed. *Creating Value in the Network Economy.* Harvard Business School Press: Cambridge, 1999.

Wlodkowski, Raymond J. "Instructional Design and Learner Motivation," in *Instructional Design: New Alternatives for Effective Education and Training.* Macmillan: New York, 1989.

Index

Abel, Robert, 41
Absolute warranty, 240
Acceptance clause, 237
Actual-knowledge warranty, 240–241
Advances against royalties, 147
Adventure games, 82
Agenda, for kickoff meeting, 164–165
Alpha version, 156, 300–301
Ambient sound, 213
American Federation of Musicians (AFM), 211–212
American Federation of Television and Radio Artists
  (AFTRA), 208, 211, 277
Animation, 205–207, 294
Anticipation, 41
Apple Computer, 39
Application. *See* Product
Appropriate technology, 172–173
Approvals, 147, 174, 289, 290, 291
Archiving, 304–306
Art, in prototype phase, 276–277
Arthur series, 146, 160
Artificial intelligence (AI), 57, 74, 79–80, 175
Art of Human–Computer Interface Design, The
  (Laurel), 39
Asset(s)
  databases of, 219–220, 221
  defined, 24
  in game design document, 139–140
  types of, 187
Asset breakdown, 25–26, 184, 185–186, 187

Asset development, 155–156, 276–277
Asteroids, 75
Attributes, of game characters, 79
Audience. *See also* Target users
  desire for control, 7–8
  for functional specification, 110
  redefining multimedia, 6–7
  viewers versus, 6–7

Backstory, in game design, 77–78
Barbie Fashion Designer, 81, 91, 160, 206
Battle of the forms, 243
Behaviors, of game characters, 79
Beta version, 156, 300–301
Bid, 151, 191–193, 235–236
Branching, 18, 20
Breakdown chart
  asset quantification, 25–26, 184, 185–186, 187
  node-by-node breakdown, 107, 108, 138
Brinson, J. Dianne, 234–268
Broadcast learning, 56
Broderbund Software, 146, 160, 174,
  201, 209
Brown, Barbara Mahone, 61
Browse Mode, 20
Browsing methods, 57
Budget
  of client, 161
  final, 223–225, 226–228
  in initial contact, 163